A Heart of Wisdom

SUNY Series in
Religious Studies

Harold Coward, Editor

A Heart of Wisdom

Religion and Human Wholeness

Maurice Friedman

STATE UNIVERSITY OF NEW YORK PRESS

Production by Ruth Fisher
Marketing by Fran Keneston

Published by
State University of New York Press, Albany

© 1992 State University of New York

Production by Ruth Fisher
Marketing by Fran Keneston

For information, address the State University of New York Press,
State University Plaza, Albany, N.Y. 12246

Library of Congress Cataloging-in-Publication Data

Friedman, Maurice S.
   A heart of wisdom : religion and human wholeness / Maurice
Friedman.
      p.   cm. — (SUNY series in religious studies)
   Includes bibliographical references and index.
   ISBN 0-7914-1215-6 (alk. paper). — ISBN 0-7914-1216-4 (pbk. :
alk. paper)
   1. Religion. 2. Religions. I. Title. II. Series.
BL48.F74 1992
200—dc20   91-42031
                                                                CIP

10 9 8 7 6 5 4 3 2 1

So teach us to number our days
That we may get a heart of wisdom.
Psalm 90

Le coeur a ses raisons
Que le raison ne connait pas.
Pascals, *Pensées*

No Break

Rabbi Mendel saw to it that his hasidim wore
nothing around the neck while praying, for, he
said, there must be no break between the heart
and the brain.
Martin Buber, *Tales of the Hasidim*

To the memory of my friend

Ben Weininger, M.D.

Who possessed a heart of wisdom
which he shared unstintingly
with countless others

CONTENTS

Part Five — Religion and Human Wholeness

ACKNOWLEDGMENTS

Grateful acknowledgment is made to the following publishers for permission to quote passages from the following books:

Jelaluddin Rumi, *This Longing: Poetry, Teaching Stories, Selected Letters*, by Coleman Barks and John Moyne (Putney, Vt: Threshold Books, 1988);

Random Books for Martin Buber, *Tales of the Hasidim: The Early Masters* and *Tales of the Hasidim: The Later Masters*, both trans. by Olga Marx (New York: Schocken Books, 1961);

Princeton University Press for Mircea Eliade, *Cosmos and History: The Myth of the Eternal Return*, trans. by Willard Trask (New York: Harper Torchbooks, 1966);

Oxford University Press for John O. Voll, "Renewal and Reform in Islamic History," Chap. 2 of John Esposito, ed., *Voices of Resurgent Islam* (New York: Oxford University Press, 1983);

Charles E. Tuttle for Paul Reps, *Zen Flesh, Zen Bones: A Collection of Zen and Pre-Zen Writings* (New York: Doubleday, Anchor Books, 1961);

New Directions for Thomas Merton, *The Way of Chuang Tzu* (New York: New Directions, 1965).

PREFACE

Thirty-five years ago when I was working on my first book, *Martin Buber: The Life of Dialogue*, Martin Buber helped me in my task by pointing out that writing is like musical composition: one has to know what goes in each segment. Today, when I am working on my twentieth book, I have rediscovered the truth of Buber's statement in a new and surprising manner.

In 1972 E. P. Dutton published my book *Touchstones of Reality: Existential Trust and the Community of Peace*. Ten years later Anima Publications published *The Human Way: A Dialogical Approach to Religion and Human Experience*, which I regarded as a sequel to *Touchstones of Reality*. In the course of discussions about a new edition of *Touchstones of Reality* and a paperback edition of *The Human Way*, I made a surprising discovery. I found I had a perspective as to what belonged where that I had not had even five years before. Looking at the two books together, I realized that even a radical revision of each would not suffice. Rather I had to take from both books (plus one chapter on "Literature and Religion" from my 1974 book *The Hidden Human Image*) what belonged to my reflections on religion and human wholeness.

As a result, *A Heart of Wisdom* now brings together more of my thought on religion and the religions than any of my earlier books and does so in a new Gestalt that I had not previously glimpsed. As such, I believe it will have a value to the reader considerably surpassing *The Human Way*, which Professor Harry Buck, director of Anima Publications, has graciously allowed to go out of print in order that I might be free to pursue the new vision that has opened up to me.

I wish to acknowledge the more than generous help of my colleague Professor Marcia Hermansen of the Department of Religious Studies of San Diego State University who has helped me leaven this book with a proper representation from Islam, which supplements my own witness to Sufi mysticism in chapter 2—"My Dialogue with the Religions."

Chapter 4 on "Jesus: Image of the Human or Image of God" is not a scholarly account of the Christian viewpoint but is instead the fruit of my own dialogue with the Gospels and with Christianity and Christians. I do not deal with that part of the Gospel record which is the foundation for the Christian experience of Jesus, namely, his resurrection and continued presence through the Holy Spirit. That makes it more of a Jewish than a Christian touchstone of reality, although one that is more open to the meeting with Jesus than that of many other Jewish writers.

Maurice Friedman
Solana Beach, California
April 1991

PART ONE

A Way That One Walks

1

Religion and the Religions

You could not in your going find the ends of the soul, though
you travelled the whole way: so deep is its Logos
                                            Heraclitus of Ephesus

What is man that Thou art mindful of him?
    And the son of man that Thou dost care for him?
                                            Psalm 8

My great teacher, Joachim Wach, defined religion as a total
response of the total being to what is experienced as ultimate reality.
"Total response" because in religion, as distinct from scientific inquiry
and aesthetic emotion, the whole being is responding and the whole
being is involved in the response. Religion as we know it has always
expressed itself in doctrinal forms as myth, creed, theology, metaphysics. It has expressed itself in practical forms as rituals, masses, and
prayer—communal and individual. It has expressed itself in social forms
as brotherhoods, churches, and sects. It is impossible, indeed, to
understand any religion except in terms of these three expressions and
their interrelations.

But for all that, one cannot reduce religion merely to these
expressions and interrelations, for their matrix is the religious reality
that is expressed, and what is expressed is not in itself directly
expressible. One of the great errors in the approach of many people
to religion is to see it as a form of philosophy or metaphysics which
is going to prove that God exists or describe his nature and attributes.

3

This is to reduce God to an object, a part of the universe, to make him subservient to our logic, and in any case has to do with the detached observer rather than the involvement of one's total being. Religion is a way that one walks. Religion is a commitment. Religion is one's basic response *whether* or not one calls oneself religious and *whether* or not one affirms the existence of God. Some of our "labyrinthine ways," whether we are fleeing "the Hound of Heaven" or not, are so far underground that we ourselves are not aware of them when we come up again.

Religion for me, accordingly, is neither an objective philosophy nor a subjective experience. It is a lived reality that is ontologically prior to its expression in creed, ritual, and group. At the same time, it is inseparable from these expressions and cannot be distilled out and objectified. The *religious* at this deepest level might be described as a basic *attitude* or relationship arising in the encounter with the whole reality directly given to one in one's existence. The task of philosophy of religion for me is a conceptual clarification and a metaphorical pointing to the religious reality that is known in the between. This clarification and pointing must take place *without* abstracting from that meeting detached statements about the nature and attributes of God and without doing injustice to the typical and the unique apprehended in the phenomenological study of the history of religions.

In entering into dialogue with the religions, therefore, we are not looking for *the* truth, either in the sense of a Platonic truth—a metaphysical absolute—or in the sense of one religion being true and the rest false, or in the sense of a "perennial philosophy" in which we can say what is the "essence" of all religions and what is only the "accidental," cultural expression. Insofar as we can enter into dialogue with it, each religion will say something to us of its uniqueness and will say something to us about our life—our life as human beings but also as the particular persons that we are. We cannot *become* Mohammed or Lao-tzu or the Buddha or Jesus, but we can meet them and know them in that meeting. We cannot be an ancient Greek, but we can respond with "pity and terror" to the downfall of Oedipus or feel in the depths of our own lives Socrates' drinking the cup of hemlock.

What is common to all great religions is that each in its own way sees the human person as a problem to his or herself. Why is the person a problem to herself? Because of the given of human existence. The awareness of self, of the passage of time, of change, in oneself, others, and the world, of the fact that one is mortal and will die, of the fact that one moves inexorably and irreversibly from youth to age, of possibility and the need for choice, of freedom and the checks on freedom by the limitation of our inner resources and the constraint of our natural and social environment, of one's dual existence in self-relationship and interpersonal relationship, in inner awareness and outer social role, of one's dual consciousness in waking and sleeping, in languor and intensity—all these in themselves make human existence problematic. Through all of them, there run discontinuities and confusions that force us to seek a reality amidst appearance, a stability amidst flux, an order amidst chaos, a meaning amidst paradoxes and incongruities. What is the self? What is time? What is reality? What is life and death? What is consciousness and what is the essence of the objective world? These questions have been an integral part of all human existence from the earliest times till today.

The Zen Buddhist asks, "When you are dead, and your body is cremated, and the ashes scattered, where are you?" "Then was not nonexistent nor existent," says the Hymn to "Creation" from the Rig-Veda, Hinduism's earliest scriptures, perhaps eighteen centuries before the Christian era. "Death was not then, nor was there aught immortal....Who verily knows and who can here declare it, whence it was born and whence comes this creation? The gods are later than this world's production...whether he formed it all or did not form it, whose eye controls the world in highest heaven, he verily knows it, or perhaps he knows not." It is not such a long way from this hymn to Alice crying in *Through the Looking Glass* because Tweedledee tells her that she is only a part of the Red King's dream and would go out "like that" if he were to wake up. Alice says, "Why, I wouldn't be crying if I were just a part of his dream!" But Tweedledum says, "Do you think these are real tears?" And she cries anew.

In the chapters that follow I offer the reader not an objective, scholarly survey of these religions with which I deal, but the fruits of my own dialogue—and the roots as well in the form of the particular passages from the scriptures of these religions that I have meditated upon and made my own.

In *A Heart of Wisdom* I approach religion from the standpoint of what I call "touchstones of reality." The metaphor of touchstones of reality implies no prior definition of reality nor any metaphysical absolute. Yet touchstones of reality cannot be reduced to any current form of subjectivism—whether it be that of cultural relativism, psychologism, Freudian psychoanalysis, behaviorism, Sartrian existentialism or linguistic analysis. There is no *touch* independent of contact with _otherness_, an otherness that transcends subjectivity even though it cannot be known without it. The coloration of the *Zeitgeist* that seals us within our cultural subjectivity is not a touchstone of reality but fool's gold. Touchstones of reality must be made true ever again by testing them in each new situation—bringing the life-stance they have produced into a moment of present reality. Unlike scientific generalizations, touchstones of reality provide valid insights confirmable in some situations but not all. Touchstones of reality are closer to events than insights. They provide no secure purchase above the stream of living. We are left with the problem of when to move in the direction of insight and abstraction and when to move back into the living waters.

The approach of touchstones of reality is nowhere more fruitful than in trying to understand religion.

When during World War II I entered my first Civilian Public Service Camp for conscientious objectors in December 1942, at West Campton, New Hampshire, the director of that camp was a young scholar, Ken Morgan, who was at that time working for the American Friends Service Committee. It was Ken Morgan who gave me a copy of Buber's *I and Thou* to read in 1944, although he confessed that he could make nothing out of it himself, and we renewed our acquaintance years later when I lectured at Colgate University where he had established an institute for world religions.

I like so much the spirit of what Ken Morgan says in his recent book *Reaching for the Moon* about dialogue with religions that I want to set some of it down here prefatory to the chapter on "Religions with Which I have Been in Dialogue":

> The most dependable guides along the different religious ways I have observed were the ones who have been moved to follow their path by the wonder, gratitude, awareness, and awe that center their attention outside themselves, guides who are trying to live in closer harmony with what they see is true, is good, is sacred.
>
> Sympathetic study of religions other than one's own helps religious seekers to see the realities of their own path more clearly, to discover new ways for humans to increase the good in their relations with each other and with the natural world, and to gain new understanding of the Sacred.[1]
>
> Some. . .say that all paths lead to God, or that we are all climbing the same mountain and will meet at the top. Others say theirs is the only Way. But when I explore Asian religious ways I find that often I am only in the foothills, with some bypaths that are dead ends, some valleys shadowed with tangled undergrowth—and that there are also many beckoning paths, often arduous, leading to awesome peaks, some hidden in clouds.
>
> When I reflect on my efforts to understand Asian religious ways I find that I have been looking for followers of religious paths. . .who are committed to live by what seems to them to be

true, who recognize some given aspects of their world as good and some of the good as sacred. I have searched for people of sensitive awareness who respond to the world with wonder and joyous appreciation for the beauty and diversity they see, with awe for the mysteries not fully grasped, and with compassionate help for the needy and suffering. I have found such persons in each religious group.[2]

PART TWO

Religions With Which I Have Been In Dialogue

2

My Dialogue with the Religions

If I use my touchstones of reality for the understanding of religion, I have used my dialogue with the religions in the first instance as a source for many of my touchstones. In this interplay the insights into the human way that came to me during my mystical years of immersion in Hinduism, early Buddhism, Taoism, and Zen have continued to grow in the forty years of study and teaching in comparative religions since that time. I prefer to label myself as a philosopher or a philosophical anthropologist rather than as a scholar of religions, if a label be needed. But as a philosopher I have always claimed the right to draw the material for my philosophizing from whatever sphere seems suitable to the questions that concern me. Since these questions are always integrally related to the problematic wholeness of the human, it is small wonder that I have continued to find in the scriptures of the great religions some of the sources of my insights.

My first serious contact with religion as an adult was with Hinduism. I began my meditations in our "Gemeinde" of four at the institute for the "feeble minded" where I worked outside of Philadelphia on detached service as a conscientious objector in the Civilian Public Service Camps during the Second World War. My first meditations were on Christian mystical texts and on Gerald Heard's nondualist books *The Creed of Christ* and *The Code of Christ*. Soon, in cooperation with my roommate who is today a swami in the Ramakrishna-Vivekananda Society, I turned full-force to *advaitin* (nondualist) Hinduism as taught by Sri Ramakrishna, Swami Nikhilananda, and Swami Yatiswarananda, a disciple of a disciple of Ramarkishna's whom I saw weekly at the Vedanta Society in Philadelphia. I meditated three hours a day and

11

might have continued in this path had I not fallen prey to what I have described elsewhere as

> the growing tension I felt between various pulls: toward active love, the search for the truth, toward meditation and spiritual exercise, and my desire for a way to express my emotions in worship. What troubled me most was the lack of a tradition or symbol to which I could wholly give myself. My attempts to meditate on Sri Ramakrishna, on Christ, and on the Buddha did not resolve my conflict.[1]

Although I knew from my studies of the theistic tradition in India, because of my work with the Ramakrishna Order, I did not bring into my own dialogue what John Hick writes of the "divine Thou" in Hinduism:

> That the Real is experienced as the divine Thou in the post-axial traditions of Semitic origin—Judaism, Christianity and Islam— need no arguing. . . But the personification of the Real is scarcely less characteristic of oriental traditions. Until comparatively recently the West tended to think of the richly pluralistic religious life of India in terms of one only of its many schools of thought, namely advaita Vedanta. This simplification was aided by the reifying effect of the western term 'Hinduism.' But neither in the past nor today has most of the wide and multifarious stream of life that we call Hinduism been other than theistic.[2]

After a lecture of mine at Pendle Hill, the Quaker study center in Wallingford, Pennsylvania, my then wife Eugenia asked me, "What touchstone of reality do you still retain from Hinduism?" My answer was that it gives existence a depth-dimension that is always there for me even when I do not spell it out—a transpersonal consciousness the reality of which I recognize, though not as the only reality. Hinduism was at one time in my life a "live option," in William James's phrase, a road that I could and did follow. I have taken a different path in the years since. Yet I believe that the options which we choose and later reject are almost as important for us as the options we ultimately choose and make our own. They remain with us, like an obligato to the melody of our lives.

To me the Hindu Upanishads' progress to absolute subjectivity can be understood in terms of our common experience in which the dreamer is more real than the dream, in which the continuity of the self is set in contrast to the flux of the world that the self witnesses, in which we are aware at times of the consciousness as detached from the senses, as when we concentrate so much on a certain matter that although our auditory senses are fully functioning, we do not hear what is going on around us. Though music is playing, we do not hear the music. Someone may even call our name, and we do not hear it. This is true with all the other senses too. One can look and yet not see anything because one is intent on something else. If we can thus withdraw the consciousness from the senses, we can conceive of the mind remaining within itself without going out to the senses. If we follow this through, we discover that consciousness is not, as we often think, simply a matter of sensation—that, apart from sensation, consciousness exists itself as something pure, something *sui generis*, something in itself. So the mystic experiences it when he reaches a state that seems beyond time, beyond place, beyond awareness of itself—a state of pure consciousness, resting and dwelling in consciousness. Yet in some way this very consciousness also enters into the perception of the world to which the mystic relates. Thus the very beginning point of the Hindu yoga of meditation is the withdrawal of consciousness from the senses into the mind, leading to inner illumination.

We are also aware of our self as detached from what we habitually associate with it—sense impressions, names, forms, social relations. Somehow each of us has a sense of ourself as transcending all these things, no-matter how aware we may be at the same time of our self as constituted within all of these things. Finally, according to mystics the world over, we find, by going within, an intensified consciousness that not only is ineffable and all-absorbing, including every other sensation, reflection, and concern, but also is a self-evident and self-validating reality of existence, compared to which our waking consciousness seems unreal. When dreaming, we feel that our dreams are real, but when waking we know that they are only dreams compared to the waking consciousness. Similarly, when we attain this higher consciousness, our waking world seems to us, in comparison, a dream. Thus the world is unreal *only* in comparison with this higher reality.

In *Through the Looking Glass*, the "Wood with no Name" is one of the eight squares through which Alice must pass before she can become Queen Alice. Alice comes on a fawn in the wood and asks it what its name is. The fawn says, "I can't remember, but I'll tell you when we get to the edge of the wood." Alice puts her arm around the neck of the fawn, and they walk together to the edge of the wood. Then the fawn comes to and says, "Why, I'm a fawn, and *you* are a little girl!" and scampers away in great fright. Thus the name gets in the way of the basic reality. Only when we progressively back away from the categories and from the world of particulars, are we ready to arrive at that awareness of identity that is at the root of the mystical experience. The philosophy itself does not give one the experience, but it may be a necessary preparation for it—for the final leap—just as in Plato's *Republic* the dialectic of the philosopher leads him out of the cave up the hill to the top of the hill where he then makes the leap to the sun, which represents the direct knowledge of the Good, the True, and the Beautiful.

Having arrived at these two separate points, the absolute subjective essence within the self and the absolute objective essence of reality, then through a combination of direct mystical experience and philosophical contemplation stimulated by that experience, the two aspects of absolute subjectivity and absolute objectivity are identified. In a lightning flash there arises the central insight of the Upanishads and of the whole nondualistic Vedanta: *Brahman is Atman, tat twam asi*— Thou art That.

This whole religious approach begins with the intense need, the wholly concentrated desire to find one's true way. "The good is one thing, the pleasant another," Death tells Nachiketas in the Nachiketas Upanishad. Those who seek after pleasure will always be deluded. To say this is to say that there is a life of appearances and a life of reality. It is to say, as Socrates says to the Athenians, "Are you not ashamed that you value the things that are *not* valuable, like money, fame, and prestige, and you do not value the things that are truly valuable? You do not value your soul." Or in the words of Jesus, "What doth it profit a man to gain the whole world if he lose his soul?" "Only when man shall roll up the sky like a hide," says an Upanishad, "will there be an end of misery, unless this truth has first been known." No greater contrast could be found to the Epicurean view that looks on pleasure as the sole meaning and the only possible fulfillment of life. The *Gayatri mantram*, perhaps the most famous Hindu prayer, begins, "From the unreal lead us to the real, from darkness to light, from death to immortality."

Perhaps the central statement in the central Hindu scripture the Bhagavad Gita is, "He who sees the action that is in inaction, the inaction that is in action is wise indeed." The "action that is in inaction" is the effectiveness of the person who does not seem to act, who does not interfere in the world arbitrarily, and yet acts out of the wholeness, the fullness, the concentration of one's being, out of the spiritual state that one has reached. The inaction that is action is the ineffectiveness of the busy, active person—the typical Western political, social worker, or anyone, for that matter, who rushes around thinking that if one does more and more things, one is accomplishing more and more. What is at stake here is not merely the accomplishment of a goal, but the total meaning. One cannot realistically speak of the goal and the way to the goal as separate entities. The Hindus speak of *apûrva*, a subtle cause. One's actions begin as gross and become subtle so that one is not aware of them. Yet they have their effect, whether for good or for evil. So to the Hindu, the old argument about means and ends is radically transformed. Everything has its effect: if one uses a good means it will have a good effect; if one uses a bad means, it will have a bad effect. The aim is not merely the piling up of external structures, moreover, but is inner spiritual growth and enlightenment.

One's reason, one's motivation, one's relation to an action determine its very nature, quality, and effectiveness. Karma yoga—the yoga of action—is action without attachment to the fruits of action. You live in the world and act, but you are not acting for the sake of the result. If you want to help others, you can only do so out of your spiritual state of being. Yet you cannot cultivate that state of being in order to help others. If you do so, you will be thinking of the fruit of the action, and therefore your state of being will not be that out of which effective help can proceed. This is a paradox. But this is the only true, the only effective action, according to the Gita. Gandhi gave an incomparable demonstration of the way this could be put into practice in his *satyagraha*, his nonviolent direct action.

> He who is ever brooding over results often loses nerve in the performance of duty. He becomes impatient and then gives vent to anger and begins to do unworthy things; he jumps from action to action, never remaining faithful to any. He who broods over results is like a man given to the objects of senses; he is ever-distracted, he says good-by to all scruples, everything is right in his estimation and he therefore resorts to means fair and foul to attain his end.[3]

The Buddha was a greater social revolutionary than Gandhi; for he rejected the Hindu caste system. For him a Brahmin was not a person who has a certain caste-mark on his forehead, but a person who is noble in character and action. In Buddhism one backs away from the world, and this backing away makes no statement and implies no assumption about the reality or unreality of the world. The emphasis here is not upon knowledge, therefore. It is not upon discovering what is the nature of the cosmos or the acosmos that includes or is identical with the human being. The emphasis here is anthropological, it is human. It makes no statement about reality, except one thing, and that is that it changes: "All things change, all things perish, all things pass away." If we try to hold on to any part of existence, we will suffer. We will suffer because the attempt to hold on goes against the fact of change. Our very enjoyment of this moment must mean our suffering and sadness in the next moment. It cannot but be so. If we were able to enjoy the moment, relate to it, and then let it go, that would be different. But something else happens. Not only do we have this momentary relationship, but then we fix it: we record the fact that this was a pleasurable sensation or that was painful. Thus, at a later time, we are drawn to this sensation or we shrink from it. As a result, we are not able to accept the simplest and most elementary fact of human existence—that all things change, perish, and pass away. Human life is a vain search for building security. We fruitlessly try to shore it up in every direction, like Kafka's mole who is never done fortifying his hole. Unable to accept her child's death, Kisogatomi went to the Buddha and pleaded, "Bring my child back to life." Eventually she realized that death is a part of all human existence, and she was able to put her child aside.

The "compassionate Buddha" always remained close to the concrete situation, to the pragmatic problem at hand, "How can I help or how can we help ourselves escape from suffering?" He began with the human, with anthropology, rather than with metaphysics or cosmology. This closeness to the concrete is renewed in sophisticated and paradoxical form in Zen—that form of Mahayana Buddhism which grew out of the most abstruse philosophies of "mind only," "the void," "suchness," and the interpenetration of all reality.

Religion is often taken to be a movement away from mundane reality to the spirit floating above it. Zen Buddhism says no such movement is possible: there is only the one spirit-sense reality. It says, secondly, that it is our reason that has created the impression that there are these separate worlds of spirit and sense-intellect. This differs strikingly from Hinduism with its statement that this world is *maya*, or illusion, and that Brahman is reality. Instead, we have the remarkable statement that the "one" and the "ten thousand things" are identical, that "nirvana *is* samsara." It is our minds that bifurcate existence into body and spirit, the one and the many. We cannot overcome our existential dilemma by fleeing from the many to the one; for this very attempt to overcome dualism leads us to still another dualism—that of the one as opposed to the many. One must instead go right to the concrete particular that is at the same the Buddha Nature. There is no process here of abstracting from concrete reality, of uncovering the essence and shucking off this world. There is no Hindu *nama-rupa*— no world of name and form which is to be understood as merely that and therefore illusion. On the contrary, the very particularity of things, their very name and form, is the only means through which one can attain enlightenment.

> When a mind is not disturbed,
> The Ten Thousand things offer no offence.
> No offence offered, and no ten thousand things.

Zen Buddhism is perhaps the most intellectual form of anti-intellectualism that exists. It goes even beyond the "neti, neti"—the "not this, not this"—of the Hindu Vedanta. For it is absolutely opposed to the discrimination of the mind; it is absolutely against the intellection that cuts us off from the concrete world. If one is so intellectual that one gets all one's emotional satisfaction thereby, one cannot be a Zen Buddhist; for one will cling to the intellect and not be willing to go beyond it. Zen is just the everyday life—pulling up carrots in the garden, peeling potatoes in the kitchen.

> Walking is Zen, sitting is Zen,
> Whether talking or remaining silent, whether moving or
>   standing quiet, the essence itself is ever at ease.

One finds the "essence" just as much in the movement of the world as in the nonmovement. In that sense, Zen is like Taoism: it does not cling to one opposite or the other. Zen was much influenced by Taoism, in fact, with its sense of "the way" and of the coincidence of opposites.

> Not knowing how near the truth is,
> People seek it far away,—what a pity!
> And straight runs the path of non-duality and non-trinity.
> Abiding with the no-particular which is in particulars,
> Whether going or returning, they remain for ever unmoved...
> This very earth is the lotus land of purity,
> And this body is the body of the Buddha.

Not only is there no illusion in this world, there is no escape from the world. The Buddha nature, the particulars and the no-particulars are all one reality.

It is impossible for us to meditate on any reality, religious or otherwise, without pointing to it. Through these pointers—words, symbols, myths, even rituals, we enable ourselves to return again and again to the insight or the contact we have achieved. But then the second step always follows: the tendency to regard the pointer as the reality and to lose what it is pointing toward. The Vedantists and the early Mahayana Buddhists were on the right track in trying to overcome the idea that things are divided up into myriads of discriminate particles, but from the Zen point of view, they did not go far enough. They turned it into an intellectual conception, and they said, "Reality is the 'not-two' " and fell into a world of intellectual discrimination between spirit and matter, the one and the many, the not-two and the ten thousand things. They could not get to the reality which is so concrete that it baffles all of our attempts to grasp it by any of these forms of mental categories. As a Zen text puts it, "They take the finger pointing to the moon for the moon itself."

The Zen Buddhist would say the same about Western attempts to identify the absolute, or God, with some particular image of God. A young man came up to me after a talk I gave on Jesus at a southern university and said to me, "Have you no faith in theology? How can you live without theology?" I replied, "My faith is not in theology. My faith is in God." He believed that only faith set down in propositions guarantees that the world is constructed so as to give one salvation and happiness in the world to come. Such a belief opens itself to any scriptural text only insofar as it can be fitted into a ready-made theological category. Perhaps the most healthy religion is the dialectic between the interpretation and the religious reality. Most great theologians make a real effort to go back again and again to the scripture and to the experience. But we ought to be aware that their turning to the text often takes place through the spectacles of their particular way of looking, their favorite way of interpreting. This is not a criticism of having the categories, but of making the categories reality, of forgetting that "the finger pointing at the moon" is not the moon.

There is much in both Zen Buddhism and Taoism which raises serious questions about the assumption of most of the intellectual currents of the nineteenth and twentieth centuries that *analysis* is the way to reach reality. If I take a thing apart into its supposed parts, have I thereby grasped this thing? Only if I assume that all things are really reducible to their component parts. That often means, only if I have already found what I believe to be the basic reality—sush as a Marxist dialectic or a form of economic determinism or Freud's or Jung's theory of the libido or the analytical categories of the linguistic philosopher.

The very different attitude of Zen is illustrated by the following:

> It is the substance that you see before you—*begin to reason about it and you at once fall into error.* . . . . like the boundless void which cannot be fathomed or measured. This universal mind alone is the Buddha and there is no distinction between the Buddha and

sentient being....you have but to recognize that *Real mind is expressed in these perceptions, but is not dependent on them on the one hand, nor separate from them on the other.* You should not start reasoning from such perceptions, nor allow your thinking to stem from them, yet you should *refrain from seeking universal mind apart from them or abandoning them* in your pursuit of the Dharma. *Neither hold to them, abandon them, dwell in them, nor cleave to them,* but exist independently of all that is above, below, or around you, *for there is nowhere in which the Way cannot be followed.*[4]

Martin Buber in *I and Thou* has a remarkably similar passage in which he says,

If you explore the life of things and of conditioned being you come to the unfathomable, if you deny the life of things and of conditioned being you stand before nothingness, if you hallow this life you meet the living God.

The way is right there before you, but you are going to miss it either if you say that perceptions are all illusion or if you take perceptions as the material for your analysis. Much of what is called "existential" philosophy in our day—Heidegger, Sartre, even Tillich—starts with existence but then goes on to analyze it into phenomenological categories. Unlike the Zen Buddhist it does not stay with the concrete but quickly leaves it to go to one realm or another and thereby perhaps loses the really existential quality that does not yield itself to analysis.

The way is not some other way, some mystical or occult path "out there" apart from the everyday world. It has to do just with the concrete here and now. Sometimes a therapist helps a schizophrenic patient involved in an inner world of fantasy by presenting himself to the patient again and again as simpler than he actually is—just as an everyday person—and that way, over a number of years, brings the patient to some contact with reality. We are all schizophrenics, the Zen Buddhist might suggest; we really do not see reality as it is. We think we do: we call the formulae of science "concrete," for example, forgetting that science, though useful, is precisely the most abstract way of apprehending nature or reality. We see everything in terms of space and time and number and miss each thing's uniqueness. We miss the startling reality of "suchness" that is simply there. Between us and it is this veil of intellection of which we are unaware. Nor is this a question of the intellectual as opposed to the ordinary person. Every person, just by virtue of being human, is almost certain to have this veil between her and reality. Enlightenment means removing, overcoming this veil, and finding the reality that is simply there. When the great Zen scholar D.T. Suzuki came to Sarah Lawrence College once to speak to our philosophy seminar, there was a Hindu woman from my class in the history of religions who joined us at supper beforehand. "Do you believe that God is in the sugar bowl?" Suzuki asked her. "Yes," she replied, and he rejoined, "So do we." "Do you believe that God is in you?" he pursued. "Yes," she again replied, and he again assented, "So do we." But then he asked her, "Do you believe the same God is in the sugar bowl and in you?" This time when she said yes, he countered, "That is where we differ!" It is not the same God, even though it is not a different one. It is neither two nor one. The Buddha Nature is to be comprehended in and through birth-and-death, and birth-and-death must somehow harbor the Buddha Nature in it. Nirvana *is* samsara.

"All things are reducible to the One," says a typical koan, "but to what will this One be reduced?" Evolution, to some people, is an explanation of how things got to be what they are, but if we do not remain content with that, where in turn does that lead us? Cause and effect, in the same way; may give us a sense of satisfaction. But if we press the question a step further and inquire, like Hume, into the reality underlying the connection between cause and effect, where does that leave us? "When you are dead, cremated, and the ashes scattered, where are you?" Where is the "I" that at this moment, in this consciousness, sees reality? The question is not, Where is this body, objectified and seen apart from you? You are still to see through your own eyes and ask yourself the question, How is it possible that the whole of reality is grasped through this "I" and yet that this "I" will cease to exist? This is the paradox of existence itself, one beyond which we cannot see.

"The bridge flows, the water remains standing," says a Zen koan. If we were floating down the stream, the bridge would flow with us; the water would not flow at all. The water flows only when we are on the bank and have a stationary position relative to its flow. Heraclitus said, "No person can step twice into the same stream." From this he concluded, "All is flux." But a disciple of his said, "No person can step once into the same stream." The observation that all is flux is only possible when you have removed yourself from the stream. If you flow with the stream, you are not going to know that the stream flows. The very statement that "all is flux" is a static statement, for it presupposes a stationary observer; it presupposes getting hold of something, trying to hold on to it, and then, as a result, observing the next moment that it is gone. This, Henri Bergson tells us, is the beginning of the great error of all Western metaphysics. This metaphysics takes the stream of reality and freezes it into a solid block (idealism) or into myriads of tiny particles (empiricism), turns it into something static and discrete. It was the standpoint of the observer, the fact that the ancient Greek was becoming more aware of the subject-object split, which made him see that all is flux and that he could not step twice into the same stream. The "same" stream is the stream as we have fixed it with our categories— so high, the water flowing so fast, and so many thousands of pebbles in the stream bed. Thus the Zen Buddhist statement, "The bridge flows and the river remains standing," means a basic reversal of our customary perspective in relation to reality over against us—a reversal in the direction of the concrete and the particular, "the one *and* the ten thousand things."

However important it is that things be consistent when we are constructing bridges and roads, when we are dealing with ultimate realities we encounter something that is necessarily paradoxical, something that pushes beyond the bounds which our categories can comprehend. For our categories are always within the given system. If we are talking about ultimates, we are talking about what transcends, includes, or undergirds the system and is not included within it. There is no basic philosophy of religion that is not paradoxical, therefore, including the nondualist philosophy of the Vedanta, founded as it is on the paradox that we not only take *maya* to be reality but that it is indeed as real as creation, for creation itself is a paradoxical union of the utter Absolute with the world of the relative. But the Zen Buddhists retain their paradoxicality right down to the particular. It is a part of their lifestyle, their touchstone of reality.

Less intense and less paradoxical than Zen, but no less a mysticism of the concrete and the particular, is Taoism. The center of Taoism is the Tao—the way of life and the human way in which one finds the "natural" course that flows with the stream rather than runs against it. Taoism accepts the opposites of *Yin* and *Yang*—feminine and masculine, dark and light, earth and heaven, receptive and active—without insisting on one or the other. It does not hold them in tension but swings easily from one to the other. Hence its action is *wu-wei*, the action of the whole being that has the appearance of nonaction because it does not intervene or interfere. This action seems most effortless just when it is most effective.

The *yin* and *yang* is also in Confucianism, but in Confucianism the active side is emphasized at the expense of the passive. Taoism gives equal place to the "feminine" virtues of receptivity and passivity. But Taoism does not insist even on these. It lets things flow between the opposites without making one or the other the basic reality. Neither is the Tao simply the unconscious or feeling, as Witter Bynner suggests in his introduction to *The Way of Life according to Lao-Tzu*. D. H. Lawrence, reacting against the domination of conscious, rational man, swung to the opposite extreme. Taoism, in contrast, does not place feeling above thought any more than it places thought above feeling. It does not need to overcorrect detached intellectuality by an emphasis on "gut-level" emotion. It knows that thought never occurs without feeling and that feeling never occurs without thought, even though we sometimes use our thoughts to mask our feelings and our feelings to mask our thoughts.

Lao-tzu's *Way of Life*, in the classic poetic translation of Witter Bynner, has proved to be of a lasting and ever-new significance for me as no other Eastern scripture has. It does not contain the mystic secret of supreme enlightenment or *nirvana* or even *satori*. Rather, like that Confucian wisdom to which it otherwise seems so opposite, it represents a path that is not far from common consiousness, a wisdom that gently informs and gently reproves just where our lives most stray from it. My own life, indeed, like that of most of the overcommitted persons of affairs whom I know, has often seemed to me what I once wrote of K., the hero of Franz Kafka's novel *The Castle*: an illustration of the very opposite of everything that Lao-tzu taught about flowing with the Tao. But this is precisely why, along with its necessary Confucian counterpart of structure, propriety, and reciprocity, Taoism speaks so powerfully to our condition.

> Existence is beyond the power of words
> To define:
> Terms may be used
> But are none of them absolute.

In the Hindu Vedanta it is only Brahman, the One without Second; in the metaphysics of Plato and Aristotle, it is only the Good or the Unmoved Mover that cannot be defined. The very nature of finite existence to these latter implies that it can be delimited into name and form, same and other, category and class. For Zen Buddhism and Taoism, in contrast, it is existence itself that is illimitable and ineffable. In Taoism both the core and the surface are essentially the same.

> If name be needed, wonder names them both:
> From wonder into wonder
> Existence opens.

Plato said that wonder is the beginning of philosophy but the philosopher, as Martin Buber has said, neutralizes his wonder in doubt. From Descartes to the present even the beginning of philosophy is doubt and not wonder. Only here and there: in Francis Thompson—"The angels keep their ancient places/ Turn but a stone and start a wing./ Tis ye, tis your estranged faces/ That miss the many-splendoured thing"—in William Blake's aphorisms—"How do you know but that every bird that wings its way through the air is a whole world of delight closed to your senses five?"—in the philosophy of religion of Abraham Heschel, who sees each thing as pointing beyond itself and grounds all knowledge, art, and religion on "the awareness of the ineffable"—is any comparable insight found in the Western world. The one "name" that does not falsify existence, dividing it up and closing it off, is wonder: "From wonder into wonder existence opens." Taoism is an existential mysticism in which the concrete, precisely in its concreteness, reveals vista upon vista to the eye of the person who meets it in openness. "The senses" as Heraclitus said, are only "bad witnesses to those who have barbarian souls."

This means no disparagement of words. Only those words that attempt to fix and delimit, to close off and confine, are unreal, not those that point beyond themselves to a concrete reality that no concept can delineate.

> Real words are not vain,
> Vain words are not real;
> And since those who argue prove nothing
> A sensible man does not argue.

Words do not control reality, they serve it—for the person who uses them in flowing openness of reciprocity, "The oracle at Delphi neither reveals nor conceals," said Heraclitus. "It indicates." The sane person, in consequence, is the one who does not try to capture existence as a whole within the limited, and limitedly useful, categories of analysis, whether scientific, psychoanalytic, or linguistic. Life reveals itself in images if one opens oneself to the image in such depth that one allows it to speak—as every image does—of its source.

> The surest test if a man be sane
> Is if he accepts life whole, as it is,
> Without needing by measure or touch to understand
> The measureless untouchable source
> Of its images...

The person who cannot do this is literally insane, like the paranoiac whose whole endeavor is to create a world of which he is totally master, totally in control. When I discovered that one of my dearest friends, of whom I had lost track, had been for three years in a mental hospital, I believed at first, as did a mutual friend, that he was actually sane. But then he told me, in connection with his plan to sue the state for a million dollars, that he knew the name, address, and phone number of the governor, the lieutenant-governor, and everyone else who might be of importance for his scheme. "If one didn't know, one would think from his letters that he was sane," our mutual friend said to me. "They are perfectly rational." "What makes you think that rationality is a sign of sanity?" I responded. Even a philosophical "world view" can easily become a form of insanity when it becomes so total that no otherness can ever find its way through its meshes.

The metaphysician discriminates between the real world and mere "appearance" or "phenomena," and he sets the goal of the true philosopher as ascending beyond the world of the senses to a face-to-face confrontation with absolute reality. Lao-tzu is content to allow ultimate reality to speak to him in the only way in which it can speak to us—through its images. This ultimate reality for him is not some unmovable, self-sufficient absolute but the core, the womb of life, that constantly gives birth to the concrete reality which, changing and evanescent though they be, are as real as the Tao that flows through them. Although "the source" appears dark emptiness," actually it:

> Brims with a quick force
> Farthest away
> And yet nearest at hand
> From oldest time unto this day,
> Charging its images with origin:
> What more need I know of the origin
> Than this?

We do not have to look beyond seeing for "the unseen" or beyond hearing for "the unheard." The true oneness "forever sends forth a succession of living things as mysterious/ As the unbegotten existence to which they return." People have called these living things "empty phenomena/ Meaningless images,/ In a mirage/ With no face to meet,/ No back to follow." But that is because they insist on setting up a dualism between "mere appearance" and some entirely hidden, unmanifested Reality. The true meaning of "phenomenon," as Martin Heidegger has pointed out in our day, is precisely that it shows forth and manifests Being, and Being is not a static absolute but the very ground of existence in time. This cannot be known through philosophical reflection alone, however, but only through the way of life of the person who allows the Tao to flow through one and between one and all beings, rounding the way of earth and of heaven. "One who is anciently aware of existence/ Is master of every moment." There is no split for one between the eternal and the present, the origin and the immediate. One's mastery is one's openness in depth to what each moment tells one of origin. Flowing with life, one "Feels no break since time beyond time/ In the way life flows."

This is Lao-tzu's "sound man," the one who, holding the door of one's tent wide to the firmament, can possess "the simple stature of a child, breathing nature," and just thereby "Become, notwith-standing,/ A man." Such a one is "at the core of life." One does not have "to run outside for better seeing." Abiding at the center of one's being, one understands the central teaching of Lao-tzu: "The way to do is to be." This does not mean passivity, for doing is still the emphasis. It means the action of the whole being in flowing interaction with everything it meets. In this flowing interaction the old paradox reemerges that we find authentic existence, realize our true selves, manifest our uniqueness not through aiming directly at it but through opening ourselves to and going out to meet what is not ourselves—immersing our selves in the stream of the Tao that is within, between, and beyond all creatures.

> A sound man by not advancing himself
> Stays the further ahead of himself
> By not confining himself to himself
> Sustains himself outside himself:
> By never being an end in himself,
> He endlessly becomes himself.[5]

Remaining at the center of one's being does not mean turning away from one's fellows, as in so many other mysticisms, but responding to them from that very core. "A sound man's heart is not shut within itself/ But is open to other people's hearts." It means too recognizing that people do not possess fixed character—good or evil, honest or dishonest—but that the way in which I approach them, the way in which I allow the Tao to flow between myself and them frees them to possibilities of goodness, trust, and openness, just as my mistrust and categorizing makes it difficult for them to break out of habitual modes of dishonesty and mistrust. "Bad people" and "liars" are not bad and dishonest the way a table is a table or a chair a chair. Approached with openness and trust, they may be able to respond in kind. Approached with hatred and distrust, they will be confirmed in the mold in which their earlier interactions have already fixed them.

Lao-tzu perhaps needs the counterbalancing of Confucius, with his emphasis upon structure and conscious intention and the recognition that since people do not reveal their feelings, the only safe guide is not to do to others what you would not want done to yourself. In some moments of life, it is structure that counts and at other, flowing. The "way of life" is a swinging interaction of the two in which structure is both created and informed by flowing, flowing both preserved and facilitated by structure. Lao-tzu, nonetheless, has the deeper insight into that willing of the whole being which, in its openness and response, means spontaneity as opposed to that willfulness which tries to impose itself upon others. Taoism is for me a profound and enduring touchstone of reality.

My first significant encounter with Jesus was through my Christian pacifist friends, my second through Christian mysticism, my third through the study of the comparative records of the Synoptic Gospels (Matthew, Mark, and Luke) in the discussion groups run by the "Sharman" method. Finally, I returned to encounter Jesus again from the standpoint of biblical, normative, and Hasidic Judaism as I had come to understand them.

I affirm the biblical covenant as a covenant of trust between God and a people, between God and every people, to be renewed in every age according to the cruel but real demands of that age. The biblical covenant is not the exclusive possession of modern Judaism any more than it is of modern Christianity. Jesus is, to me, one of the unique bearers of the covenant, as are Abraham, Job, Isaiah, and the Baal Shem Tov. He is not to me *the* unique bearer; for no one moment of history may do the work of all other moments. If it comes down to us in its uniqueness, it must be taken up into the uniqueness of this new historical hour. Jesus is not an image of God to me. The paradox of our being created in God's image lies in the fact that it is precisely God's imagelessness which is imitated and represented in the uniqueness of each new person. But Jesus *is* an image of the human to me—along with Job and Saint Francis, Socrates and Lao-tzu, the Buddha and Albert Camus. Even Jesus' denials were a part of his faithfulness to the covenant, his immediacy of relation to the Father, his concern for "the Kingdom." His "take no thought for the morrow" is an unforgettable renewal of biblical *emunah*, as is that verse without whose commonsense wisdom and whose intimations of the morrow's grace I could hardly live from one day to the next: "Sufficient unto the day is the evil thereof." Jesus' life and his crucifixion are not, for me, the fulfillment of "prophecy," but a true incarnation of the "suffering servant," who has never long been absent—from Abraham to the "Job of Auschwitz."

Jesus' unconditional trust is a demand for wholeness that carries forward the biblical covenant as, for me at least, Paul's either-ors of flesh versus spirit and law versus grace do not. Paul is a figure for whom I have an admiration amounting to awe. He was no mere organizer but a unique religious genius, no mere rhetorician but a person of great passion and anguish—perhaps the first truly modern, truly divided person, who came to Christ in a great turning of mystic faith that rings down through the ages. But I cannot witness for Paul as I can for Jesus, since the "new covenant" of Paul represents, for me, and I think even for him, a break with the old. There is literally no end to the witnesses I might make to this or that strand of Christianity which has, in my dialogue with it, become for me one of my touchstones of reality: Saint Augustine crying out to the "Ancient of Days" that burst his deafness and shattered his blindness; Meister Eckhart confessing that when God laughs at the soul and the soul laughs back at God, the Trinity is born; Saint Francis singing his Hymn to the Sun; Brother Lawrence picking up straws for the love of God; the fourteenth-century Brethren of the Common Life renewing Christianity in an unprecedented mystical, communal fervor; Jacob Boehme, George Fox, Blaise Pascal, Thomas Vaughn, Francis Thompson, and Thomas Kelly—powerful witnesses and contenders for faith down through the ages.

Although I have studied Islam in general, it is Sufi mysticism—the meat in the Islamic walnut shell, to use a Sufi metaphor—that has again and again won my heart. A great favorite of mine for years has been the "Invocations" of 'Abdullah Ansari, a Persian Sufi of the eleventh century of the common era. These invocations are an excellent example of what the Hindus would call Bhakti, or devotional, yoga, but they have a flavor that is unique to Sufism:

> My being or not being is of little worth...
> O God, may my brain reel with thoughts of Thee,
> May my heart thrill with the mysteries of Thy grace,
> May my tongue move only to utter Thy praise...
> Whom Thou intoxicatest with Thy love
> On him bestoweth Thou both the worlds.
> But Thy mad devotee,
> What use hath he for both the worlds?
> O Lord, give me a heart
> That I may pour it out in thanksgiving.
> Give me life that I may spend it
> in working for the salvation of the world....
> The flame of Thy love glows in the darkness of my night.
> O Lord, though the blue flower be poisonous

It is of Thy garden,
And if 'Abdullah be a sinner
He is of Thy people....
O Lord, every one desires to behold Thee,
I desire that Thou mayest cast a glance at me....
If in Hell I obtain union with Thee
What care I for those who dwell in Paradise?
And were I called to Heaven without Thee
The pleasures of Paradise would then
Be worse than the fires of Hell.
O Lord, prayer at Thy gate is a mere formality:
Thou knowest what Thy slave desires....
If thou wishest to become a man in the world,
...learn to feel for others.[6]

I also treasure many of the insights of the thirteenth-century Sufi mystic Jelaluddin Rumi:

> Some devout people should stay weak and poor. If they become successful in the world, they abandon acts of self-denial and lose their spiritual power....
> Choice is the salt on acts of worship. If worship were compulsory, God would not be glorified. Muhammad said, "Whoever knows God, stammers." Speaking is like an astrolabe pointing at the sky. How much, really, can such a device know? Especially of that Other Sky, to which this one is a piece of straw? That Other Sun, in which this is a fleck of dust?...What is the body? That shadow of a shadow of your love, that somehow contains the entire universe....His desire is for influence and power, blind and rushing to sell to anyone. Whereas patience and self-denial try to find the buyer that has already bought them, the owner...
> Anyone who loves Your making is full of Glory. Anyone who loves what You have made is not a true believer....A revealer of mystery and that which is revealed are the same. Seed, sowing, growing, harvest, One Presence....Those who live in Union become pregnant with the feelings and words of invisible forms! Their amazed mouths open. Their eyes withdraw....God's silence is necessary, because of humankind's faintheartedness....The Priest may explain about the ritual prayer: It begins with "praise" and ends with "peace." But the True Sheikh says, *Prayer is union with God, so that no one is there but God.*[7]

We don't need wine to get drunk,
or instruments and singing to feel ecstatic.
No poets, no leaders, no songs,
Yet we jump around totally wild....

Someone who sees you and does not laugh out loud,
or fall silent, or explode in pieces,
is nothing more than the cement
and stone of his own prison....
Being is not what it seems,
nor non-being. The world's
existence is not
in the world....

Inside water, a waterwheel turns.
A star circulates with the moon.
We live in the night ocean wondering,
What are these lights?...

What I most want
is to spring out of this personality,
then to sit apart from that leaping.
I've lived too long where I can be reached....

Burning with longing-fire,
Wanting to sleep with my head on your doorsill,
my living is composed only of this trying
to be in your presence....

I have lived on the lip
of insanity, wanting to know reasons,
knocking on a door. It opens.
I've been knocking from the inside!...

My work is to carry this love
as comfort for those who long for you,
to go everywhere you've walked
and gaze at the pressed-down dirty.[8]

My mother comes from two distinguished lines of Lubavitcher (Habad) Hasidim, yet neither in my home nor in the Reform Temple to which I belonged in Tulsa, Oklahoma, did I even hear of Hasidism until I was twenty-four years old. The first Hasidic book that I read was an early attempt at the translation of Martin Buber's *The Legend of the Baal-Shem*. This was the first Jewish book that had had any impact on me since I was a child, the first that spoke to me as a mature, thinking person. As I look back on this impact, it was that of the Baal Shem Tov as an image of the human that superseded—without displacing—Saint Francis, the Buddha, Sri Ramakrishna, and Jesus in my allegiance.

In Hasidism I found an image of an active love and fervent devotion no longer coupled with self-denial or metaphysical theorizing about unity with the divine. After my immersion in the individualistic and world-denying forms of mysticism that I had found in Hinduism, Buddhism, and Christianity, Hasidism spoke to me in compelling accents of a wholehearted service of God that did not mean turning away from my fellows and from the world. All that was asked was to do everything one did with one's whole strength—not the denial of self and the extirpation of the passions but the fulfillment of self and the direction of passion in a communal mysticism of humility, love, prayer, and joy. After my concern for techniques of spiritual perfection, I now learned that fulfillment and redemption do "not take place through formulae or through any kind of prescribed and special action," but through the *kavana* that one brings to one's every act. "It is not the matter of the action, but only its dedication that is decisive." A new image of the human offered itself to me, that of the zaddik—the humble person, the loving person, the helper:

> Mixing with all and untouched by all, devoted to the multitude and collected in his uniqueness, fulfilling on the rocky summits of solitude the bond with the infinite and in the valley of life the bond with the earthly.... He knows that all is in God and greets His messengers as trusted friends.[9]

Hasidism has spoken most strongly to me through *The Tales of the Hasidim*—the "legendary anecdotes" that bear true witness in stammering tongue to the life of the Hasidim as Martin Buber has presented it to us. If I am asked about the uniqueness of Hasidic mysticism, I do not give a definition: I tell a tale. I can best witness, I believe, to the way in which Hasidism speaks to my condition and to the condition of our contemporaries through the tales themselves.[10]

My devotion to Hasidism does not mean a rejection of the other religions with which I have been in dialogue. Brought up in a liberal Judaism of a very thin variety, I could never have returned to Judaism and established a new and deeper relationship with it had I not gone through Hinduism, Buddhism, Zen, Taoism, and Christian mysticism.[11] Nor have I lost these other touchstones. They are part of the way in which I came to Hasidism and relate to it.

3

The Biblical Covenant:
Exile, Contending, and Trust

So teach us to number our days
That we may get a heart of wisdom.
Psalm 90/12

"I who am dust and ashes have taken it upon myself to argue
with the Lord. Will the Lord of justice not do justice?"
Genesis

You must not hate your brother in your heart ...you shall
not take vengeance...you shall love your neighbor as
yourself: I am the Lord.
Leviticus 19:17–18

A large general contrast that one could make with some
justification between Hinduism and Buddhism and the so-called—
Western religions—Zoroastrianism, Judaism, Christianity, Islam—is that
the latter have a central concept of revelation whereas the former speak
in terms of illumination or "enlightenment." The reason for this
difference is a profound one; for they differ basically in two respects.
One is in their view of the ultimate nature of reality, of the relation of
God, the human, and the world. The tendency in much, although not
all, Hinduism and Buddhism is to see this as one reality, as one basic
Absolute, and this means that at the profoundest level, God, the world,
and the human are not separate. Everything is God, if by "God" you

31

no longer mean a God "out there," but *Brahman*, ultimate reality, the One without Second. In such a situation, revelation is not needed. What is needed is enlightenment, illumination; that is, the discovery of the absolute reality that is already here. The movement toward this Absolute is often seen under the aspect of *samadhi* or *satori*—a mystical or spiritual consciousness, "enlightenment." If we attain a certain state of spiritual consciousness, of spiritual being, then what already *is* the basic reality will be open to us so that nothing changes except us, except our relation to it. The veil is torn asunder, the illusion is pierced. Name and form and time and place, change and individuation are all seen either as illusion or as dependent reality. The essence of them all is the Absolute that is also the Absolute in us.

In the Hindu Upanishads we find a progression from gods who were attached to nature, to gods who were behind nature, to the creative power (*prakriti*) that runs throughout nature, finally to the conception of an Absolute beyond change, yet somehow lying within, or underlying, or being the reality behind all name and form and change, behind all that we know of objective nature. There is also an inward progress in which what is taken to be the self, the personal self—this body, this name, the person, personality—is unmasked as not being the real self. The real self is found deeper in consciousness itself. From individual consciousness we come to that deep consciousness that is somehow the all-consciousness, the underlying consciousness in every self. It is not as if each of us has a different consciousness. We discover that the consciousness in each of us is identical with that in the other. Since this is so, we cannot talk of revelation since there is nothing to reveal. There is only something to uncover, something to discover, something to move toward, and we discover it primarily moving inward, by sinking into this spiritual consciousness, by the type of spiritual exercises that enable us to withdraw the senses, to concentrate, to smooth the waves of the mind, to enable the spiritual energy to arise until finally illumination is secured.

The basic view of the Western religions is that God, world, and the human are separate, although related. God, world, and the human are not reducible to one reality; yet they stand in relation to each other. The way whereby one comes to know the divine, therefore, cannot be merely opening up, unfolding, illumination. A gap has to be bridged, otherness has to be transcended. Revelation means not only that we go forth to meet the divine, but that in some sense the divine comes to meet us. Divine reality can approach us, can address us, can accost us, can demand of us, and our response becomes then the beginning of our way, the beginning of religious reality. This is why these are primarily history religions. This does not mean they reject nature. Far from it. The Hebrew Bible is full of the glory of God in nature—nature declaring the glory of God. Yet it is primarily through history that God speaks to the human being because history is none other than the concrete significance of this time, this place, this situation. In this time, place, and situation, in this concrete context, revelation comes not as some universal, which is always there for me to apprehend at each moment but does not itself move to meet me, but as the Eternal entering into time, as the human meeting the Eternal in a moment of time, in a moment of history, whether it is the personal history of the individual or the history of a group of people.

The very beginning of understanding the problem of revelation is understanding that God is not reducible to the world and the human or the world alone or the human alone, any more than the human can be reduced to the world or the world to the human. This paradoxical view of God as in relation to the human and yet apart from it is the very meaning of the term "creation"—not that God was some carpenter who at one time made an immense bird cage in which all of us now dwell, but that, transcending cause and effect, transcending space and time, not taking place as a cause in time, but creating, as it were, the very order of cause and time, creating anew at every moment, sustaining at every moment, Transcendence enters into relation with the world— sets it free and remains in relation with it. It is not a question of whether God *is* a person, in the sense of being like a human being. It is the question of whether reality is seen as a meeting with transcendent reality *within* which meeting nature and the cosmos arise. Or whether it is the other way around: whether the cosmos becomes the all-inclusive in which the human and God are set.

The Hindu notion of creation as "the play of the gods," or *lila*, has been rightly interpreted by Alan Watts and others as "sitting lightly to the world," though this attitude only truly comes to those who have gone through and beyond the order and attained enlightenment. The history religions, in contrast—Judaism, Christianity, and Islam—speak not of divine sport, *lila*, but of divine destiny—in the sense that God himself has a stake in creation, in history. History here is not the cyclical history that we see in the notion of the *kalpas* and *yugas* of Hinduism and the great Year of ancient Greek religion. Rather it is linear, a line that reaches from creation to redemption, even though neither the beginning nor the end can be understood as a moment of time. Instead of an event being merely a part of a cycle or spiral, every event has its own uniqueness and its own meaning. As Martin Buber puts it, "Meaning is open and accessible in the lived concrete." We do not have to put away the world of the senses, or nature, or time, or history to find this meaning.

There is a basic trust in Hinduism, Buddhism, and Taoism—a trust which says that this world is not a place in which we are hopelessly lost. But there is a special emphasis on trust in the Hebrew Bible—a trust or faithfulness, *emunah*—that does not necessarily have a faith content. This trust does not mean security. The "happy man" in Psalm 1 is not assured of immortality in the world to come or of many sheep, goats, and camels in this life. He is compared to a tree planted by streams of water that brings forth fruit in its season. He has found a true existence that the sinner, however wealthy and prosperous, does not have. That is why the latter is compared to "chaff blown by the wind": dry and rootless, he loses his way; he has no way.

Thus at the center of the faith of biblical Judaism stands not belief in the ordinary sense of the terms but trust—trust that no exile from the presence of God is permanent, that each person and each generation is able to come into contact with reality. In the life of the individuals as of generations, it is the movement of time—the facts of change and death—that most threatens this trust. Every great religion, culture, and philosophy has observed that "all is flux" and that we ourselves are a part of this flux. The conclusions that have been drawn from this fact, however, are as different as the world views of those who have drawn the conclusions. The response of the biblical person has not taken the form of a cyclical order of time or an unchanging absolute, like the Greek, nor of the dismissal of time and change as *maya*, or illusion, like the Hindu, nor of the notion that one may flow with time, like the Taoist. One stands face to face with the changing creation and receives each new moment as an address of God—the revelation that comes to one through the unique present.

To stand before eternity is to be aware of one's own mortality:

> For a thousand years in thy sight
> are but as yesterday when it is past, . . .
> men . . . are like a dream, like grass . . .
> in the morning it flourishes and is renewed;
> in the evening it fades and withers. . . .
>   our years come to an end like a sigh. . . .
> yet their span is but toil and trouble;
>   they are soon gone, and we fly away. (Ps. 90:4–10)

This is the universal human condition—a condition that has tempted some to see existence as unreal or as an ephemeral reflection of reality and others to "eat, drink, and be merry, for tomorrow we die." The psalmist, in contrast, prays that one may withstand this reality and heighten it, that one may make one's existence real by meeting each new moment with the whole of one's being:

> So teach us to number our days
> That we may get a heart of wisdom (Ps. 90:12)

In the beautiful poem of Ecclesiastes from the later Wisdom literature, time has become a cycle that goes round and round and will not reach a meaning. Even when at the end of the poem we are told to remember the Creator in the days of our youth, there is still no suggestion that we shall find meaning here, in the actual flow of time, but only somewhere above. But in the Psalms and in the Book of Job, there is a wrestling for meaning despite the passage of time.

It is not only human mortality, however, but the suffering of the innocent and the prosperity of the wicked that leads to the tempering of trust in Job and in the Psalms. The reaffirmation of trust takes place out of an immediate sense of exile. When God no longer prepares a table for the good person in the presence of his enemies, when the good person sees not the recompense of the wicked, but their prosperity and their arrogance, his trust is shaken. He cannot bear the fact that the presence of God is emptied out of the world, that the sinners who cannot stand in the judgment are nonetheless confirmed by the congregation, and divine and social reality are split asunder. The world is not built In such a way that the natural and moral order correspond. Neither the author of the Book of Job nor of Psalms 73 and 82 can say with the earlier Psalmist, "I am old and have been young, and never yet have I seen the righteous begging for bread." It is not true. The righteous suffer and the wicked prosper. It is out of this situation that Job cries out and contends with a strength perhaps unequalled in any of the world's religious scriptures.

The basic paradox of the Hebrew Bible is the dialogue between eternal God and mortal human being, between the imageless Absolute and the human being who is created in God's "image." If that dialogue is to take place, it must take place not in eternity but in the present—in the unique situation of a limited person who was born yesterday and will die tomorrow. Jacob wrestles with the angel, and Job wrestles with God to receive the blessing of this dialogue on which the very meaning of their existence depends. Job holds fast to his trust in the real God whom he meets in the dreadful fate that has befallen him, and he holds fast to the facts of his innocence and his suffering. At the heart of the Book of Job stands neither "blind faith" nor denial of God, but trusting and contending, recognizing his dependence on God yet standing firm on the ground of his created freedom.

Job wanted a dialogue with God, but when this dialogue comes, it dismays him by forcing him to recognize that the partner with whom he speaks is the Creator who at each moment creates the ground of existence and transcends it.

"Where were you when I laid the foundation of the earth?
Tell me, if you have understanding...
when the morning stars sang together,
and all the sons of God shouted for joy?" (38:37)

The reality of creation is the reality of the otherness that we cannot remove into our rational comprehension of the world. We seek to "anthropomorphize" creation—to rationalize reality to fit our moral conceptions. Despite our power to "comprehend" the world, it has a reality independent of us. The real God is not the God whom we remove into the sphere of our own spirit and thought, but the creator who speaks to us through creatures that exist for their own sake and not just for human purposes.

What Job asks for he does receive: not an explanation of why he suffers, but that at last this God who has become far from him comes to him, speaks to him out of the whirlwind and says, "Now I will speak and you reply." Then Job says, "Before I had heard of you with the hearing of the ear, but now my eye sees you." When Job earlier makes the statement, "I know that my redeemer lives," he couples it with the statement, "And I will see him, even out of my flesh"—when my skin is stripped away by disease—I will see him, "my eyes and not another." That is what does happen to Job in the end. Had Job *not* contended, had he followed the advice of his friends and accepted his suffering humbly as his due or God's will, he would not have known the terrible and blessed experience of God coming to meet him as he went forth to meet God.[1]

The meaning of the biblical dialogue is not what we get from God—whether it be "peace of mind," "peace of soul," "successful living," or "positive thinking"—but our walking with God on this earth. The trust at the heart of this walking with God is tried, and we are exiled by the facts of the passage of time, sickness, and death and by the very social order that we build. There is the possibility of renewing this trust, but only if we can bring the exile into the dialogue with God, not if we turn away from the exile or overlook it. What happened to Job can and does happen, in more or less concentrated form, to any of us. Instead of turning Job's situation into the abstract metaphysical problem of evil we should encounter it as a touchstone of reality. For the real question—the question that lies at the inmost core of our very existence—is not Why? but How? How can we live in a world in which Auschwitz and Hiroshima happen? How can we find the resources once more to go out to a meeting with anyone or anything?

In moving to so-called Western religion, we have not left the paradox which transcends Aristotle's law of contradiction, i.e., that a thing is either A or not-A. If we speak of God creating the world and yet remaining in relationship with it, we have already gone beyond this law. Even if we speak of two people talking with each other, we imply an interhuman reality incomprehensible in terms of Aristotle's logic. If they were entirely other than each other, they could not talk, and if they were the same, they would not need to talk. Nor is it the sameness in each that speaks but one whole person to another, really other, whole person. Starting with trust as grounded in this paradoxical combination of separateness and relationship—arrows going apart and arrows coming together—we must recognize exile as inevitable.

In biblical Judaism trust and exile are inseparably coupled with rebellion. The story of Adam and Eve is not, as Nietzsche thought, "slavish Semitic obedience." On the contrary, the very meaning of the story is that the human being becomes human in rebelling against God, in ceasing to be a child and eating of the fruit of the tree of the knowledge of good and evil. Similarly the most famous statement of trust in the Book of Job—"He may slay me. I await it."—is followed by the statement, "But I will argue my ways to his face. This is my comfort, that a hypocrite cannot come before him." To bring each new situation into the dialogue with God means both faithfulness and contending. There can be no question here of "blind faith." When Kierkegaard made the story of Abraham's temptation to sacrifice Isaac the very paradigm of unquestioning obedience, he disregarded the story that appears just two chapters earlier in Genesis. Abraham not only pleads for the people of Sodom lest the innocent be destroyed with the guilty, but he contends with the Lord and demands that he be faithful to his own way of justice: "I who am dust and ashes have taken it upon myself to argue with the Lord. Will the Lord of justice not do justice?"

In Kierkegaard's interpretation of Abraham's "temptation" to sacrifice Isaac, moral responsibility disappears in favor of a "teleological suspension of the ethical" and an "absolute duty to the Absolute." In the actual story, however, Abraham does not sacrifice Isaac, but is only brought to that readiness that enables him to renew his *covenant* with God by bringing into it his relation to this unexpected son of his old age. The special covenant between God and Israel is the demand placed on Israel that it become "a kingdom of priests and a holy nation" (Exodus) through bringing every aspect of its existence—personal, social, economic, political, international—into its dialogue with God. Here social responsibility is not only the responsibility of one person to another, but the responsibility of a people as a people for its corporate existence. The prophets, accordingly, call the people to account not just as individuals who have strayed from the paths of righteousness, but as the Israel that has turned aside from the task for which it was "chosen"—the task of becoming a true people that realizes justice, righteousness, and loving kindness in genuine communal life and makes real the kingship of God in the social sphere as well as in the cultic and the specifically religious.

The covenant exists only in the mutuality of the address from God and the people's turning toward God. This covenant is no legal contract that can be made once for all; for it does not concern a part of the people's existence, but the whole. Therefore, with Israel as with Abraham, the covenant must be renewed again and again in each new existential and historical situation. The God who speaks to the people correspondingly, is not a cosmic God who guarantees a universal moral order, but the God of the Ten Commandments whose "Thou shalt" is apprehended by the individual person and by the group only in the unique, concrete situation—the ever-renewed demand of the ever new present. It is only modern consciousness that has converted these commands into the impersonal "one must" of the social norm. The "ought" implicit in the command can be derived only from the responsibility of the person to what claims one in the particular situation in which one finds oneself. One does not *apply* the Ten Commandments to the situation: one *rehears* them as utterly unique, present commands. Only through this "rehearing" do injunctions such as not to kill, not to steal, and not to bear false witness take on concrete meaning. You cannot "deal lovingly" with your neighbor as "one equal to yourself" as a general principle, but only in a mutual relationship in the concrete, particular situation.

Far from being opposites, "Love your neighbor as yourself" and "an eye for an eye and a tooth for a tooth" are the direct and indirect statements of the same principle. "An eye for an eye and a tooth for a tooth" is *not* the expression of a vengeful God, but a primitive statement of basic social democracy in which no person is held of greater worth than another, because each is created in the image of God. Such equality of person and person existed nowhere outside of Israel in the ancient world. Throughout all history, indeed, the natural *inequality* of human beings has justified razing a whole city to revenge the murder of one privileged person; countless other persons have been exterminated with impunity because they were slaves or serfs or members of an "inferior race." "An eye for an eye" is not a religious rite, but a social law based on a fundamental conception of social justice. No society has ever got further than this principle in its actual administration of justice (despite all the talk about a higher "law of love"), and many still are not up to it.

What keeps "an eye for an eye" from deteriorating into an abstract principle that ignores the uniqueness of each person and each situation is, "Deal lovingly with your neighbor as one equal to yourself." Justice, which regulates the indirect relations of persons, and love, which channels the direct, do not oppose, but complement, each other. The Ten Commandments proceed from the relationship to the God whom the people met in history ("I am the Lord your God who brought you out of the land of Egypt, out of the house of bondage") and on this basis point to the demands of the covenant in the meeting between person and person. In Exodus, the same book of the Bible in which the Ten Commandments first appear, this recognition of the equality of one's fellow before God is extended to all persons on that simple human basis of reciprocity that underlies the Golden Rule—seeing oneself in the situation of the other: "You shall not wrong a stranger or oppress him, for you were strangers in the land of Egypt" (22:21). "You know the heart of a stranger, for you were strangers in the land of Egypt" (23:9). The person confronting you may be weak and powerless, but even so she remains in dialogue with God and God will hear her cry: "You shall not afflict any widow or orphan...I will surely hear their cry" (22:22–23). "If ever you take your neighbor's garment in pledge, you shall restore it to him before the sun goes down; for that is his only covering, it is the mantle for his body; in what else shall he sleep? And if he cries to me, I will hear, for I am compassionate" (22:26–27). The compassion of God to us is also the compassion that we must exercise to our fellow, even to our enemy: "If you meet your enemy's ox or his ass going astray, you shall bring it back to him. If you see the ass of one who hates you lying under its burden, you shall refrain from leaving him with it, you shall help him to lift it up" (23:3–5).

The *doing* of the Torah grows first out of the *hearing* in the dialogue with God, the social responsibility out of the covenantal relationship. "You shall be holy; for I the Lord your God am holy" (Lev. 19). "The wages of a hired servant shall not remain with you all night until the morning. You shall not curse the deaf or put a stumbling block before the blind, but you shall fear your God: I am the Lord" (Lev. 19:13–14). The "fear of the Lord" is not the fear of punishment, but the awe before the Creator and his creation, before the otherness of the other person who cannot be treated as a mere extension of my own subjectivity. "The fear of the Lord" is not only "the beginning of wisdom," as the Book of Job says; it is also the beginning of the love of God and the love of the human being. "You must not hate your brother in your heart...you shall not take vengeance...you shall love your neighbor as yourself: I am the Lord" (Lev. 19:17–18).

To love your neighbor as yourself does not mean selflessness nor does it mean identification or empathy with your neighbor. It means, rather, meeting the other as a unique person of value in herself and experiencing the relationship from her side as well as from your own. This means that the command "Deal lovingly with your neighbor as one equal to yourself" is never an external command that I transfer from my relation to God to my relation to the human being. Rather it is precisely in meeting the other that I meet God, and in the moment when I have to do with you, there is no other way to this meeting. "The stranger who sojourns with you shall be to you as the native among you, and you shall love him as yourself; for you were strangers in the land of Egypt: I am the Lord your God" (Lev. 19:33–34).

The Torah is not, as has been thought from Saint Paul to Freud, a series of harsh laws, impossible of fulfillment, setting a standard of perfection that none can live up to and thereby condemning all alike to be sinners.

> This commandment which I command you this day is not too hard for you, neither is it far off. It is not in heaven, that you should say, "Who will go up for us to heaven and bring it to us, that we may hear it and do it?..." But the word is very near you; it is in your mouth and in your heart, so that you can do it. (Deut. 30:11–14)

It is the sufficient amount that is asked of one each day. This way of hearing and responding in the concrete present is the way of authentic existence for the individual and the people: "See, I have set before you this day life and good, death and evil. Therefore choose life" (Deut. 30:15). No external sanction or social contract is needed here as a basis for moral action and social responsibility. They are of intrinsic value as the path that the human being walks with God in history.

The prophetic protest is always essentially a call to turn back to God with one's whole existence. This turning (*teshuvah*) means shouldering anew the task of the covenant—the task of making real the kingship of God through becoming a true people in every aspect of communal and individual life. When the people follow a neighboring kingdom in sacrificing their firstborn children to the god Moloch, the prophet Micah tells them that something very much less and very much more is demanded of them, namely, their whole existence: "to do justice, and to love kindness and to walk humbly with your God" (Micah 6:7–8). In the Book of Amos similarly, it is not "religion" but true community that is called for. The demand that Amos places on the nations in the name of God is the demand of the "covenant of brotherhood." It is out of this context that the vision of the Messiah arises, the "anointed one" through whom God will be with us (Immanuel) since through his leadership the true king will lead the people, or the remnant who have remained faithful, to make real the kingship of God. His reign will be characterized by peace, justice, and righteousness; in other words, by leading the people back to the task of the covenant. "With righteousness he shall judge the poor, and decide with equity for the meek of the earth" (Is. 1:4). The "suffering servant" of Deutero-Isaiah is no king but a prophet, but he, too, is seen as continuing the work of the covenant: "I have kept you and given you as a covenant to the people, to establish the land, to apportion the desolate heritage; saying to the prisoners, 'Come forth,' to those who are in darkness, 'Appear' " (Is. 49:8–9). Even the anonymous suffering and death of this man for which the people despise and reject him, believing him smitten by God (chap, 53), must be understood within the context of social responsibility. The person who remains an integral part of the community, while at the same time remaining faithful to the covenant from which the community has turned away, suffers much more than the lonely mystic who cuts himself off from responsibility for the community in which he dwells. By standing one's ground and bearing this terrible suffering, the "servant" carries social responsibility into the depths of tragedy where political success and effectiveness give way before the direct communal reality that works in the hidden ground springs of history.

The covenant is not theology. It has to do with human history, with real situations. In one historical situation Amos emphasizes *zedakah*, righteousness; in another Hosea emphasizes *hesed*, loving kindness: "I will heal your backslidings, I will love you freely"; in still another Isaiah emphasizes *kedoshah*, holiness. The word of demand and the word of comfort are both real covenantal words. It is not a question of what sort of God each prophet believed in but of the situation into which God speaks. That is why every Bible that translates the Tetragrammaton, the ineffable and unpronounceable name of God, as Jehovah or Yahweh, including the *Jerusalem Bible*, completely misses the imageless God who is not known in himself but only in his relation with human history. This God does not say, "I am that I am," but, as Buber translates it, "I shall be there *as* I shall be there."

4

Jesus: Image of the Human or Image of God?

"Take no thought for the morrow, for the morrow shall take thought for itself. . . .The kingdom of heaven is among you."

The Sermon on the Mount

"Why callest thou me good? Only God is good. . . .If I bear witness to myself and not to him who sent me, I witness false."

The Gospel according to John

"It is better to marry than to burn."—**Saint Paul**

Biblical Judaism is the mother of both rabbinical Judaism and orthodox Christianity and, by the same token, the grandmother or great-grandmother of modern Judaism and modern Christianity. Despite the continuity of the name and people, it should not surprise us, therefore, that there is much in present day Judaism that is farther from biblical Judaism than the teachings of Jesus who stood within the living tradition of biblical and early rabbinic Judaism.

In all of my encounters with Christianity, the Sermon on the Mount (Matthew 5–7) has had an important place. This is not because I imagine that Jesus gave this sermon as such. The evidence, on the contrary, is that it is made up of many fragments, and I am inclined to credit the Sharmon approach which suggests that Luke's "Blessed are you poor" is more probably the form in which Jesus would have addressed the simple fisher folk he was supposed to have been talking

43

to in Galilee than Matthew's "Blessed are the poor in spirit."[1] For all this, I have come back to the Sermon on the Mount again and again because it forms a whole, because it is central to so much of Christianity, and because it raises such basic problems.

One of the most basic is the use of the phrase "the kingdom of heaven." This is often taken by Christians to refer, as a matter of course, to heaven in the Christian sense. I am more inclined to believe, both from the usage of the day and the context in which it is used, that it refers to *Malchut Shamayim*, a common synonym for God. Certainly the emphasis in later Christianity upon this world's being a forecourt for the sake of gaining admission to heaven is hardly borne out by Jesus' emphasis upon the present. "Take no thought for the morrow, for the morrow shall take thought for itself... / Sufficient unto the day is the evil thereof." To be sure, this passage is prefaced by a contrast between laying up treasures on earth where thieves break in and rust destroys, but the meaning of this passage is made unmistakable when Jesus adds, immediately afterward, "No man can serve God and mammon. If the eye be single, the whole body is full of light." Jesus' emphasis is clearly upon loving God with all one's heart, soul, mind, and might, and such love means an unconditional trust that does not suffer the present moment to be used as a mere means to a future end. Jesus does not disparage the need for food, clothing, and shelter. Rather he says, "Your heavenly father knows you need these things," and adds, "Seek you first the Kingdom of God and all these things shall be added unto you." The Kingdom of God, or the Kingdom of Heaven, is not thought of here as an afterlife but as finding authentic existence in the present through bringing one's life into dialogue with God. "You are the salt of the earth," says Jesus. "If the salt hath lost its savor, wherewith shall it be salted?" We are the beings who give special meaning to the earth, yet if we have lost that authentic humanity that makes us human, nothing else—neither prosperity nor power nor prestige—can make up for this lack. For Jesus the Kingdom of Heaven is in us, and it is also among us.

Jesus begins the Sermon on the Mount with a series of paradoxes, on the basic of which some have assumed a dualism between the material and the spiritual. But little or nothing in all of the Synoptic Gospels confirms this interpretation. Rather, as Jesus says, "narrow is the way, and strait is the gate": the road to authentic existence is a difficult one—and yet so easy since it means a trust that leaves to God the "morrow" as do the lilies of the field. This trust is a continuation of the biblical *emunah*, that unconditional trust in the relationship with God which characterizes Psalm 23 ("Though I walk through the valley of the shadow of death, I shall fear no evil") and Psalm 91 ("He shall not suffer thy foot to stumble"). It is this latter verse that Satan quotes to Jesus as the second of the temptations in the wilderness. He takes him to the top of the Temple and invites him to throw himself down as proof that it is he of whom this was said. Jesus' reply, "Thou shalt not tempt God," is not only a quote from Deuteronomy, referring to the people's tempting Moses to strike the rock with his staff and produce water; it is also thoroughly biblical in spirit. *Emunah* is not a magic security, a guarantee that God will *have* to protect his favored one. It is a trust that remains constant even when we walk, as we must, through the valley of the shadow of death.

What are we to make of the series of contrasts in the Sermon on the Mount: "You have heard it said...But I say unto you..."? Most of them are from the direction of outer action to inner intention, but one of them at least (that concerning divorce) is in the opposite direction. The emphasis on *kavana,* or inner intention, was nothing new in Judaism, either in the Pentateuch or in the Prophets or in the Pharisees. What appears new is the valuing of purity of intention above purity of action. "Who shall stand on God's holy hill?" asks Psalm 24. "He who has clean hands and a pure heart"—not one or the other but both. Does Jesus in fact mean what Paul later taught in *Romans*—a dualism between the outer action "that killeth" and the inner spirit "that quickeneth"? "You have heard it said that you shall not commit adultery, but I say unto you that he who looks at a woman to lust after her has already committed adultery with her in his heart." What are we to make of this statement? If it be taken as the realism that "as a man thinketh, so he is," we can only call it a fair extension of what the commandment already implies. If we take it as a call to kill all lust within the soul, it becomes a counsel of perfection appropriate to the Christian saint but not to the Jewish image of the human as forever tempted anew by the "evil urge" whose passion one must direct into the service of God. If we take it to mean that adultery is all right just so long as it is not committed with an impure heart, we fall into an antinomian gnosticism that is clearly far from Jesus' intention. If we take it to apply to the Christian image of the human in general, we run head on against a strand in Christianity that sees the human being as given over to "original sin," associated by Saint Augustine with lust. In *Romans* Paul urges the average individual to compromise since "it is better to marry than to burn" whereas in Ephesians he urges husbands to love their wives as their own bodies, as Christ loved and cleansed the Church.

How in the midst of all this are we to get back to what Jesus himself meant? I do not know. It has always seemed to me that Jesus never spoke against sex or marriage as such, but rather asked his disciples for total allegiance in response to the unusual demands of the hour.

This is that "ethic of perfection" to which Albert Schweitzer points as associated with the expectation of a speedy coming of the kingdom. Nor can I see Jesus' statement as so much opposing as supplementing the commandment he cites. The Jewish position, in any case, occupies a middle point—one in which purity of heart can never be attained entirely since temptation and the "evil urge" remain real, yet one in which the "evil urge" never becomes an "original sin" that necessitates human sinfulness unless and until one is redeemed by unmerited grace.

Whatever the difference between the everyday ethic of the Pharisees and Jesus' ethic of perfection and whatever his notions about his own messiahship, Jesus did not call on his disciples to have faith in him but in God. Paul also knew trust in God—the first Epistle to the Corinthians is a great statement of it—but it is a trust that is always "through Jesus Christ our Lord." Due to his profound experience of inner division and the still more profound conversion experience that delivered him from it, it is in this form only that Paul knows the love of God, and it is in this form only that he sees others as knowing it. The immediacy between God and the human is now broken by original sin, and it may only be restored by faith in Christ. "Wherefore, as by one man sin entered into the world, and death by sin; and so death passed upon all men, for that all have sinned" (Rom. 5:12). The "law" is no longer the Torah which guides us in our dialogue with God but a part of a fearful dialectic in which our consciousness of the law makes us "exceedingly sinful" so that only unmerited grace can redeem us. This means, for those who remain faithful to the God of Jesus but do not belong to the "household of faith" in Christ, the abolition of that immediacy between God and the human that had been the essence of the covenant and the kingship of God. The law was added to the promise to Abraham, says Paul in Galatians, because of transgressions, till the offspring should come to whom the promise had been made— Christ; "and it was ordained by angels through an intermediary" (like the Gnostic archons). "The scripture consigned all things to sin, that what was promised to faith in Jesus Christ might be given to those who believe...the law was our custodian until Christ came, that we might be justified by faith" (Gal 3:17–24). " 'I am the door' it now runs (John 10:9)" writes Buber in his contrast between the *trust* (*emunah*) of Jesus and the *faith* with a knowledge content (*pistis*) of John and Paul. "It avails nothing, as Jesus thought, to knock where one stands before the 'narrow door'); it avails nothing, as the Pharisees thought, to step into the open door; entrance is only for those who believe in 'the door.'[2]

Both types of faith are present in full strength in Christianity. Consider the use of miracles in the New Testament. We are told that when Jesus was crucified and gave up the ghost, the veil of the Temple was rent and many other wonders happened "in order that you might believe." Jesus, however, speaks differently of miracles. He tells the woman who touches his robe and is healed of an issue of blood that it is her faith that has made her whole, and he tells his disciples that if they have but as much faith as a grain of seed, they can move mountains. In other words, for Jesus miracles are not the cause of faith but at most the product of faith.

Idolatry does not arise through images of God but through any one image being taken to be God. Certainly the imagelessness of God has been a central emphasis in Judaism, yet there has been no lack in Judaism of Talmudists, philosophers, and *halachists* who have wanted to fix God in one image or another. The problem is not whether the imageless God reveals himself, as he must if there is to be a relationship to him, but whether these revelations are taken as universal, objective attributes of God or as God's relationship to human beings in concrete situations, capable of being transformed and renewed in still other concrete situations.

A few years ago I took part in a remarkable dialogue with an English Quaker who was at that time perhaps the leading theologian in the Society of Friends. The dialogue was before an audience, but the audience was not invited to take part in order that the dialogue might not turn into a debate. So far from seeing Christ as an article of faith that one must hold to, the theologian fully subscribed to Buber's I-Thou trust as the center of the relationship to God or Christ. What is more, in contrast to *both* the universalists and the fundamentalists among the Friends, he and I saw eye to eye on the meaning of the Bible as a history of unique moments of revelation, as demand and response in concrete historical situations. He did not deny the revelation of God at other times and situations than that of Christ, nor could I remain indifferent to his witness to Christ: it was a deeply moving statement from a truly religious person that I could not fail to honor. In short, his point of view was much closer to mine than to that of many Quakers, and my point of view was much closer to his than to that of many Jews.

Where then was the difference between us? At one point only, and it is a point that perhaps illuminates the subtle difference between image and imagelessness of God in Judaism and Christianity. If he had only wished to witness that for him the fullest, most complete, and most perfect revelation of God was in Christ, I should not have been troubled by this witness, even if I could not share it. But when he objectified his witness into the theological statement that Christ *is* the fullest conceivable revelation of God, he had in that moment gone over from *trust* to *belief*. "You are my witnesses, saith the Lord," we read in Isaiah, and the Talmud adds, "If you are not my witnesses, than I as it were, am not the Lord." What is this but a reiteration of the covenantal relationship in which we witness for God through bringing every aspect of our lives into dialogue with him? But the Jehovah's Witnesses have objectified this "witness" into something that can be handed out in pamphlets, memorized speeches, and phonograph records. Just such objectification takes place if one claims that the Jews *are* the "chosen people" in abstraction from the covenant—that dynamic of relationship and falling away from relationship which led Hosea to name his son *Lo-Ami*, "Not my People," when Israel had turned away from God.

Martin Buber contrasts the prophet who *speaks* to the people in the historical situation and calls for a decision that may affect the character of the next hour with the apocalyptic *writer* who sees the future as already fixed and is only concerned with foreseeing it. Jesus, in my view, stands in the tradition of the prophets who called on the people to turn back (*teshuvah*) and thought they had the power to do so. Paul, on the other hand, despairs of himself and of others and sees the initiative as necessarily coming from God—not just in the address to us but even in the grace that enables us to respond to that address. "Put off your old nature which belongs to your former manner of life and is corrupt through deceitful lusts and be renewed in the spirit of your minds, and put on the new nature, created after the likeness of God in true righteousness and holiness" (Eph. 4:22-24). The contemporary Pauline theologian, Emil Brunner, sees us as sundered from God by our original sin: God bridges the gap with his grace while we receive but cannot initiate.

Paul's cosmic view of all becoming sinful through the giving of the law at Sinai and of being redeemed from sin only at Golgotha removes from those who have not taken on a new nature in Christ the possibility of turning back to God and receiving forgiveness that is always open in the Hebrew Bible. Insofar as Pauline Christianity has held us unable to do any good thing of ourselves and has seen us as entirely dependent upon the grace that comes through Christ, the apocalyptic lineaments of the despair of history and the "Good News" coming from the supernatural breaking into history are there.

Very often, of course, as in the thought of Reinhold Niebuhr, both elements are subtly mixed. Niebuhr strongly objects to what he regards as Paul Tillich's equation of creation with the Fall. Creation is good, says Niebuhr, and the Fall comes not through man's existence as flesh but through his will that tries to absolutize what is in fact only relative. Niebuhr rejects "original sin" as any biological inheritance *à la* Augustine, but he affirms it as our social inheritance and as the sinful overstepping of creaturely limitations that, not necessarily but most probably, we will fall into again and again.

Insofar as modern Judaism has turned from the literal belief in the coming of the messiah at a specific time, it has turned from the apocalpytic. Insofar, however, as it has turned to a "messianism" that is equivalent to progress toward universal ideals, it has *not* turned toward the prophetic. It is a lamentable fact that a great deal of modern Jewish thinking is far less concerned with the prophetic reality of historical demand and decision than a great deal of modern Christian thought.

Israel, to the Hebrew Bible, means the actual people Israel who became a people through the Sinai Covenant and who remain one insofar as they are faithful to this covenant. This covenant, as we have seen, is to become "a kingdom of priests and a holy people." A holy people does not mean a collection of well-meaning individuals but a true community: imitating God's justice, righteousness, and holiness in the life between person and person *and* in the social, political, economic, and international life of the people. There is no distinction here between the religious and the social since the religious for the Hebrew Bible is not a separate dimension transcending history but the demand that the Transcendent places on the human in history. The unity of these two spheres, which have come apart in modern life and thought, is clearly grasped by Jesus when he gives as the first commandment, "Thou shalt love the Lord thy God with all thy heart, soul, mind, and might," and as the second, "which is like unto the first," "Thou shalt love thy neighbor as thyself." Many uninformed Christians do not realize that these two commandments were quoted by Jesus from Deuteronomy and Leviticus. It was with amazement, however, that I heard so eminent a Christian minister and thinker as Pastor Martin Niemoeller say that what was unique in Jesus' teaching was putting the two commandments together. From the Lord's reply to Cain, "Thy brother's blood cries out to me from the ground," to "Thou shalt love thy neighbor as thyself. I am the Lord," these two dimensions have always been joined in the Hebrew Bible, as in Judaism in general.

If we recognize this, we still have the question of how the old and new covenants differ, since Jesus himself stood so clearly in the tradition of the biblical covenant when he cited these two commandments together. In terms of Jesus himself, it must be said that he addressed his hearers more often as individuals rather than as the people of Israel. So far as orthodox Christianity's understanding of the Covenant and Israel is concerned, however, the difference is a more radical one. For Christianity there is a new Israel, an invisible Church, that unites all who have been reborn in Christ. This new Israel differs from the old in that it is not an actual community able to respond to a demand placed upon it as a people, but a spiritual band of widely separated individuals whose communal and social lives are lived in practical distinction from their membership in the invisible Church. The one covenant is associated with a task—the realization of the kingship of God through which Israel may serve as the beginning of the kingdom of God. The other is associated with a fulfilled reality—the partaking in the redemption through Christ that is already there for all who share in this communion.

The understanding of the messiah is a corollary of the understanding of Israel and the covenant. For biblical Judaism the messiah is not a divine figure who can bring redemption in himself but a person who can lead the people or a remnant of the people in turning back to God, fulfilling the covenants and making real the kingship of God. This is evident from the passages on Immanuel in Isaiah in which Immanuel is associated with the tasks of justice and righteousness to which the prophets had continually called the kings. It is also clear in Deutero-Isaiah where the suffering servant takes over this task of leading the remnant in the renewal of the covenant. The suffering of the servant may best be understood, in my opinion, not as vicarious suffering for others but as the terrible suffering that the hidden servant takes on himself by turning back to God while remaining a member of a faithless community.

The Christian conception of the messiah is very different. The root of the word in "the anointed" no longer signifies a tie to the task of realizing the kingship of God. Instead Christ is the divine figure, the Son of God, who in his oneness with God steps on the other side of the divine-human dialogue and effects a redemption that takes the place of rather than fulfills the task of becoming "a holy people." This is not the messiah who leads humans to the redemptive turning but the messiah who has already redeemed them through his crucifixion and resurrection if they are ready to accept this grace through their faith in Christ. One of the saddest aspects of the Jewish-Christian dialogue is the failure of even such eminent Christian thinkers as Jacques Maritain to recognize the essential difference between these two concepts of the messiah. As a result, they regularly attribute the Jewish rejection of Christ to a desire for a materialistic messiah who will lead them to worldly victory. This dualism between the spiritual and the material is so strongly ingrained in some strains of Christianity that it is difficult for many Christians to understand the Jewish concept of the messiah, to which such a dualism is entirely foreign.

But how about Jesus himself? Did he think of himself as the messiah in the Jewish sense or the Christian sense? The texts are far from clear, but it is as unthinkable to me that Jesus thought of himself as the messiah in the Christian sense as that he said, "Take up your cross and follow me," with foreknowledge of the central significance of the cross after his own crucifixion, or that he said to Peter, "On this rock I found my church," and meant by it the Roman Catholic Church, a type of religious structure then entirely unknown in the world.

Did Jesus think of himself as the messiah in the Jewish sense? Here too the texts are not clear. Buber thinks that Jesus' "Thou sayest it" in reply to Pilate suggests that he saw himself, in the pattern of the apocryphal texts, as the suffering servant who has had a preexistence in heaven. To me the most intriguing interchange is the one in which he asks the disciples who people say he is and then asks them who they think he is. "Christ, the Son of the Living God," says Peter, and "Jesus charged them that they tell no man of it." Seen in retrospect, the question is one of what category Jesus fits into. Seen from within as a present event, it cannot be that, for the category does not exist. What do the forty days' wrestling with Satan in the wilderness mean but the temptation of a person who knows himself called and yet must discover again in each new situation just what it means that he is called? When I. S. Eliot's Thomas à Becket is martyred, the category of the martyr, the objective and selfless instrument of God, is there ready-made for him to fill. Jesus, on the contrary, had to go through the terrible tension of a unique call that he could not know objectively but only as he responded with his whole being to the unheard of demand of the new moment. When he prays in the Garden of Gethsemane, "Father, if it be thy will may this cup be taken from me," he is not, like Eliot's Thomas, a person who has lost his own will in the will of God. Rather he is a person in anguish who wills to live, if it be God's will, but who is ready to accept God's will if it is not. And when he prays on the cross, "Eli, Eli, lama sabachtani!" he is not merely reciting a psalm, as those who wish to see him as very God but not as very man suppose; he is experiencing again the terrible anguish of the unique vocation in which he has answered the call but in this moment experiences no confirming answer.

It has been customary for many liberal Jews to wish to show their broadmindedness toward Jesus by enrolling him in the ranks of "the prophets" or "teachers" of Israel. In a broad sense of the terms, we can agree with this. But he was no prophet in the exact meaning of the term, and though he was certainly a teacher, he played a unique role in his life that bursts the bounds of any such category. A common Jewish protest against Jesus is that he spoke in his own name—"But I say unto you"—and not in the name of God, as did the prophets. At the end of the Sermon on the Mount, we read that the people were astonished, "for he taught them as one who had authority, and not as their scribes." But the prophets also taught with authority and not as the scribes. "I am no prophet and no son of a prophet," says Amos, "but when the lion roars who can but tremble and when the Lord God speaks who can but prophesy?" Jeremiah never tires of belaboring the false prophets while being able to evince no authority of his own other than, "Of a truth the Lord hath sent me," Still, they do speak in the name of God, and even Moses, who is pictured as closer to God than any human, spoke to the people only in the name of God and not in his own name.

But does Jesus speak in his own name as if he were God? The texts do not bear this out. "Not every one who says to me, 'Lord, Lord,' shall enter the kingdom of heaven, but he who does the will of my Father who is in heaven," says Jesus in the Sermon on the Mount. And even in John, the most theological of the Gospels, it says, "Why callest thou me good? Only God is good," and "If I bear witness to myself and not to him who sent me, I witness false." When Jesus cites the two main commandments, he speaks of loving God rather than of loving or believing in himself. Jesus' awareness of a unique calling undoubtedly contributed to the ring of authority in his voice. But equally important, surely, is the reaction against the Scribes who carried on tradition without *kavana*, or inner intention, and the fact that, as George Foote Moore has pointed out, this was the age of an individual piety to our Father in Heaven—a piety which Jesus exemplified in a unique and uniquely intense way.

One of the most important stumbling blocks in the relation of the contemporary Jew to Christianity is the widespread tendency to regard "an eye for an eye and a tooth for a tooth" as a description of a vengeful God and the tendency to contrast this passage with "love thy neighbor as thyself," as if the latter did not also come from Leviticus but originated in the New Testament. Christianity has rejected the Marcionite gnosticism that wished to cut off the Old Testament as the product of an evil Creator God, but there has lingered in Christianity just enough of the Gnostic apologetic to stamp indelibly in the popular mind the notion that the God of the Old Testament is a God of wrath as opposed to the Christian God of love. The texts, of course, do not bear this out. There is no end of "gnashing of teeth and wailing in the outer darkness" in the New Testament whereas in the Old there is no suggestion of a hell where the wicked are punished. The lovingkindness, mercy, and compassion of God are emphasized in countless passages throughout the Hebrew Bible, and God's wrath is seen as but minor in comparison. "For a little while I hid my face in wrath but with long-suffering compassion I have loved thee," says Deutero- or Trito- Isaiah. And there are a thousand sayings of the Talmudic Fathers and of the Hasidim that one might adduce in addition.

No amount of citing texts is going to remove this mind-set, however. It can only be removed, if at all, by a new way of thinking. Our mention of the Gnostics gives us a clue to a basic way of thinking about this problem. That is in terms of the meaning of God's oneness in biblical Judaism. "I the Lord make peace and create evil," says Deutero-Isaiah, probably in conscious opposition to whatever Zoroastrian dualism had entered the culture. To affirm God's oneness is to affirm that there is no realm or power separate from God, that there is no "devil" in the Christian sense, that Satan is nothing other than God himself tempting us, and tempting us not to damnation but in order that we may realize hitherto unfulfilled possibilities of dialogue with God. It is this basic esistential trust that underlies the *emunah* that says, "I shall fear no evil for thou art with me." Job, to be sure, was tempted in such a way that he saw God as mocking the calamity of the guiltless, but he never "appealed from God to God," as the scholar Robert Pfeiffer assumes in his interpretation of "I know that my redeemer liveth." Even in the tension between his trust in God and his insistence on justice, Job never ceases to affirm the dialogue with God into which *all* the evil that he experiences must be brought.

When it is no longer possible to hold this tension, then Job's question does indeed lead to the Gnostic dualism in which creation and the God of creation are seen as evil, and redemption is redemption *from* rather than *of* the evil of creation. This is the the dualism that is embodied in Dostoevsky's "Legend of the Grand Inquisitor" in *The Brothers Karamazov* in which the merciless justice of Ivan's Inquisitor is complemented by the completely unconditional forgiveness of his Christ, who places no demand of wholeness or authentic existence on the Inquisitor but leaves him sundered into a being whose actions betray Christ while Christ's kiss "glows in his heart." "My God is a nicer God than Amos's," said a freshman student in one of my classes. "Why is your God nicer than Amos's?" I asked. "Because he forgives *everything*," she replied. I thought about this for a moment and then asked her, "If he forgives everything, then what is there to forgive?" The answer was obvious—it was the guilt she had accumulated in that other, everyday sphere of life ruled over by parents and teachers and withdrawn from God's mercy! Even if she had not confessed that she kept her God in the closet when she was a child, it would be evident that we are confronted here with the sort of practical dualism that leads guilt-ridden people like Ivan to imagine, in utmost contrast to Jesus himself, a Christ who forgives everything and demands nothing. Surely it is such a dualism between God and creation that leads Kierkegaard to his unbiblical "suspension of the ethical" and his equally unbiblical picture of Abraham as the "knight of faith" who renounces and receives back the finite (Isaac) in lonely relation with the Transcendent.

The true mercy of God in the Hebrew Bible is that he cares that we become human, that we live a true life, that Israel make real the covenant and the kingship of God by becoming a holy people. It is this caring and concern that lies behind God's anger. It is a demand placed in a situation rather than an attribute of God. The meaning of human life is found in the dialogue with God; the meaning of Israel's existence as a people is found in the covenant. For God not to ask Israel "Where art thou?" as he asked Adam, would be a "mercy" that was no mercy, for it would abandon Israel to meaningless and inauthentic existence. God's calling to account is his mercy. It is no cutting off such as the Gnostic dualists fear. Adam and Eve must leave the Garden of Eden, Cain must become a wanderer on the face of the earth, Jacob must flee from Esau's wrath in the wilderness, Moses must stop short of the Promised Land, the suffering servant must die in disease and ignominy, Israel must be defeated and dispersed, but God is with them all in their exile. To seek a God who is all-merciful in the face of an existence that is anything but would be to settle for a practical dualism in which God must make up for the Godforsaken creation in which we are flung. To accept the real terrors of existence and bring them into the dialogue with God is to understand, as Job did at last, the mercy that is contained even in God's anger. Not to understand conceptually, of course, but in the uniqueness of one's dialogue with God.

If one defines Jewish messianism in terms of becoming a holy people in real community, one must say that an impressive number of small Christian brotherhood groups—such as the Friends, the Brethren, and the Mennonites—come much nearer to this goal than the modern Jewish community center, which often has all the aspects of real living together except actual community, on the one hand, and the centrality of the covenant, on the other. Nonetheless, we cannot regard the Christian brotherhood group, in its Anabaptist and Quaker forms, as the true inheritor of the biblical covenant, for it stands on the ground not of an uncompleted task but of the already accomplished redemption in which it is the presence of Christ that unites and transforms.

When we look at modern Christianity, we are bewildered by its variety and seek in vain to find a key that unites it in all its differences. This same variety extends to contemporary Christian thought, but here at least one key comes to our service: the understanding of Christianity as a mixture of the biblical and the Greek, in which the proportions and method of the mixture determine some of the most outstanding differences. When we then look at the spectrum of modern Judaism, we find almost as great a range if not so much variety, and when we look at contemporary Jewish thought, we find some of the very issues in the mixture of the biblical and the Greek that we have found in contemporary Christian thought.

A helpful approach to this mixture of the biblical and the Greek is the contrast between two types of knowing: *emunah* and *gnosis*, the direct knowing of trust and the contemplative, comprehensive, or indirect knowing of philosophical and theosophical faith. We shall certainly not be able to apply this typology as a simple key to the differences between Judaism and Christianity since a great deal of Christianity has been characterized by the simple knowing of a trust relationship whereas *gnosis* has again and again entered into Judaism, from Philo's Platonizing allegory of the Bible through the Merkabah mystics, to the medieval Jewish philosophers and the Kabbala.

For the Judaism of the Hebrew Bible, of Hasidism, and of such contemporary philosophers of Judaism as Martin Buber, Franz Rosenzweig, and Abraham Heschel knowing is, to begin with, a reciprocal contact, as when "Adam knew Eve" or God knew the prophet Hosea. This knowing takes place within the relationship of trust, the biblical *emunah*. Faith and knowing are not opposites or separate spheres for these types of Judaism, therefore, as they so often are in Christianity. The biblical human being does not find *Torah*, or guidance, in the order of the cosmos—the Greek *moira*—but in the unmediated dialogue with God who alone causes the sun to rise up and seals the stars. "He goeth by me and I perceive him not." Therefore, the beginning of wisdom for the Hebrew Bible is not *gnosis*—whether that means theology, cosmology, ontology, or even Plato's poetic vision of the Good—but "fear of the Lord," awe before the Reality that we can meet but cannot comprehend. This awe does not mean primitive superstition, as the Russian Orthodox philosopher Nicolas Berdyaev thinks, but the givenness of existence itself, which leads Heschel to declare that the beginning of religion, knowledge, and art is awareness of the ineffable. "All religious reality," writes Buber, "begins with the 'fear of God' "; this is the dark gate through which the person of *emunah* "steps forth directed and assigned to the concrete, contextual situations of his existence."[3]

The fear of the Lord has never led in Judaism, as it has in some types of Christianity, to putting away knowing. It has led, rather, to the Talmudist's recognition that that wisdom which is not grounded in existence will not stand, to the essential Talmudic teaching that all argument which takes place "for the sake of Heaven" endures, even though opposite and mutually incompatible points of view are put forward, to the recognition that the *doing* of the people in the covenant with God comes before the hearing, that the hearing of what is asked cames out of entering into the dialogue with God. This is a truth which one does not possess but to which one relates. It is not knowledge of God as he is in himself—neither proof of his existence nor description of his nature and attributes. Revelation to it is never something objective that God hands over to us, any more than it is a mere subjective inspiration. It is address and response in which, as Heschel points out, the response is as much a part of the revelation as the address. It is the Word of God, but this Word is not Karl Barth's Word that comes from the distance of the Wholly Other. God and the human may be radically separate, but as Franz Rosenzweig has said in criticism of Harnack and Barth, the Word of God and the human word are the same. They *must* be the same for the very meaning and existence of the word. The word does not exist in some hypostasized substantiality, like the Logos of Plato, but is a lived reality of the "between." It comes to us not out of the hyperborean blue but in the concrete, contextual situations of history.

The meaning of history, in consequence, is not an objective one that may be seen from above, but that of dialogue. The meaning of history tells me only what history's challenge is to me, what its claim is on me. This is not subjectivity. It is, rather, the refusal to lose sight of the given of our concrete situation—our existence face to face with a reality that comes to meet us and to which we can respond but which we cannot subsume under a single order or process or the chain of cause and effect. To preserve the existential reality of the present means to preserve history as dialogue. "Lord of the world," said the great Hasidic *zaddik* Rabbi Levi Yitzhak of Berditchev, "I do not beg you to reveal to me the secret of your ways—I could not bear it. But show me one thing; show it to me more clearly and more deeply: show me what this, which is happening at this very moment, means to me, what it demands of me, what you Lord of the world, are telling me by way of it." Levi Yitzhak concludes this prayer with the cry, "Ah, it is not why I suffer, that I wish to know, but only whether I suffer for your sake."[4] "Why I suffer" means here *gnosis*—an objective knowledge of the order of things that would enable Levi Yitzhak to place his suffering in relation to the overall scheme of cause and effect, reward and punishment. "That I suffer for thy sake" means the meaning found in the dialogue itself—a meaning which cannot be divorced from that dialogue and objectified but which is, nonetheless, a real knowing and not just a statement of blind faith. It is *emunah*, and the knowing that arises from this *emunah* is the open, dialogical knowing of the prophet rather than the closed monological knowing of the apocalyptic writer or the isolated philosopher.

5

Hasidism

"When I get to heaven, they will not ask me, 'Why were you not Moses?' but 'Why were you not Zusya?' "

"There is no rung of human life on which we cannot find the holiness of God everywhere and at all times."

"This is the service of men in the world to the very hour of their death: to struggle with the extraneous, and time after time to uplift and fit it into the nature of the Divine Name."
Martin Buber, *The Tales of the Hasidim*

Hasidism is the popular mystical movement of East European Jewry in the eighteenth and nineteenth centuries. The Hebrew word *hasid* mean "pious." It is derived from the noun *hesed*, meaning loving kindness, mercy, or grace. The Hasidic movement arose in Poland in the eighteenth century, and, despite bitter persecution at the hands of traditional rabbinism, spread rapidly among the Jews of eastern Europe until it included almost half of them in its ranks. Hasidism is really a continuation in many senses of biblical and rabbinical Judaism. While it is not a continuation of Christianity, many people have been startled by the resemblances between Hasidism and early Christianity, in particular between the founder of Hasidism—the Baal Shem Tov, or Good Master of the Name of God—and Jesus. Both spoke to the common, the ordinary folk; both represented something of a revolt against an overemphasis on learning; both tried to renew the spirit from within the tradition rather than destroying, cutting off, and radically changing the tradition.

The Hasidim founded real communities, each with its own *rebbe*. The *rebbe*, the leader of the community, was also called the *zaddik*, the righteous or justified person. "The world stands because of the *zaddik*," says the Talmud, and in Jewish legend this has grown into the myth of the thirty-six hidden *zaddikim* of each generation—the *lamedvovnikim*— without whom the world could not stand. Each one of these *zaddikim* had his own unique teaching that he gave to his community. Originally, as it was passed down from generation to generation, the leadership devolved not so much on those who could receive a doctrine but on those who could embody a way of life. So the first effect of the *zaddik* was to bring the people to immediacy in relationship to God. Later, when hereditary dynasties of Hasidim arose and the *rebbes* lived in great palaces and were surrounded by awe and superstition, the *zaddik* became almost a mediator between the people and God—the very opposite of his original function.

Hasidism, like Zen Buddhism, grew out of the most abstruse speculation—first the medieval Kabbala of the Zohar ("The Book of Splendor") and later the Lurian Kabbala that arose after the Jews were exiled from Spain in 1492. If you go today to Israel and go up the mountains opposite the Sea of Galilee, winding round and round you finally reach, near the top, *Zfat*, or Safed where the Lurian Kabbala arose. There Jewish mystics strove to bring the Messiah down. At one point in 1544, they all stood on the rooftops expecting that at that hour the Messiah would come. There developed in the Lurian Kabbala a marvelous gnostic doctrine in which the fall was not, as in the Zohar, a gradual emanation of ten *Sephiroth*. It was instead an event, a happening, in which heavenly vessels were so full of grace that they burst and the sparks of divine light fell downward to earth and were surrounded by shells of darkness. The *tikkun*, or restoration, meant accordingly freeing these sparks from their shells so that they could rise upward to their divine source. This could be done through *kavanot*—magical, mystical intentions with which one prayed and acted. It was believed that one could help bring the Messiah down through the part in the restoration that one's *kavanot* made possible. This led to the pseudo-messianic movement of Sabbatai Zvi, which ended disastrously when Sabbatai Zvi was forcibly converted to Islam. Out of all this ferment and the Chmielnieski Cossack massacres of hundreds of thousands of Jews in village after village in Eastern Europe was kindled the movement founded by Israel ben Eliezer (1700–1760), the Baal Shem Tov. The Baal Shem said, "I have come to teach you a new way, and it is not fasting and penance but joy in God, in Israel, and in the Torah."

Hasidism is a mysticism that does not hold chastity to be the highest virtue. On the contrary, it sees marriage as the highest form of life. It is a mysticism that does not turn away from community or put aside the life of the senses. Community is to be hallowed, the life of the senses celebrated and sanctified. Hasidism supplemented *kavanot* with *kavana*: it stressed the consecration and direction of the whole person as well as special mystical techniques.

The Baal Shem pointed out that Isaac and Jacob had to find their own unique relationship to God and could not base their searching on that of Abraham alone. The Besht's relationship to God was the meaning and goal of his strivings compared to which no future life was of importance. He did not emphasize mystical exercises but wholehearted turning to God. He preferred a passionate opponent to a lukewarm adherent. "For the passionate opponent may come over and bring all his passion with him. But from a lukewarm adherent there is nothing more to be hoped." He turned away from asceticism and mortification of the flesh to the joyful recognition that each person is a son of the King. But he did not mistake the son for the King. His last words were, "Let not the foot of pride come near me!"

In the end the most important heritage that Hasidism has bequeathed us is not its doctrine and teachings but its image of the human—the image of the Besht, the maggid of Mezritch, Levi Yitzhak of Berditchev, Nachman of Brazlav, Shneur Zalman of Ladi, the "Yehudi" of Pzhysha, and a host of other zaddikim, each with unique relationship to God and to his particular community.

One can find motifs in Hasidism that add up to a teaching—a human way, a way of life. But these motifs are very closely interrelated, and they are not so much parts of a system as they are wisdom. For example, Hasidism emphasizes the uniqueness of the person without stressing self-realization. "When I get to heaven," said Rabbi Zusya, they will not ask me: 'Why were you not Moses?' but 'Why were you not Zusya?' " We are called to become what we in our created uniqueness can become—not just to fulfill our social duty or realize our talent or potentialities, but to become the unique person we are called to be. This is not an already existing uniqueness that we can fulfill through "self-expression" or "self-realization." We have to realize our uniqueness in response to the world. A part of this response, for Zusya, was the fact that Moses was there for him—not as a model to imitate but as an image of the human that arose in dialogue and that entered into his own becoming. Why did you not become what only you could become? does not mean, Why were you not *different* from others, but Why did

you not fulfill the creative task you have become aware of as yours
alone?

> Rabbi Pinhas said: "When a man embarks on something
> great, in the spirit of truth, he need not be afraid that another
> may imitate him. But if he does not do it in the spirit of truth,
> but plans to do it in a way no one could imitate, then he drags
> the great down to the lowest level—and everyone can do the
> same."[1]

There is a great tendency in our culture to exalt the different and to
confuse the different with the unique. The "different" is merely a term
of comparison. The unique is something valued in and for itself. This
is very important; for the search for originality, which is so strong in
our day, usually takes the form of a different twist or a new wrinkle.
What we ought to be concerned about is our faithful response. If we
respond really faithfully, this will bring out our own uniqueness.

This also means, of course, that I must stand my ground and
witness for that unique creation which I am. When the servant forgot
to give Mendel a spoon, Rabbi Elimelech said, "Look, Mendel, you must
learn to ask for a spoon and if need be, for a plate too!" Mendel took
the words of his teacher to heart and his fortunes began to mend. This
is related to the contending with God which is essential to biblical faith.
"Every man should have two pockets to use as the occasion demands,"
said Rabbi Bunam, "in one of which are the words, 'For my sake the
world was created' and in the other the words, 'I am earth and ashes.' "
This balance—neither affirming yourself absolutely nor denying yourself
absolutely but recognizing that you are given a created ground on which
to stand and from which to move to meet the world—is the true humility
of Hasidism. "If God so desires, let him take our life," said the rabbi
of Ger, "but he must leave us that with which we love him—he must
leave us our heart." Usually, it is not God who takes away our heart
but we ourselves—by living in such a way that there are no free
moments in which our heart might open itself to the address of the
world and respond. "A human being who has not a single hour for
his own every day," said Rabbi Moshe Leib, "is no human being." This
is for me the most painful of all the Hasidic sayings; for I encounter
it again and again as a judgment on my way of life and on that of most
of my contemporaries! The fact that we ourselves have chosen our form
of slavery does not make it any less slavery.

To realize one's uniqueness rules out every form of imitation, even
of Abraham, Isaac, and Jacob. "Each one of us in his own way shall
devise something new in the light of teachings and of service," said

the maggid (preacher) of Zlotchov, "and do what has not yet been done." When a son who inherited his father's congregation was reproached by his disciples with conducting himself differently from his father, he retorted: "I do just as my father did. He did not imitate and I do not imitate." The relationship between person and person was central to Hasidism, but only in spontaneous address and response and not in that invidious comparison and contrast that leads people to call one person "superior" to another. When someone praised one person to Rabbi Mendel of Kotzk at the expense of another, Rabbi Mendel said: "If I am I because I am I, and you are you because you are you, then I am I and you are you. But if I am I because you are you, and you are you because I am I, then I am not I, and you are not you." When Rabbi Abraham was asked why people feel so crowded despite the fact that the sages say that everything, the human being included, has its place, he replied, "Because each wants to occupy the place of the other." Uniqueness does not preclude dialogue. On the contrary, it is precisely through each one standing one's own ground and yet moving to meet the other that genuine dialogue from ground to ground takes place. For a person for whom there is no dialogue, even the ground of life itself crumbles away. After the death of Rabbi Moshe of Kobryn, a friend said: "If there had been someone to whom he could have talked, he would still be alive."

When asked for one general way to the service of God, the Seer of Lublin replied:

> It is impossible to tell men what way they should take. For one way to serve God is through the teaching, another through prayer, another through fasting, and still another through eating. Everyone should carefully observe what way his heart draws him to, and then choose this way with all his strength.[2]

Hasidism is like Hinduism in not having any one way that the person should walk. But the way for the Hasid is not a matter of one's caste duty or even one's *dharma* or *karma* but of one's personal uniqueness, one's "I" in the deepest sense of that term. To speak of the heart drawing us does not mean the facile impulse of the moment. Our "I" is not our image of ourselves but the deepest stirring within ourselves. That stirring, in its response, becomes our way.

That is why the "evil" urge is so important to Hasidism. In the Book of Genesis this word for "urge" appears as "imaginings." Before the Flood, the Lord gives "For the imagining of man's heart are evil from his youth onward" as his reason for destroying the world by flood. Yet after the Flood, the same reason is given for never again destroying the world by flood. For these same "imaginings," although evil from youth on, *can* be directed to God. Similarly, the Talmud says one must love God with *both* urges, the good and the "evil." Without the evil urge no one could have a business or raise a family. That means the "evil" urge is not evil in itself. It is evil only when it is not given direction. It is evil only when it is not given the personal meaning of our unique response to the situation. It is needed for our service. The person who succeeds in being "good" by repressing the "evil" urge is not serving God with all one's heart, soul, and might.

The "evil" urge is the passion, the power that is given us to serve God. We cannot extirpate it or do away with it. When it seems to make us fail, it does so because we have tried to impose upon ourselves and our environment what we are determined to be. The "evil" urge is that something more in us which taps us on the shoulder and recalls us to ourselves. Often we have so lost touch with ourselves that we do not know what way our heart draws us to. It is then that precisely the "evil" urge which seems to wish to lead us astray comes to our rescue. By its very tempting of us, it tells us that we have left ourselves out of our own projects, that our deepest passion has not been given direction, that our decisions have not been made with our whole being. "He who still harbors an evil urge is at great advantage," said one Hasidic rabbi, "for he can serve God with it. He can gather all his passion and warmth and pour them into the service of God. . . .What counts is to restrain the blaze in the hour of desire and let it flow into the hours of prayer and service." This does not mean the repression of desire but giving it meaningful direction.

The "evil" urge was thus potentially good to the Hasidim, yet they had no illusions about its being an easy matter to give the "evil" urge direction. The Maggid of Mezritch was recognized as the successor to the Baal Shem because he answered the question of how one can break pride by saying that no one can break it: "We must struggle with it all the days of our life." Similarly the rabbi of Rizhyn said to a young man who wanted help in breaking his evil impulse: "You will break your back and your hip, yet you will not break an impulse. But if you pray and learn and work in all seriousness, the evil in your impulses will vanish of itself." Sometimes the result is more of a draw, as when Rabbi Moshe of Kobryn compared the service of God to walking over a freshly plowed field in which furrows alternate with ridges: "Now you go up, now you go down, now the Evil Urge gets a hold on you, now you get a hold on him. Just you see to it that it is you who deal the last blow!"

You cannot get a hold on the evil urge through self-mortification, however. The maggid of Koznitz said to a man who wore nothing but a sack and fasted from one sabbath to the next, "The Evil Urge is tricking you into that sack. He who pretends to fast...but secretly eats a little something every day, is spiritually better off than you, for he is only deceiving others, while you are deceiving yourself." When another Hasid, known for the harsh penances he imposed on himself, came to visit the maggid of Zlotchov, the latter said to him, "Yudel, you are wearing a hair shirt against your flesh. If you were not given to sudden anger, you would not need it, and since you are given to sudden anger, it will not help you." Worse and more harmful than the sin a person plunges into when one gives way to the evil urge is the despondency that overtakes one by way of one's sinning. Once one sees oneself as a sinner, then the evil urge really has one in its power. Instead of sinning and then saying, "But I won't sin again," like the cheerful sinner of whom the Seer of Lublin was so fond, one gives way to the image of oneself as a sinner and loses what resources one might have had to direct the evil urge into the service of God.

The power of the evil urge is the power of desire—desire for something that turns out to be nothing. The Evil Urge goes around the world with his fist closed, and everyone thinks that in that fist is just what he wants most in the world and follows after it. But the Evil Urge opens his fist, and it is empty. Once some disciples of Rabbi Pinhas ceased talking in embarrassment when he entered the House of Study. When he asked them what they were talking about, they said, "Rabbi, we were saying how afraid we are that the Evil Urge will pursue us." "Don't worry," he replied. "You have not gotten high enough for it to pursue you. For the time being you are still pursuing it." This is how it is with most of us. We can feel for the person who came to ask the Seer of Lublin to help him against alien thoughts that intruded on him while he prayed. Even after the rabbi had told him what to do, the man went on asking questions until finally the rabbi said:

> I don't know why you keep complaining to me of alien thoughts. To him who has holy thoughts, an impure thought comes at times, and such a thought is called "alien." But you—you have just your own usual thoughts. To whom do you want to ascribe them?[3]

How does one serve God with the "evil" urge? Not through turning away from everyday life in the world but through bringing right dedication—*kavana*—to everything one does, through responding with one's whole being to the unique claim of unique situations. This means bringing all of one's passion into meaningful relationship with the people one meets and the situations one encounters. "What are all *kavanot* [special magical and mystical intentions]," exclaimed the Baal

Shem, "compared with one really heart-felt grief!" "Every lock has the key that is fitted to it and opens it," said the maggid of Mezritch:

> But there are strong thieves who know how to open without keys. They break the lock. So every mystery in the world can be unriddled by the particular kind of meditation fitted to it. But God loves the thief who breaks the lock open: I mean *the man who breaks his heart for God.*[4]

In Hasidism it is not the doctrine that is important but the way of life, the image of the human. Rabbi Leib, son of Sara, said he went to see the maggid of Mezritch not to hear him say Torah but to watch the way in which he laced and unlaced his felt boots. The caption of this tale is "Not to Say Torah but to Be Torah." Words are of importance when they manifest life, not when they take its place. This applies most clearly of all to prayer. The Baal Shem once refused to enter a synagogue because it was crowded from floor to ceiling and from wall to wall with prayers that had been uttered without real devotion. Even the right mood is of no avail if the motivation is wrong: the one who prays in sorrow because of the bleakness that burdens one's spirit does not know the real fear of God, and the one who prays in joy because of the radiance of one's spirit does not know the love of God. One's "fear is the burden of sadness, and his love is nothing but empty joy." Honest grief, in contrast, is that of one who knows what one lacks, while the truly joyful person is like someone whose house has burned down and who begins to build anew out of the deep need of one's soul: "Over every stone that is laid, his heart rejoices."

Once the maggid of Mezritch let a sigh escape when, as a young man, he was poor and his baby was too weak even to cry. Instantly a voice said, "You have lost your share in the world to come." "Good," exclaimed the maggid. "Now I can begin to serve in good earnest!" *Kavana* does not mean that what is important is "purity of heart" but that one must bring oneself with all one's possibility of response into every action. This is the Hasidic image of the human: "Only he who brings himself to the Lord as an offering may be called man." This bringing oneself is no once-for-all commitment but an ever-renewed finding of direction, a responding to the call in each new hour. After the death of Rabbi Moshe of Kobryn, a disciple replied to the question, "What was most important to your teacher?" with the answer, "Whatever he happened to be doing at the moment."

From *kavana* we can understand the unique approach of Hasidism to love and to helping one's fellow. The Hasidim rejected emphatically the image of the helper who stands above the person one wants to help and reaches down a helping hand. "If you want to raise a man from mud and filth," said Rabbi Shelomo of Karlin, "you must go all the way down yourself, down into mud and filth. Then take hold of him with strong hands and pull him and yourself out into the light." This does not mean that you imitate his sins, but you must open yourself to the reality of the evil into which he has fallen and not try to bestow charity from above while keeping your soul free from any thing that might disturb it. Rabbi Moshe Leib of Sasov learned to love when he went to an inn and heard one drunken peasant ask another, "Do you love me?" "Certainly I love you," replied the second. "I love you like a brother." But the first shook his head and insisted, "You don't love me. You don't know what I lack. You don't know what I need." The second peasant fell into sullen silence, but Rabbi Moshe Leib understood: "To know the need of men and to bear the burden of their sorrow, that is the true love of men." This love only exists in mutual relationship, in that dialogue in which one experiences the other side of the relationship, knows the other from within. One needs to be loved not in one's universal humanity or divinity but in one's uniqueness, including what one lacks.

Rabbi Moshe Leib not only understood this; he lived it. He shared so earnestly in the spiritual and physical sufferings of others that their suffering became his own. When someone once expressed astonishment at this capacity to share in another's troubles, he replied, "What do you mean 'share'? It is my own sorrow; how can I help but suffer it?" The Yehudi, the "holy Jew," was asked why the stork is called devout or loving (*hasidah*) in the Talmud because he gives so much love to his mate and his young but is classed in the Scriptures with the unclean birds. The Yehudi answered: "Because he gives love only to his own." We must love the other—the stranger, the enemy—even as we love our family. In both cases our love must be an openness and response to the unique person that we meet. Mixed with this insistence on concreteness is a good measure of Hasidic realism and humor, as in the story that the rabbi of Zans used to tell about himself:

> In my youth when I was fired with the love of God, I thought I would convert the whole world to God. But I soon discovered that it would be quite enough to convert the people who lived in my town, and I tried for a long time, but did not succeed. Then I realized that my program was still much too ambitious, and I concentrated on the persons in my own household. But I could not convert them either. Finally it dawned on me: I must work upon myself, so that I may give true service to God. But I did not accomplish even this.[5]

The title of this tale is "Resignation," resignation without any admixture of bitterness, despair, disillusionment, defeat.

The Hasidic demand that we discover and perform our own created task, that we channel the passion of the "evil" urge into the realization of our personal uniqueness, that we act and love with *kavana*, or inner intention, implies the strongest possible rejection of all those ways whereby we divide our lives into airtight compartments and escape becoming whole. Becoming whole does not mean "spiritual" wholeness or the wholeness of the individual Self within the unconscious (to use the language of Jung). It means that personal wholeness the necessary corollary of which is the wholeness of our lives. When Menahem Mendel of Kotzk asked a fellow disciple of Rabbi Bunam, "To what purpose was man created?" the latter replied, "So that he might perfect his soul." "No, indeed," said the Kotzker. "He was created so that he might lift up the heavens!" Our true wholeness is not the perfection of our "immortal soul" but the fulfillment of our created task. Only the latter brings our personal uniqueness into being in integral relation with the creation over against which we are set. Our existence does not take place *within* ourselves but in *relationship* to what is *not* ourselves. To make our goal spiritual perfection, consequently, means a foreshortening of our personal existence.

The rabbi of Kotzk explained the biblical injunction, "Ye shall be holy unto me," as the demand not for perfection but for authentic humanity: "You shall be holy unto me, but as men. You shall be humanly holy unto me." We are not asked to be saints or supermen but to be holy in the measure and manner of the human, in the measure and manner of our unique personal resources. This is a seemingly easier demand than perfection but in fact it is harder; for it asks you to do what you really can do rather than despair over what you cannot. We take our ideas and ideals with grim seriousness, says Martin Buber, but we do not allow them to have a binding claim upon our everyday lives. "No amount of hypocritical piety has ever reached this concentrated degree of inauthenticity!" Our wretchedness is due to the fact that we do not open our lives to the holy, Buber adds and concludes: "A life that is not open to the holy is not only unworthy of spirit, it is unworthy of life." This is not a question of being punished for being "unworthy." It is a matter of the meaning of life itself.

To open our lives to the holy does not mean to rise above our situation. It means to bring our situation into dialogue with God. The openness to the holy does not mean leaving the everyday for a higher spiritual sphere but "hallowing the everyday" through a genuine openness to what meets you. "Whoever says that the words of the Torah are one thing and the words of the world another," said Rabbi Pinhas of Koretz, "must be regarded as a man who denies God." C. H. Dodd, the biblical scholar, said, "Most people seem to think that everything that happened in the Bible happened on Sunday."

If there ought be no dualism of "sacred" words and "secular" words, neither ought there be a dualism between words and silence. When the Yehudi discovered that a young man had taken a vow of silence for three years except for the Torah and prayer, he called the young man to him and asked him why it was that he did not see a single word of his in the world of truth. When the young man justified his silence by talking of the "vanity of speech," the Yehudi warned him that he who only learns and prays is murdering the world of his own soul. "What do you mean by the 'vanity of speech'?" continued the Yehudi, almost in the language of Lao-tzu. "Whatever you have to say can be vanity or it can be truth."

The rabbi of Rizhyn imposed upon a confirmed sinner a terrible penance: "From now until you die, you shall not utter a single word of prayer with empty lips; but you shall preserve the fullness of every word." The sinner himself had brought the rabbi the list of his sins to have penance imposed on him. The rabbi's response not only demanded a sincere inner repentance but a wholehearted turning of his existence. Only thus could a person who was used to living moment by moment in inner division bring the whole of one's intention and the whole of one's life into prayer. What does it amount to that they expound the Torah!" cried Rabbi Leib, son of Sara. "A man should see to it that all his actions are a Torah and that he himself becomes so entirely a Torah that one can learn from his habits and his motions and his motionless clinging to God."

"Man is like a tree," said Rabbi Uri of Strelisk. "If you stand in front of a tree and watch it incessantly to see how it grows and to see how much it grows, you will see nothing at all. But tend to it all times, prune the runners and keep the vermin from it and, all in good time, it will come into its growth." "It is the same with man," he added. "All that is necessary is for him to overcome his obstacles and he will thrive and grow. But it is not right to examine him every hour to see how much has been added to his growth." If there is any single evil in our culture that overtops all others, it is this one of examining and measuring people all the time to see how far along they have come in school, in training, in business and professional life, in maturity, in self-realization, in comparison with their brothers and sisters, their classmates, their colleagues and fellow workers, or their neighbors. Even our "spiritual life" comes fully equipped, like Benjamin Franklin's chart of virtues, with measuring rods to show whether we have learned "receptive listening," realized our potential, grown in Christian humility and the love of God, or advanced in mystical contemplation or saintly perfection! The more we try to discover how far along we are and what progress we have made, the more we will get in our own way.

The only true growth is that which comes through spontaneity, through a response so great and wholehearted that we forget to be concerned about ourselves. A great violinist may negotiate for what he is to be paid for a concert, but each time he draws the bow over the strings, he does not think of how much money he is making! Rabbi Hayyim of Krosno became so absorbed in watching a rope-dancer that his disciples asked him what it was that riveted his gaze to this foolish performance.

> "This man," he said, "is risking his life, and I cannot say why. But I am quite sure that while he is walking the rope he is not thinking of the fact that he is earning a hundred gulden by what he is doing, for if he did, he would fall."[6]

Although Hasidism grows out of a theosophy—knowledge about God—and a very detailed one, the Hasidim tended to lay greater stress on simple devotion to God. One consequence of this stress was that for the Hasidim, as for biblical faith, God's hiding was as real as his revealing himself, and when God hid himself, it was difficult to maintain one's trust. The favorite disciple of Rabbi Pinhas complained to him that it was very difficult in adversity to retain perfect faith in the belief that God provides for every human being. "It actually seems as if God were hiding his face from such an unhappy being," he exclaimed. "It ceases to be a hiding," replied Rabbi Pinhas, "if you know it is hiding." Shneur Zalman, the rav of Northern White Russia and the founder of the Habad, or Lubavitcher, Hasidim, once asked a disciple, "Moshe, what do we mean when we say 'God'?" The disciple was silent. After the rav had asked him a second and third time without response, he demanded the reason for his silence. "Because I do not know," replied the youth. "Do you think I know?" said the rav. "But I must say it, for it is so, and therefore I must say it: He is definitely there, and except for Him nothing is definitely there—and this is He." The rav could not define God, or describe his attributes, or even assert his existence in the abstract. But he could and did point in his dialogue with his disciple to meeting God in our actual existence in all its particularity.

A similar dialogue took place between Rabbi Bunam and his disciple Rabbi Hanokh. For a year the latter had wanted to talk with Bunam every time he went into his house but did not feel he was man enough. Once though, when he was walking across a field and weeping, he knew that he must run to his rabbi without delay. Bunam asked him, "Why are you weeping?" "I am after all alive in this world," he confessed, "a being created with all the senses and all the limbs, but I do not know what it is I was created for and what I am good for in this world." His master did not reply by showing him the meaning of his life or confirming his value in the world but by revealing that this torment was one that he too could neither resolve nor dismiss: "Little fool," said Bunam, "That's the same question I have carried around with me all my life. You will come and eat the evening meal with me."

Revelation, to the Hasidim, did not mean the incursion of the supernatural, but openness to the wonder of the everyday—"the enormous lights and miracles" with which the world is filled. Once a naturalist came from a great distance to see the Baal Shem and said: "My investigations show that in the course of nature the Red Sea had to divide at the very hour the children of Israel passed through it. Now what about that famous miracle!" "Don't you know that God created nature?" answered the Baal Shem. "And he created it so, that at the hour the children of Israel passed through the Red Sea, it had to divide. That is the great and famous miracle!" "Miracle" is simply the wonder of the unique that points us back to the wonder of the everyday. If you fell through the ice and were saved at the last second from drowning, your knowledge of all the laws of heat and friction that might account for the ice melting at just that rate would not diminish by one jot the sense of wonder you would feel.

The rabbi of Kobryn taught:

> God says to man, as he said to Moses: "Put off thy shoes from thy feet"—put off the habitual which encloses your foot, and you will know that the place on which you are now standing is holy ground. For there is no rung of human life on which we cannot find the holiness of God everywhere and at all times.[7]

The true opposite of "the habitual" is not the extraordinary or the unusual but the fresh, the open, the ever-new of the person who hallows the everyday. When Rabbi Bunam was asked why the first of the Ten Commandments speaks of God bringing us out of the land of Egypt rather than of God creating heaven and earth, he expounded: " 'Heaven and earth!' Then man might have said: 'Heaven—that is too much for me.' So God said to man: I am the one who fished you out of the mud. Now you come here and listen to me!' "

It is only as persons that we can enter with our whole being into the dialogue with God that takes place in the heart of the everyday.

To enter this dialogue means to hear and respond to God's "Torah," his guidance and direction in each hour of our lives. But it does not mean to freeze the Torah into a fixed, objective, universal law that demands only our external obedience and not our unique response to a unique situation. The rabbi of Kotzk heard his disciples discussing why it is written: "Take heed unto yourselves, lest ye forget the covenant of the Lord your God, which He made with you, and make you a graven image, even in the likeness of any thing which the Lord thy God hath bidden thee," and not, as they would have expected, "Which the Lord thy God hath forbidden thee." The zaddik declared: "The Torah warns us not to make a graven image of any thing the Lord our God has bidden us." Even divine Law and divinely sanctioned morality may become an idol that hides from us the face of God. By the same token, we cannot limit the address of the Torah to the Scriptures; for the word of the Creator speaks forth from the creation and the creatures each day anew. We can learn not only from what God has created but from what man has made, the rabbi of Sadagora declared to his disciples.

> "What we can learn from a train?"—one hasid asked dubiously.
> "That because of one second one can miss everything."
> "And from the telegraph?"
> "That every word is counted and charged."
> "And the telephone?"
> "That what we say here is heard there."[8]

In the fifth chapter of his classic little book *The Way of Man according to the Teachings of the Hasidim*, Martin Buber retells Rabbi Bunam's story of Reb Eisik, son of Reb Yekel, who lived in Kracow but who dreamt three times that there was a treasure buried beneath a bridge in Prague and finally set out and walked the whole enormous distance to Prague. He found the bridge but was afraid to approach it because of the soldiers who guarded it until the captain of the guard noticed him and asked him kindly what it was he wanted. When he had told the captain his dream, the latter exclaimed, "And so to please the dream, you poor fellow wore out your shoes to come here!" If he had had faith in dreams, continued the captain, he would have had to go to Kracow when once a dream told him to go there and dig for treasure under the stove in the room of a Jew—Eisik, son of Yekel. When Rabbi Eisik heard this, he bowed, traveled home, dug up the treasure from under the stove, and built with it a house of prayer. The moral of this story, says Buber, is that the fulfillment of existence is only possible "here where one stands," in the environment which one feels to be natural, in the situation which has been assigned as one's fate, in the things that happen to one and claim one day after day. If we had power over the ends of the world and knew the secrets of the upper world, they would not give us that fulfillment of existence that a quiet, devoted relationship to nearby life can give us.

There is another aspect to this tale that Buber does not bring out, but which the life of most of us shows to be essential. Perhaps if we had not gone to "Prague," we should not have discovered that the treasure was hidden beneath our own hearth. There is meaning in our searching, even when it takes us far afield, if it enables us to come back home to the unique task that awaits us. A young person raised in Judaism or Christianity is often barred from any genuine relationship to these religions by the fact that they are associated in his or her mind with the parents against whom one must rebel, with a social system the injustice of which is manifest, and often in addition with a shoddy way of presenting the religion that seems more concerned with group belonging or social snobbery than with anything genuinely religious. Such a person might find liberation in the teachings of Eastern religions encountered in a relatively pure state unencumbered by relatives and institutions. After these have liberated one, one may be able to go back to find the treasure under one's own hearth. When one does come back, it is with a new relationship such as only the fact of distancing makes possible. And if one does not come back, one still relates to whatever one finds from the ground of one's original roots.

If the human being, to Hasidism, is a partner of the Creator, a co-creator who helps complete the creation by lifting the fallen sparks in the circle of existence allotted to one, one is by the same token a co-redeemer. The rabbi of Kotzk surprised a number of learned visitors with the question, "Where is the dwelling of God?" "What a question!" they laughed. "Is not the whole world full of his glory!" But he answered: "God dwells where man lets him in." Rabbi Nachman of Bratzlav, the great grandson of the Baal Shem, pictured human existence in terms of an *Angst* as strong as any that Kierkegaard ever depicted:

> Let everyone cry out to God and lift his heart up to him as if he were hanging by a hair, and a tempest were raging to the very heart of heaven, and he were at a loss for what to do, and there were hardly time to cry out. It is a time when no counsel indeed can help a man and he has no refuge save to remain in his loneliness and lift his eyes and his heart up to God and cry out to him. And this should be done at all times, for in the world man is in great danger.[9]

But this very *Angst,* this very loneliness becomes redemptive, as Buber suggests by entitling the following saying of Rabbi Nachman "The Kingdom of God":

> Those who do not walk in loneliness will be bewildered when the Messiah comes and they are called; but we shall be like a man who has been asleep and whose spirit is tranquil and composed.[10]

The first saying is entitled "Prayer." Those who walk in loneliness do not wall themselves in in "demonic shut-in-ness," as Kierkegaard would say. They cry out to God. Even when they do not know how to pray, the silence beneath their words cries out:

> We know very well how we ought to pray; and still we cry for help in the need of the moment. The soul wishes us to cry out in spiritual need, but we are not able to express what the soul means. And so we pray that God may accept our call for help, but also that he, who knows that which is hidden, may hear the silent cry of the soul.[11]

In the end redemption is neither the action of the human alone nor of the divine alone but the completion of the dialogue between them. As Martin Buber says in the last sentence of *I and Thou,* "The event that from the side of the world is called turning is called from God's side redemption." If human turning and divine redemption are two sides of one event, then the opposition that is so common between human action and divine grace is a false one. This is not a matter of abstract theology, however, but of wholly concrete situations in which at times human beings have the resources to begin the turning and at other times not. Nowhere has this lability of the human situation vis à vis God been put more vividly than in a tale entitled "Turning and Redemption":

> The rabbi of Rizhyn laid the fingers of his right hand on the table after the morning meal, and said: "God says to Israel: 'Return unto me. . .and I will return unto you.' " Then he turned his right hand palm up and said: "But we children of Israel reply: 'Turn Thou us unto Thee, O lord, and we shall be turned; renew our days as of old.' For our exile is heavy on us and we have not the strength to return to you of ourselves." And then he turned his hand palm down again and said: "But the Holy One, blessed be he, says: 'First you must return unto me.' " Four times the rabbi of Rizhyn

turned his hand, palm up and palm down. But in the end he said: "The children of Israel are right, though, because it is true that the waves of anguish close over them, and they cannot govern their hearts and turn to God."[12]

This is not a statement about sinful human nature and our dependence upon divine grace. It is a dialogue between the human and the divine taking place in a concrete historical situation, the situation of exile when the resources to be "humanly holy" by serving God with the "evil" urge were at their lowest ebb and the silent need of the soul cried out to God from beneath the waves of anguish. The love between person and God, like the love between person and person, is not a matter of merit or unearned grace but of the "between": If one loves less, then the other should love more for the sake of the relationship itself. It is in this spirit that we must understand one of the most moving of the Hasidic tales—one that at first glance gives the mistaken appearance of being close to the Pauline dualism between grace and law. This tale is entitled "The Judgment of the Messiah":

A young man who lived in the days of the Great Maggid had quitted his father-in-law's house to go to the maggid. They had fetched him back and he had pledged on a handclasp that he would stay at home. Yet shortly thereafter he was gone. Now his father-in-law got the rav of the town to declare that this broken promise was cause for divorce. The young man was thus deprived of all means of subsistence. Soon he fell ill and died.

When the zaddik had finished his story, he added. "And now, my good men, when the Messiah comes, the young man will hale his father-in-law before his court of justice. The father-in-law will quote the rav of the town, and the rav will quote a passage from the commentary on the *Shulhan Arukh* [the "Table of the Laws" codified by Joseph Karo in the sixteenth century]. Then the Messiah will ask the young man why after giving his hand on it that he would remain at home he broke his promise just the same, and the young man will say, 'I just had to go to the rabbi!' In the end the Messiah will pronounce judgment. To the father-in-law he will say: 'You took the rav's word as your authority and so you are justified.' And to the rav he will say: 'You took the law as your authority and so you are justified.'

"And then he will add: 'But I have come for those who are not justified.' "[13]

Hasidism not only stresses the love and mercy of God; it shows that to be a Hasid, a loyal follower of God, means to love one's fellows and even one's enemies. It is a living embodiment of the dictum to "deal lovingly with thy neighbor as one like thyself." As such it demonstrates, as no amount of pointing to Leviticus can, that this injunction was taken over by Jesus from the Judaism in which he himself stood.

The love of Hasidism is not a spiritualized love but a love of the whole person. By the same token, it is not a purely forgiving love but one that places a real demand upon the other—the demand of the relationship itself. The "hallowing of the everyday" means making the concrete relations of one's life essential, and real relationship includes both mutuality and passion. Mutuality means that love does not simply flow forth from the loving person to others; rather it moves back and forth within the dialogue between them as the fullest expression of that dialogue. Passion means that one does not suppress one's humanity before bringing oneself into relation with others, but on the contrary directs one's "evil" urge into that relationship in such a way that, without losing its force, it ceases to be evil. It is in this sense that Hasidism represents a sanctification of the profane in which every natural urge is waiting to be hallowed and the profane itself just a name for what has not yet become open to the holy.

This concrete and realistic approach to the "evil urge" is vividly illustrated by a story of the Baal Shem's called "The Limits of Advice." When the disciples of the Baal Shem asked him how to know whether a celebrated scholar whom they proposed to visit was a true zaddik, he answered:

> Ask him to advise you what to do to keep unholy thoughts from disturbing you in your prayers and studies. If he gives you advice, then you will know that he belongs to those who are of no account. For this is the service of men in the world to the very hour of their death: to struggle time after time with the extraneous, and time after time to uplift and fit it into the nature of the Divine Name.[14]

So often the religious is conceived of as putting aside the extraneous and the profane and turning to the holy and the pure. But here the extraneous is precisely that which has something to ask of us. Once a group of Hasidim started to pray in one place and then went to another, at which the first place cried out: "What is wrong with me that you went to another place? And if I am evil, is it not up to you to redeem me?" The rav of White Russia once asked his son, "With what do you pray?" To which the son replied, "I pray with the verse, 'May every high place become low.' " Then the son asked his father,

"With what do you pray?" The rav answered: "I pray with the floor and with the bench."

Jesus offered his disciples a counsel of perfection—"But I say unto you that he who looks at a woman to lust after her in his heart has already committed adultery." Paul, in contrast, saw not only temptation but sin as inevitable—"Of myself [in my flesh] I can do no good thing." "The evil that I would not do I do." In between the teaching that one can overcome temptation altogether and become "pure in heart" and that which sees the human being as naturally sinful is the teaching, already present in the Bible and the Talmud but given strongest emphasis and exemplification in Hasidism, that the daily renewal of creation also means the daily renewal of temptation and with it the strength and the grace to direct that temptation into the service of God through an essential and meaningful relation with the world.

Particularly significant for the current constellation of religious philosophy and metaphysics in the Western world of thought is the Hasidic doctrine of *tzimtzum*—the metaphor of God's self-limitation in the act of creation that Hasidism takes over from the Lurian Kabbala. The highest reality of the divine, as Hasidism reinterprets *tzimtzum*, is not Meister Eckhart's impersonal Godhead but the Absolute who makes himself into a Person in order to bring us into relationship with him. "On account of his great love," says the maggid of Mezritch, "God limits his illuminating power in order that, like a father with his son, he may bring man stage by stage to where he may receive the revelation of the limitless original God."[15] God's relation to creation is a voluntary contraction that in no way limits his absoluteness.

Father John M. Oesterreicher, the editor of the series of Catholic "Judaeo-Christian Studies," *The Bridge,* sees the Hasidic doctrine of *tzimtzum* as an inferior conception that derogates God's glory—a depreciation based upon a substantive and static misreading of the concept. Seen in its true dynamic and interactive character, *tzimtzum* stands as one of the greatest reformulations of the biblical understanding of creation. It shows God as at once separate from the world and from the human and yet in relationship to them, and in such a way that neither the separateness nor the togetherness can be shown as either temporally or logically prior. Creation, in this view, is the radical fact which establishes and reestablishes the world and behind which we cannot look to any primal state before creation or godhead before God. In our own existence we can neither begin with our separate existence as persons and then deduce our relations to others nor begin with our relations with others and then deduce our uniqueness as separate persons. Rather we must begin with both at once.

In our relation to God, similarly, we cannot go back behind creation to some more basic fact. Yet this is just what not only the mystics but also the theologians and the metaphysicians constantly attempt to do. Through a logical analysis of the relationship between the human and the divine, they separate out the two factors of separateness and relatedness and then make one or the other of them prior. Paul Tillich rightly attacks the theists for making God a person beside other persons. But what he offers instead is no more satisfactory—a "Ground of Being" that satisfies our logic's desire for a reality undergirding human relation with God and that at the same time forgives and accepts as only a personal God could do! Alfred North Whitehead and Charles Hartshorne, on the other hand, say that since God cannot logically be both absolute and in relation, they prefer to sacrifice the Absolute in favor of an imperfectly actual God who attains his completion only through dialectical interaction with the world. The Hasidic understanding of the relation of God and the world does not have to fall into these logical either-or's. It can be a paradox because it sticks to the concrete given of our existence in which the seemingly irreconcilable opposites produced by our analytical thought exist together as one whole. In this it is like Zen.

Hasidism, in my opinion, has a contribution of the greatest significance to make. It calls us to a realization of the covenant—a reminder that to become a "holy people" means not just becoming a collection of well-meaning individuals but a never-ending realization of righteousness, justice, and loving kindness in true community. This is a task that not only Jews but Christians and indeed people of any religion and culture may and must shoulder. Nor is it a task that is really exemplified in any aspect of modern Judaism. In the Israeli kibbutz this community exists without the relationship to a divine center that in Hasidism built community out of a wholly personal mode of faith. In the Jewish communities of the diaspora, on the other hand, this center exists without the community—since a modern temple or synagogue with all its multifarious activities is a cultural and social center to be sure, and at times a religious one too, but not a real community where people live and work together. Among the Hasidim of Israel and of America, there seems to be both center and community. Yet the task of hallowing the everyday has fallen into abeyance in favor of a special sphere in which the holy is protected from the contamination of the profane. The Hasidism of the Baal Shem may point the way to a true covenant community that does not now exist.

PART THREE

Religious Communication

6

The Meeting of Religion and Human Experience

Walking is Zen. Sitting is Zen.

"What is all this talk of praying 'earnestly'!" the rabbi of
Kobryn called to his Hasidim. "Is there anything at all that
one ought not to do earnestly?"

In religion our whole being responds and is involved in the
response. We respond to what we perceive as "ultimate reality." But
we do not know this ultimate reality by prior metaphysical or theological
definition. We know it only as we enter into dialogue with it, only as
we meet it in and through the concrete situations of our lives. Therefore,
it is not the "object" that we meet which is ultimate but the reality of
the meeting itself.

Religion, as we have said, is the way that one walks, a basic
commitment in life itself. It expresses itself, as we have seen, in doctrinal
forms such as myth, creed, theology, and metaphysics; in practical forms
such as liturgy, ritual, prayer; and in social forms such as fellowships,
churches, sects, and denominations. For all that, we cannot reduce
religion to any one of these expressions or even to all of them taken
together and their interrelations. The matrix of all of these expressions
is our ultimate meeting itself, and this is not in itself directly expressible.
What is more, the expressions of religion inevitably come loose from
their mooring, become detached and independent. When this happens,
it is necessary to return to the original immediacy, to reestablish the
ultimate meeting that creed, ritual, and social form no longer lead us
back to.

Our approach to religion and human experience is then a dialogical one. I use the word *dialogue* here not in the sense of two people speaking, but in the sense of openness, directness, mutuality, and presentness. Dialogue means here a mutual knowing, a knowing in direct contact in contrast to a detached subject's knowledge of an object. It may arise in the dialogue between person and person, including the sharing that I call "a dialogue of touchstones." But it may also arise in our meeting with any nonhuman reality, the sunset over the ocean, a ghost pine on Point Lobos, the cry of the loon, the grandeur of the mountains, and the aggravations of everyday toil. It may also come in that indirect dialogue we know as art—paintings, sculpture, poetry, dance, and orchestral and chamber music.

Not all religion is dialogue, of course, and neither is all knowing or, for that matter, all human experience. In one sense, human experience includes just everything in a person's life, inner and outer, conscious and unconscious, waking reality, fantasy, or dream. In another, it may be limited to what is singled out from among the stream of happenings, that which has an impact and stands out for itself. When we say, "I had an experience," we mean just that: something surfaces from the general flux as an event in itself and does so precisely because it impinges on us in some way, whether through the feelings it arouses—pleasure, pain, joy, misery—or through the significance we attach to it, or through the wonder that it evokes. Although we certainly are not consciously aware of all the experiences that happen to us, we can, nonetheless, say that experience is that which we become aware of.

One of the most puzzling difficulties in any attempt to arrive at a phenomenology of human experience is the subtle change in the meaning and emphasis of the term over the last century and a half. In a picaresque novel, say one by Charles Dickens, *experience* means the external happenings in the life of Mr. Pickwick or David Copperfield. Today, experience is often thought of as essentially an internal matter. If one speaks of drug experiences, "the Jimi Hendrix experience," sex or love experiences, one means primarily the experience of being "turned on." "I saw you last night and got that old feeling." If the song concludes, "That old feeling is still in my heart," that is as it should be; for, essentially, it is the feeling *within* me that I am concerned with, not what is *between* me and you. The feeling may be so expansive that it seems to include us both, as in the song "Marie Elena": "A love like mine is great enough for two. To share this love is really all I ask of you." But a love that demands so little, and so much, is the love of one's own feelings that Marie Elena arouses and occasions, not a love *between* Marie Elena and me. If "altered states of consciousness" is substituted for love, the situation is in no way changed. My concern with the reality that I meet is at best incidental. Either it and the meeting with it are the mere occasions for my elevations and ecstasies or these altered states of consciousness are held to be the higher reality itself. Consciousness, and in particular "higher consciousness," has become for many the new, self-evident touchstone of reality.

A look at dreams may further illustrate our problem. Dreams are regarded by Freudians and Jungians alike as "within," the pure raw material of the unconscious. Yet if we look at dreams more closely, we shall see that this cannot possibly be the case. Researchers tell us that we "dream" all the time. But when I tell you that I had a dream last night, I am not referring to some activity that can be picked up through appropriate electrodes placed in my brain and connected with an encephalograph, but to a series of events that I remember precisely because their impact on me enables me to lift them out of the general flow. In this sense, dreams are exactly the same as any other experience. We "have" the dream through remembering it and, perhaps in addition, writing it down and or recounting it to others. But in that remembering, writing, and recounting, three other things are taking place. First, we cut the dream loose from the aura of less well-remembered "dream events" as well as from emotions and sensations that cling to it but cannot be communicated. By the same token, we give the dream a form, a *Gestalt*, that enables us to contemplate it as a whole in itself. Second, we transfer the dream from the peculiar logic of our sleeping world to the very different logic of our waking consciousness and, in so doing, shape and elaborate it. We also elaborate it through our own first thoughts and feelings about it *and*, equally importantly, through our anticipations of whom we might tell it to. If we tell it to our therapist, we are likely to find ourselves highlighting those aspects that fit his or her school of psychology, whether Freudian, Jungian, Adlerian, Gestalt, or whatever. Third, and most important of all, having set the dream over against us, thus having isolated, shaped, and elaborated it and given it form as an independent opposite, we enter into dialogue with it. From now on, it becomes one of the realities that addresses us in the world, just as surely and as concretely as any external happening.

From this illustration it should be clear that we cannot understand experience either as merely external or internal or even as a sum of the two, with some part of each experience the one and some part the other. Experience in the truest sense is itself an event of the "between." It is our meeting with whatever accosts us in the situation in which we find ourselves, dragon, damsel, or dream. One of the things that makes it difficult to understand this, as we have said, is our habit of regarding experience as something that takes place inside ourselves. Another is the pseudo-objectification that arises from our identifying experience with experiential and experiential with science. The so-called empirical sciences do, indeed, have a foundation in our experience. Yet they become sciences precisely by abstracting from the concrete uniqueness of the experienced event and turning what is thus abstracted into data that can be set into relation to other data through placing them into categories of class, condition, cause, or field of operation and interaction.

If there are difficulties that attend any phenomenology of human experience, there are still greater difficulties which attend a phenomenology of religious experience. When William James wrote his great classic, *The Varieties of Religious Experience,* he presented with admirable openness a whole range of "religious experiences" from mysticism and drugs to saintliness and conversion. Though his conclusion was pragmatic ("Religion is real because it has real effects."), it was not yet subjective in the way that religious experience has since tended to become. Today a religious experience is less something that seizes one on one's way than it is an experience that one "has," often by willfully setting out to have it. This is so much the case that I am often inclined to jettison the term *religious experience* entirely in favor of *religious reality* or *religious event* or any other term that might help liberate us from the bondage of the new subjectivism.

Another, older problem in the phenomenology of religious experience arises from the tendency to regard religion as a special experience to be set alongside sensory experience, aesthetic experience, sexual experience, or the like. If we do that, we give up once for all the claim that religion has to do with human wholeness in favor of seeing religion as one special sphere of life, perhaps that of mystic ecstasy, higher consciousness, fervent devotion, contemplation, trance, or even, as some would hold today, schizophrenia! Religion then becomes related to special times and places—Easter Sunday and Yom Kippur, the church or synagogue. As the "upper story" of our lives, it then usually has less claim on our total response than an absorbing piece of theater or symphony orchestra concert, or even a very good dinner or an engrossing game of football. It becomes, indeed, with all its prescribed creeds and rituals, downright tedious and boring.

On the other hand, if we seek to make religion equal to the sum total of human experience, we have either robbed religion of its reality entirely or we have reduced it to John Dewey's "common faith," a vague idealism superimposed upon experience as the "religious" dimension of everyday life. For the whole to be greater than the sum of its parts, that whole must have a wholeness that is integral to it. It must come together into a whole the way the various notes of a composition come together, when performed, to become a piano concerto or a string quartet. If religion is a way that we walk, then the whole of human life is included in it. Yet that life comes to wholeness not additively or by abstraction but only in the upsurging of events in which all the moments of the past are caught up into the present and given new reality by it. Such an event could be an hour of prayer at a time of great need—when we are facing death or are facing the death of loved ones. Or it could be a moment of breathtaking awe before a waterfall or in the midst of a raging storm at sea. Or it could be an action in which we gather together all the past meanings of our life in one great hour of devotion or sacrifice. In all cases, it is an event in which we attain selflessness not by giving up the self, as the ascetics suggest that we do, but by the totality of our response. In such a totality we are taken out of ourselves, called out by something to which we respond so fully and spontaneously that our self is neither our aim nor our concern but only the self-understood and self-evident ground of our responding.

To understand religion in this sense, we must unify our phenomenology of human experience and our phenomenology of religion into a phenomenology of the *meeting* of religion and experience. Here we risk confusion because we have already defined experience as, in one sense, itself a product of meeting. It is also the springboard and base for future meetings. We go out from our present experience to meet the new that befalls us. We bring our experience with us into what we meet. We meet that experience itself in our reflections on it and our concern with it—as in holding in our mind a dream or a personal exchange that has touched our heart, not analyzing it but letting it speak to us and letting ourselves answer this address.

We can clear up our confusion further if we recognize that *religion* is often treated as being the external forms that seem to the observer to make up religion—ritual, organization, creed—and experience is often seen as the subjective aspect of our existence—our feelings, our consciousness, or even our unique participation in an event common to ourselves and others. Looked at in this way, we could then speak of the meeting of religion and experience as a way of pointing to the reality of the between that cannot be caught in the objective forms of religion or the subjective forms of experience. Only in this way, perhaps, can we point ourselves back—and forward—to that "ultimate response to what is encountered as ultimate" which we have tentatively defined as religion.

Yet we shall not be satisfied with approaching religion through a double negative—*not* objective and *not* subjective—or even by defining religion as a dialogical reality that the objective expressions and the subjective experiences are merely the byproducts of and accompaniments to. We shall want, instead, to speak of this dialogical reality itself and in its own terms as an event of meeting that comes to light *before* our abstractions into external and internal, objective and subjective, thought and feeling, and the like. To do this we must turn to that neglected reality I call the *via humana*.

7

The Via Humana

Rabbi Leib, the son of Sarah, said, "I did not go to the Maggid of Mezritch to hear him say Torah, but to see how he unlaces his felt shoes and laces them up again."

It is written: "And ye shall be holy men unto Me." The rabbi of Kotzk explained: "Ye shall be holy unto me, but as men, ye shall be humanly holy unto me."[1]

In the chapter on religious symbolism in *Touchstones of Reality*, I coin the term the *via humana* to set in contrast with the two traditicrnal approaches—the *via positiva*, which describes the attributes of God, and the *via negativa*, which emphasizes the utter unknowability of God and speaks only of what God is not:

> The importance of touchstones of reality as an approach is that it does not claim to be the absolute truth, but it also does not abandon us to some completely subjective relativism. It witnesses to as much reality as we can witness to at that moment. In opposition to both the *via negativa* and the *via positiva*, therefore, I would make bold to call touchstones of reality the *via humana*. Only through it can we keep close to the concrete reality, without pursuing theology at the expense of the fully human or humanism at the expense of closing man off from the nameless reality that he meets in his meeting with everyday life.[2]

In using the *via humana* as the title of this chapter, I am taking
it out of the context of theology and religious symbolism and giving
it the broader meaning of the dialogical approach to religion and human
experience—the way that we walk in the concrete situations of our
existence. If we wish to put this in a theological context, we might speak
of theology as biography, theology as event. But to do so already
changes radically the traditional meaning of theology. It no longer rests
upon a set of traditional interpretations of "sacred history" and biblical
events. Rather it is the event itself that again and again gives rise to
religious meaning, and only out of that meaning, apprehended in our
own history and the history of past generations that we have made
present to ourselves, do religious symbols and theological interpretations arise. For this reason, I have found it difficult to go along with
those of my friends who call for a return to theology as an antidote
to the excessive naturalism and restrictive "humanism" of the recent
past. I believe in a larger humanism that is defined not by negation
of transcendent reality but precisely by the fact that it negates nothing
and is open to the concrete and unique, even if it should manifest itself,
as William James puts it, "in the very dirt of private fact."

With these cautions in mind, what can we say of *theology as event*?
First, that it is much more modest than traditional theology and
metaphysics in that it claims to know nothing about what God is "in
Himself." This is not such a great sacrifice as it might at first appear
if one holds, as I do, that the philosopher does not have access to
absolute Truth but only a relation to truth and the revelations of which
the theologian speaks do not put us in firm possession of the "essence"
of God but speak to us in and out of particular historical situations.

I received a few years ago an invitation from a colleague to a
chanukkat habayit, a dedication of a new household. As I reflect on the
meaning of the word *chanukah*, almost lost sight of in the lighting of
candles and cooking of lotkes at the Jewish festival by that name, I am
struck by the fact that it was a celebration *millennia afterwards* of the
rededication of a profaned temple that itself no longer exists and has
not existed for two thousand years! David was forbidden to build
himself a temple but had only the wandering ark. When King Solomon
built his temple, one of the wonders of the ancient world, it signaled
the beginning of the deterioration of biblical Judaism from the covenant
with God that the people entered into with their whole personal and
social existence to the dualism in which God was served only with holy
rites—incense, ritual, and sacrifice—and no longer with everyday life.
It is against just this dualism that the prophets of the Hebrew Bible
inveighed—one after the other in each historical situation. Nonetheless,
for the millennium and more than the First and Second Temple lasted,

the temple was the sacral center of religious life in the land. People went up to it from all over the land once a year, bringing their offerings, coming to be forgiven, purified, reconciled, atoned. When the Maccabees drove the idolatrous vestments of Hellenistic culture out of the temple, they felt that they were restoring the holiness which dwelled in the temple. Yet in modern Judaism the historical event stands out far beyond the original significance of the rewedding of sacred act and sacred place. The destruction of the temple is mourned, to be sure, on the ninth of Av. Yet it is mourned not as the ritual center of Judaism but as the symbol of an event, the Diaspora, the *galut*, the great scattering, the millennia of exile that separated the people from their religious covenant, from the land, and from one another.

We can also say of theology as event that it makes a staggering claim, namely, that it is in our lives that we apprehend the divine—not through sacred times and places and rituals alone but in the everyday happening, the "days of our years." Christianity says this in the most dramatic way of all—that God has become incarnated in a human being like ourselves, that he has suffered and died and been resurrected, and that our access to the divine is through the celebration, the creative remembering of just those events. But Judaism says it too; for Judaism is a religion of events, and each of its great holidays is a celebration of events. The Ten Commandments do not begin with the proclamation of God as Cosmic King or even Creator but as Historical Redeemer.

The Book of Deuteronomy reaffirms the biblical covenant by demanding that the individual and the people love God with all their heart, soul, and might. This, as Jesus rightly said, implies and includes the famous injunction in Leviticus, to "love your neighbor as yourself," that is to deal lovingly with the person with whom you have to do as one equal to yourself. Instead of the revelation being safeguarded by removing it to an impossible transcendence, what is stressed is the reality of present dialogue and the immediacy of the demand God places on us. When Moses gave the Israelites the Torah, they responded, *Na'aseh v'nishmah*: "We shall do and we shall hear"—out of our doing itself. The revelation is not given to us before history but in the midst of history, and it is in our dialogue with history, with the events great and small that make up our lives, that we learn what it is that we are commanded to do. This applies to the everyday as much as to the great crises in history.

An important part of most religions is prayer, but prayer is also an event and issues into events. For the Hasidim, God himself is prayer, but that is only true when true praying happens as a dialogical reality. "Nicholas was born in answer to prayer," says Benjamin Britten's *St. Nicholas Cantata*. This does not mean, as we might think, that our prayers are "answered" in the sense that we are given what we pray for. The people did not know who Nicholas was until he was in their midst. Yet praying itself is a powerful event, and out of prayer the reality between God and the human is changed.

To speak of religion as event in no way means to reduce religion to ethics. It means only that our total existence is involved in religion, that it is *not* some sacred upper story that has nothing to do with the rest of our lives. One of my students was once profoundly troubled because in teaching the Sermon on the Mount, I raised the question of whether the students thought Jesus' injunction to turn the other cheek and walk the second mile was in accord with human nature as we are coming to understand it from modern psychology. She was not troubled because this is a troublesome question, as it is indeed, but because she had never thought of the Sermon on the Mount as a teaching that she might follow. For her it was only a part of the image of Christ's perfection! When Jesus ceases to be an image of the human and becomes instead an image of the divine, the way in which our existence is involved, if we are Christians, is likely radically to change, though not the fact of that involvement.

A similar development takes place in Buddhism. Whether or not Gautama actually went through the noble Eightfold Path himself before attaining enlightenment, it seems certain that he or some of his disciples devised the Eightfold Path as a mnemonic guide to others who are following the path to enlightenment and Nirvana. It is unthinkable that this Path was taught simply as an adornment to the image of the Buddha's perfection. Later when the Buddha came to be worshiped, the marks of perfection were quite other, physical ones, or they were stories of his sacrifice of himself in previous birth, as in the Jatatka Tales. But even when Mahayana Buddhism developed the concepts of Buddhahood, Transcendent Wisdom, and salvation through the grace of the Bodhisattva, none of these implied a moving of religion from the ground of existence to that of a timeless ideal or spiritual upper story. The whole existence was still claimed, though in a radically different way.

This is equally evident in Taoism and Confucianism. Whether the *Tao-Te-Ching* be translated as "The Canon of Reason and Virtue" or as "The Way of Life," it is still manifestly a way that a person walks. It is not an isolated ethic; for its central concern is with the Tao that rounds the way of heaven and earth and is the way of the person. At first glance the Analects of Confucius might appear more as pure ethics, or even etiquette, yet its link with the heaven that "knew" Confucius when no one else knew him is as unmistakable as its concern with the whole of human life. In Hinduism the ethical occasionally appears like a stage one must attain or go through to reach higher spiritual paths. Yet the four yogas, or *margas*, of discrimination, action, devotion, and meditation themselves constitute a total way of life.

Basic to the Hebrew Bible, as to the Vedanta's conception of *Nirguna* Brahman and Lao-tzu's understanding of the Tao, is that "God" is imageless. The *via negativa* of the mystics stresses again and again our inability to describe or conceptualize the God whom we can somehow meet in our lives. Yet the Bible speaks of our being created in God's image. If we place these two thoughts together, we arrive at the paradox that we are created in the image of the imageless God. If we hold the tension of this paradox and even deepen it, we shall deepen our understanding of the *via humana*. All religions and philosophies have come to a blank wall in trying to explain the relation of Being to Becoming, the One to the Many, the Uncreated Creator to the Creation, Eternity to Time. Yet the paradox we are faced with goes even beyond this problem, insuperable as it is. For we are asking how it is possible that Eternity has to do with us, human beings, mortals, living and dying in our time-bound, culture conditioned, geographically and economically constricted lives. We are not asking for an answer in any metaphysical sense but rather for the credibility of a claim—the claim that it is not by leaving the perishable for the constant, transiency for permanency that we make contact with the Eternal, but through the events of our changing, vacillating existence. In contrast to the old metaphysics, like that of Plato, we do not seek an ideal world above the moving images of time. Neither do we seek, like the new metaphysics of Martin Heidegger, for a Being or Truth that is to be revealed, or "unconcealed," in the phenomena of time. We seek rather for the reality of mutual contact, a happening that becomes for us a witness and for which we can ourselves witness.

To understand the *via humana*, the claim that "meaning is open and accessible in the lived concrete" is to grasp the central biblical paradox that we have already adumbrated: that we are created in the image of an imageless God whom we cannot define or describe, imitate, or model ourselves after yet can relate to, meet, "know" in the direct, unmediated knowing of mutual contact in the events of our lives. To plumb this paradox is not an excursus in biblical theology; for essentially the same claim stands behind all religion. All religion is founded on the basic truth that this world is not a place in which we are hopelessly lost, that evil or illusory as the world may be, and sinful or ignorant as we are, there is a way, a path, that leads from darkness to light, from lostness to salvation, from evil to redemption.

To say that we were created in God's image confers a meaning and dignity on us that seems to contrast oddly with the fragility, instability, and complexity of our existence. It repeats the Psalmist's cry: "When I behold the heavens, the work of your hands, the sun and the stars that thou has placed there, what is man that you think of him and the son of man that you keep watch on him? Yet you have placed him just a little lower than God." Pascal experienced terror before the infinity of the stars and the silent spaces between them. Yet he could also affirm the human being as a finite middle between the infinite and the infinitesimal: not everything but also not nothing. Modern man, in contrast, sees only the terrifying vision of infinity, "the heartless voids and immensities that threaten us from behind with the thought of annihilation when beholding the white depths of the Milky Way" (Melville).

> This August night in a rift of cloud
> Antares reddens,
> Great one,
> Lord among lost kingdoms

wrote the American poet Robinson Jeffers in his long poem "Night."

> But to you, O night, what?
> Not a spark,
> Not a flicker of a spark,
> Dim coals from a sandpit
> The bedouins wandered from at dawn.

For us to reaffirm that we are created in God's image means to stand our ground before an infinity that we can neither encompass nor comprehend. It means to enclose the awful silence of the spaces between the stars in renewed and deepened existential trust.

This trust will fail us if we are content to leave our affirmation in the form of some abstract essence of "human nature"—"that of God in every man," "a spark of the divine," "man's essential goodness." The real power of the creation in God's image is that somehow we can imitate God's ways in relation to us, that we can become like the Eternal which we can only meet in the dimness of time. To do this we need not shed our mortal clothes as impediments but live a truly human life, authenticate our humanity as persons called to become what each of us, in our created uniqueness, can become. What is actual and what is potential must become transfigured by a direction through which our divine essence can permeate our existence. It is my concern with this direction that has led me to occupy myself with the "human image" over a span of a quarter of a century.

Whatever may be the case with religion, the religious person has always been aware of the central importance of our images of true human existence. This is because the religious life is not in the first instance affirmation of a creed nor is it philosophy or *gnosis*—an attempt to know *about* the world or God—but a way that the human person walks *with* God, a flowing with the Tao, a discovery of "the action that is in inaction, the inaction that is in action." For the religious person, it is not enough to have a philosophy of life: one must live one's philosophy. "Not to say Torah but to be Torah"—this is the existential demand that all religion ultimately places on us. Philosophies of religion are ultimately meaningless abstractions if we divorce them from the living Buddha, Lao-tzu, Confucius, Jesus, Mohammed, Moses, St. Francis, and the Baal-Shem-Tov. Swami Prabhavananda and Christopher Isherwood claim in their introduction to the Bhagavad-Gita, the Hindu "Song of God," that it does not matter whether Christ or Krishna really lived because we have their teachings and they are universal. In so doing they miss the central reality from which all religious teachings spring and to which they again and again point back: the image of the human. The historical Krishna is not so important to Hinduism as the historical Jesus is to Christianity. But even so a one-time historical human image stands behind the avatar.

For the *via humana* the only truth that we can hope to possess is a human one. To say this implies no degradation of truth or even relativization. It does imply a humanization of truth, one that robs it of its false claim to literalness, dogma, and absoluteness. We cannot possess the Absolute, but we can stand in relation to it, and our human truth is the product of that relation. Meaning, to the *via humana*, does not lie in any *Weltanschauung*, or world view, but in existential trust. This test is not a trust that something is the case nor is it any evolutionary process, however attractive that view is to us moderns. We cannot possess even human truth as a secure continuity, but we can have relationship with it. We can allow it to be the finger pointing at the moon, or the way in which the Maggid laces and unlaces his felt shoes.

From this standpoint, the conscious and verbal affirmation of the existence of God is less important than our deeply rooted human attitude or life-stance. Martin Buber wrote me that I should not call Albert Camus an atheist but one of those philosophers who destroy the images of God that no longer do justice to him in order that the religious person may set out across the darkness to a new meeting with the nameless Meeter. Camus told R. W. B. Lewis that he would not mind being called religious in Buber's sense of the I-Thou relationship. Both Camus and Buber, the "atheist" and the theist, are paradigms of that human image that I call the Modern Job—one who trusts and contends within the Dialogue with the Absurd.

The Hebrew Bible speaks of God hiding his face. This means in our terms that we can no longer find a touchstone of reality, that we can no longer find a meaning, a contact. There are periods in history, such as the present, when the existential trust that underlies the courage to respond no longer seems possible, when the meeting with present reality in the everyday is lost in a welter of mistrust—psychological, political, social, existential. The fact that we have a ground to stand on means nothing if we cannot use that ground to go out to meet a genuine other. The Job of Auschwitz had to face a reality that is by its very nature unfaceable. *The Diary of Anne Frank* can move millions, but the extermination of six million to eleven million unique persons exceeds our capacity to understand or even imagine. We live in the era of Auschwitz, Hiroshima, Vietnam—an era in which the social cement that held society together has been dissolved and the most ordinary social confidence is no longer present. We could not imagine in advance that people would systematically turn other persons into cakes of soap or irradiate people in such a way that they would die on the spot or slowly and horribly over a great many years. Yet now that this has happened, reality creates possibility, and the unthinkable is no longer unthinkable.

I have spoken in other writings of a Dialogue with the Absurd implying that it is sometimes possible, without making the absurd anything other than absurd, to enter into dialogue with it, to find meaning in this dialogue. But this Dialogue with the Absurd does not in any way mean that the inconceivable horror that it has been our fate to witness and live through is anything other than just that. Any view enables us to be comfortable with the destruction and endless suffering of countless of our contemporaries is surely a deception.

If the Modern Job, the Job of Auschwitz, nonetheless remains in dialogue with God or, like Doctor Rieux, the hero of Camus' novel *The Plaque*, in dialogue with the absurd, it is not an affirmation that really everything is for the best. It is existential trust that just in this terrible world and here only is reality. Rather than leave this world of illusion for some supposed oneness with the cosmic All or the God within, it is better to stand one's ground and contend as long as one has life and breath with which to contend.

8

Religious Symbolism and "Universal" Religion

The truth is one. Men call it by different names.

The Vedanta

That which alone is One does and does not want to be called Zeus.
The oracle at Delphi neither reveals nor conceals. It indicates.

Heraclitus of Ephesus

They take the finger pointing at the moon for the moon itself.

Zen saying

Can we extract a universal religion or essence from the religions with which we have entered into dialogue? Can we content ourselves with being eclectics who take a bit from here and a bit from there? Or must we make a decision between climbing one ladder or the other?

There is quite a range of people who have suggested that we can get hold of a universal religion, that it is something, indeed, that we moderns must do. We are confronted as no previous age has ever been with the variety of cultures and religions. We are in a position to distill the essence from this variety, they say, and we owe it to ourselves and humankind to do so—to ourselves for the sake of truth and to humankind for the sake of ending those endless internecine wars that people wage with one another because they do not believe the same thing. In particular, there are many in our age who claim to have rediscovered the secret of the mystics who offer us, in one form or another, keys with which to uncover their hidden treasures of meaning. Seeing the essential unity in the varied forms of religion, they quicken our hope for a universal religion that will unite all generations and all cultures in a common brotherhood. Aldous Huxley, Gerald Heard, Ananda Coomaraswamy, Carl Jung, Henri Bergson, Erich Fromm, Bahai, the Ramakrishna Society—these are but a few of the many thinkers and groups who seem to be moving in that direction. "The truth is one," says the Vedantist. "Men call it by different names."

The danger of these attempts lies in the tendency of these thinkers to fall into a relativistic pansymbolism that affirms all religious manifestations indiscriminately, or naively to overlook the really important differences between religions and force them into a mold quite foreign to their spirit. As soon as we say that this or that is the "essence" of all religions and all the rest is only "manifestation," we are, of course, making a selection. Every particular formulation of a universal religion runs the danger of being an expression of a particular culture, even when one is least aware of it. Take, for example, the Ethical Culture Society. The members of this society are much to be praised for the seriousness of their ethical concern and the seriousness with which they have gone about realizing it. But when they claim that the essence of all religions is ethical and that the ethical is essentially the same in all religions, they say something that is patently untrue to anyone who knows a number of religions well. They do not say it knowing it to be untrue, however. It is because they are, in fact, so very American, Western, and more or less modern that they see it that way. It is a perfect example of seeing the whole world through the lenses of one's particular culture.

The only way we can keep our foothold on the narrow path between the forbidding cliff of a too rigid literalism and the abyss of a too flexible symbolism is by an examination of the problems of religious symbolism. The symbolic is not a negation of the literal but another and deeper level. The "intrinsic symbol" points to some object that can also be known literally and directly without the aid of symbols. The "insight symbol," on the other hand, points to a referent that cannot be known literally and in itself because it is beyond the rational or the empirical or because it is utterly transcendent and unconditioned. Thus the cross in its Christian usage is an intrinsic symbol that points to the suffering of Jesus and the way of life of those who seek to follow him. But the sufferings of Jesus are themselves used as an insight symbol for a hidden process of redemption that can never be known directly and nonsymblically, yet is nonetheless an article of faith with the majority of Christian sects. The concept of God as a loving father, the concept of the Holy Spirit as the wind that bloweth where it listeth, the concept of Christ as the Word, the Jewish concept of the Shekinah or Glory of God, which is exiled from the Infinite, the Hindu concept of the avatar or incarnation of the Absolute—these are all insight symbols, and it is symbols such as these that form the primary material of all religions.

If we recognize the central significance of insight symbols in all religions, we must also recognize the importance and the difficulty of proper interpretation of these symbols. It is on the basis of a careless, too easy, and one-sided interpretation of these symbols that many forms of occultism and universalist religion thrive, even as many religious sects keep their ranks by a too literal, exclusivist, or traditionally distorted interpretation. Every true symbol speaks to us in its own name, and yet it informs us that it is merely a re-presentation of something beyond it. For this reason we cannot entirely accept it as true or reject it as false. The same applies to myth. People find it much too simple to say that a "myth" is something that is untrue. That is not so. On the contrary, many myths contain a truth that we cannot get in any other way. It is a dramatic capturing of truth in an event rather than in a concept. But that does not mean that a myth is "literally true" any more than it is "literally false." A myth is a way of thinking, pointing, speaking that altogether eludes the criteria of "literalness"; nor can it be entirely captured within the category of the "symbolic" since it speaks out of events in time and involves the listening in the happening itself as many symbols do not.

The paradox of symbol interpretation lies in the fact that all symbols need to be interpreted and expanded, yet in this process much of the concrete reality that we held by the tight mesh of myth and symbol falls out of the frame of rational categories. The only fruitful course, then, is a dialectic between symbol and interpretation or, to speak more accurately, between one type of symbol and another—that of poetry and that of philosophy, that of religion and that of metaphysics, that of myth and that of concept—for, in matters relating to the transcendent, even the most literal and rational language can only be symbolic.

Positive theology undertakes to describe the attributes of God, believing that these attributes, even if anthropomorphic in character, have at least analogical significance in pointing to something that is actually true of God. It aims to divest theology of the cruder anthropomorphisms and yet to retain those anthropomorphic images, such as the Wisdom, Justice, and Mercy of God, that are insight symbols behind which we cannot see. Negative theology, on the other hand, emphasizes the utter unknowability and transcendence of God and contents itself with statements not of God's perfection but of all the many things God

is not. This is the *via negativa* of Plotinus and the *neti, neti* of the Hindu
Vedantist. For this school, God is not good but is more than good; he
is not being but the ground and abyss of all being; he has neither
attributes nor qualities and is unutterably beyond human comprehension. Even to speak of him as person is symbolical and misleading, and
for this reason many mystics distinguish between the personal God and
the Godhead, the Ground, the Eternal, or the Infinite.

It is in the differing conceptions of God that we see most clearly
the fallacy of those who seek a universal essence in all religions and
ignore the very real conflicts between religions as to the nature of God.
Even in the final stage of the great religions there is no agreement as
to whether God is to be ultimately understood as Thou, I, He, or It.
To the mystic, time and space sink into unreality before the awful being
of Eternity; but to the prophet and the Jewish or Christian theologian,
the events of history are of the greatest significance and a God who
does not in some sense enter into time is felt to be an unreal, philosophical absolute. Again there is a radical difference between those who
conceive of God as entirely transcendent and wholly Other, as Barth
and the neo-orthodox theologians have tended to do; the dualists, who
divide the universe between good and evil, light and darkness, God
and the devil; the pantheists, who see God as entirely immanent in
the world; and the panentheists and mystics, who see God as both
immanent in the world and at the same time utterly transcendent. If
this last position is paradoxical, it is also the one that many of the
profoundest religious thinkers of all ages have come to.

We confront another paradox when we attempt to decide whether
God is personal or impersonal. If it is impossible for us to conceive
of God as really like a human being, on the one hand, it is equally
impossible for us to conceive him as entirely impersonal in the way
that we regard the rest of the world that is not human. If we do the
former, we are uneasily conscious of the fact that our God is an idol
that we have created in our own image. If we do the latter, we lose God
altogether in some monism of matter, energy, or abstract consciousness.
This paradox is often solved or at least transformed by referring to God
as the superpersonal or as the Absolute that appears personal when
turned in the direction of the human. One of the profoundest expressions of the later concept is Martin Buber's description of God as the
"absolute person," who "if he is not a person in himself...so to speak,
becomes one in creating man, in order to love man and be loved by
him."

Buber's approach to God as absolute Person finds a profound echo
in John Hick's book *An Interprepretation of Religion*:

...the Real is personal not *an sich* but in interaction with human (and/or other finite) persons.

Personality, then, is not a substance but a network of relationships consisting in the ways in which one is seen by, acts upon and is responded to by others...One's *persona* in relation to a particular group or individual is not an extrinsic mask that one puts on: it *is* oneself within that system of relationships...

The analogy is however only partial in that, when we speak of different *personae* of the same human self, that self is a particular finite system of character dispositions, whereas when we speak of the *personae* of the Real, the Real *an sich* is not a greater self or a divine dispositional system, but the ultimate ground, transcending human conceptuality, of the range of *personae* and *impersonae* through which humans are related to it. However, despite this limitation of the analogy, the notion of a divine *persona* expresses well the way in which the gods are formed in interaction with their worshippers. For they are at the same time both idealised projections of the character of those worshippers *and* manifestations of the Real. A divine *persona* arises at the interface between the Real and the human spirit, and is thus a joint product of transcendent presence and earthly imagination, of divine revelation and human seeking.

Such an image or *persona* is not permanent and unchanging. On the contrary, it may well undergo development in the course of a faith-community's religious history, mediating a more or, as the case may be, less authentic awareness of the Real.[1]

Religious symbols do not give us an objective knowledge, says Tillich, but only a real awareness. Through religious symbols we experience the unconditioned as the boundary and source of everything conditioned, but the knowledge we attain of God through these symbols is not a theoretical, but an existential, truth, that is, a truth to which one must surrender in order to experience it.

If all our knowledge of the divine is symbolical, what, then, are the possibilities of getting direct contract with God or at least of discovering what part of the symbol is true and what part fiction? This is a question that cannot be answered with assurance. Every religious person tends to make her own interpretation of insight symbols on the basis of her religious tradition and one's religious experience, and, by this same token, those who have neither tradition nor experience usually draw a blank when confronted with such symbols. The mystic claims to get beyond all symbols in direct contact with God, and the Hindu Vedantist claims that all religious traditions and all religious

paths—those of devotion, discrimination, meditation, and action—lead
to the same Absolute. But even the mystic and the Vedantist express
themselves symbolically and mythically when they try to characterize
what it is that they experience in their direct contact with the Divine.
Aldous Huxley has called this mystical contact "unitive knowledge"—
the union of subject and object in which one loses consciousness of
one's self in the great consciousness of the Divine. But if this is so, it
also follows that when one returns to objective self-consciousness, one
can find no literal or undistorted way of describing what one has
experienced. Neither Huxley nor his philosophical counterpart, W. T.
Stace, seems adequately aware of the difference between mystical
experience and mystical philosophy or of the fact that experience can
quite properly be interpreted in terms of quite different philosophies,
each with equal metaphysical claim. No interpretation is going to add
up logically, for we are beyond the order of where logic holds. The
relationship of the One and the Many will always baffle the human
mind. It cannot help but do so. Neither monism nor nondualism
necessarily follows from mystical experience, nor is the abstract concept
of nonduality the only or best means of representing the experience
in which the intensity of reciprocal relationship temporarily submerges
the awareness of one's self as a separate person, so that, as T. S. Eliot
says, "you are the music while the music lasts."

Because we cannot get beyond the symbolical in our description
of the divine, all religions are constantly faced by the problem of idolatry
and demonism—elevating to the status of the unconditioned and
absolute that which is only conditioned and relative.

What then is our hope for attaining a universal, if still symbolic,
essence of religion? Thinkers like Whitehead and Urban would bid us
look in the direction of metaphysics, and here surely we shall find
universal concepts, if any place. Yet metaphysics is, at its height,
inevitably symbolic. It provides us with insight symbols that we cannot
see beyond, but metaphysicians are by no means agreed, and their
differences stem as much from differences in their basic insights and
assumptions as from the differences in their logic. Moreover, metaphysics always runs the danger of emptying the religious symbol of
its living content and turning it into an "It"—a philosophical absolute
with which no one could be in meaningful existential relation.

Even less promising are the efforts of such thinkers as Huxley,
Coomaraswamy, Stace, and Jung. Huxley follows the modern Vedantists
of the Ramakrishna Society in asserting that the identity of Brahman
and Atman, the Absolute and innermost soul, is the essence of all
religions. Like them, he distorts all other religions in favor of one and
makes a futile attempt to formulate a mystical essence that cannot be

formulated. Coomaraswamy bases his perennial philosophy on the myth of the dragon and the dragon-slayer—the emergence of the many from the One and the reentrance of the many into the One. He, too, sets up a false universal that is contrary to the spirit of many religions.

W. T. Stace's *Time and Eternity* contains a more systematic, but ultimately no more satisfactory "perennial philosophy." Here God and the mystic are identical within the mystical experience of the infinite and eternal that intersects time but is not in time. Not only are all mystical experiences identical, but all mystics are identical within this experience. "There is, from within, no relation at all between one mystic experience and another, and therefore no likeness or unlikeness, *and therefore no concept*" (italics mine). But this statement is itself a concept, and no less so for being a concept of the absence of concept. Nor is Stace justified in identifying this concept with the nonsymbolic and nonconceptual reality to which it refers, for it operates in the realm of subject and object in which even the memory of the mystical experience cannot guarantee the validity of the leap from experience to expression in this and only this way. Stacey's claim that "the eternal moment. . .is the one God. . .one self-identical point. . .which is everywhere, coextensive with the universe" is not derived from the mystical experience itself, for this experience gives the mystic no information that he may carry away with him about the nature of God and the universe. It is derived rather from metaphysical speculation, stimulated, no doubt, by Stace's own mystical experience and his sympathetic reading of certain kinds of mystical philosophy.

Still less is the order of the world and scale of being with which Stace explains the intersection of the timeless with time a valid conclusion of mystical experience per se. How does Stace know that the divine order and the natural order coalesce in the mystical moment and "God is totally God"? Is the mystical experience the proof of the truth of these metaphysical statements or are the statements intended to be only symbols of the mystical experience? In either case we are faced with an immense gap between an experience that is defined as beyond discursive thought and a world-picture that presupposes stages in God's self-realization and the separate, yet overlapping, existence of natural and divine orders.

Stace's uncritical identification of mystical experience and mystical symbol finds a corollary in his still more questionable attempt to solve the problem of how one may judge the adequacy of religious symbols. The "more adequate" symbols, we are told, are those that are "higher" on the stage of consciousness, with the highest of all being the mystic who is one with God. "The relation between the symbol and the symbolizandum is not that of resemblance, but that of greater or less *nearness* to the full self-realization of God." This "criterion," far from being easy to interpret, as Stace suggests, can hardly be applied at all, for it begs all the essential questions. It provides no support other than mere assertion for Stace's claim that "to find the scale of values...we have to look...to the eternal moment as viewed from within,...to the experience of the mystic." Nor does it provide any criterion as to which type of mystic experience is "higher," which type nearer "to the full self-realization of God." It assumes, but in no way supports, the nondualist mystical philosophy that Stace, unlike most mystics in the history of religions, holds to be the most valid interpretation of mystical experience. Finally, and most remarkable of all, it clearly depends for its truth upon an articulation of stages and degrees of mystic experience that only a mystic who had reached the "highest" level could properly make! Since Stace would hardly claim to have reached the highest level himself, what entitles him to judge which mystics have attained a "higher" stage of consciousness than others and which have came "nearer" to "God's self-realization"? Certainly not the testimonies of the mystics themselves, for they are by no means in agreement as to which experiences, symbols, and philosophies are the highest, nor can we divorce their statements from their immersion in particular cultures and religious traditions that lead them to interpret their mystical experiences in terms of one symbol or philosophy rather than another. The apparent tolerance of the modern Vedantists for all forms and manifestations of religion masks a value hierarchy in which the nondualist stands higher than the qualified nondualist, the yoga of discrimination than the yoga of action or worship, the impersonal Absolute than the God who can enter into personal relations with us humans.

Jung substitutes for the intended meaning of the religious symbol an unconscious process in which the individual reconciles himself with the collective unconscious and thus attains both personal integration and spiritual power. Jung has made a real contribution to the understanding of comparative religions insofar as he has substituted the insight symbol for the Freudian sign as the proper means of interpretation. He is guilty, however, of religious vitalism and relativism. Ultimately, "personal integration" is meaningless unless it is in terms of something. Jung's "collective unconscious" fails to provide an adequate integrating center because, for all its great energy, it does and must fall short of any conception of God as really transcendent and unconditioned. Unlimited psychic energy cannot be identified with the divine without running the risk of falling into a demonic identification of spirituality and psychic power that leaves unanswered the question of motivation of the will. This criticism can be leveled against many of the forms of occultism, spiritualism, and scientific mysticism that are in vogue today.

Jung's psychology of religion is only one among many manifestations of the strong modern tendency to reduce religion to symbolism, in which the "symbol" no longer corresponds to a transcendent reality or derives from a meeting with the divine but is merely a manifestation of the psyche or an imaginative projection of human ideals and aspirations. When Jung advises his Catholic patient to go to the confessional, the pragmatic effect for which Jung hopes depends upon the patient's believing in the objective reality of divine forgiveness and not himself being a Jungian! "In earlier times, symbolism was regarded as a form of *religious thinking*," writes Abraham J. Heschel in *Man's Quest for God.* "In modern times religion is regarded as *a form of symbolic thinking.*" This reversal of roles "regards religion as a *fiction*, useful to society or to man's personal well-being. Religion is, then, no longer a relationship of man to God but a relationship of man to the symbol of his highest ideals." No pragmatic "will to believe" can make such "symbols" believable. No psychological or social need to act "as if" these symbols had some reality independent of us can enable us to worship them.

"Symbols can be taken seriously," writes Heschel, "only if we are convinced of man's ability to create legitimate symbols, namely, of his ability to capture the invisible in the visible, the absolute in the relative." Heschel's insistence that our indirect symbolic knowledge must be constantly referred back to the direct knowledge of religious reality is of the utmost importance as a corrective to the tendencies toward an idolatry that fixes the divine in the objective, visible symbol, toward a relativism that accepts all symbols as equally valid, and toward a subjectivism that reduces religion to "mere" symbolism. But is Heschel justified in treating the real symbol as a static, visible object that represents and gives direct knowledge of an invisible divine object rather than as something that communicates the relation between the human and the divine? Metaphysical analogies, as Dorothy Emmet has shown, are analogies between relationships rather than between one object that is familiar and known as it is in itself and one that is either abstract or unknown. To say "the Lord is my Shepherd" does not mean that the shepherd is a known, visible object corresponding to an unknown, invisible God. It means that my relationship to God is, in one of its aspects, analogous to the relationship of a good shepherd to his sheep (a shepherd such as we can imagine the young David to have been and not some modern employee of a slaughterhouse!). Heschel himself treats symbols in this active, relational way when he speaks of the human as a symbols of God and interprets our being created in the image of God as our potentiality of becoming like God through imitating his mercy and love. "What is necessary is not *to have a symbol* but *to be a symbol*," writes Heschel. "In this spirit all objects and all actions are not symbols in themselves but ways and means of enhancing the living symbolism of man."

The "nonsymbolic" knowledge to which Heschel refers is, in the first instance, "the awareness of the ineffable," and it is this awareness, in his opinion, that represents the one universal element in all religions—the essence of religious experience which is both the source and the criterion of religious symbols. The sense of the ineffable alone leads us to meaning—meaning that can never be truly expressed but only indicated. We encounter the ineffable as a powerful presence outside us, a spiritual suggestiveness of reality that gives certainty without knowledge. The ineffable is the "something more" in all things that gives them transcendent significance. It is an allusiveness of all beings, which teaches us that "to be, is to stand for." We do not proceed from God's essence to his presence but from his presence to his essence. The transcendent significance in things and self is not a mystery at the edge of being but that which we are immediately and concretely given with the things themselves, an awareness that is within all our experience, closer to us than the experience itself.

The "awareness of the ineffable" is not the knowledge of God as an object but of ourselves as known by God, embraced by his inner life. We know only our relation with God, and we discover this relation when we perceive ourselves as perceived by him and respond to his demand. We come to understand the wonder as a question that God asks of us, and through this question and our response, we come to the awareness of God "in which the ineffable in us communes with the ineffable beyond us."

Heschel frequently falls into a tendency to identify his categories and symbols of the ineffable with the ineffable itself. "The categories of religious thinking...are unique," he writes, and "on a level that is...immediate, ineffable, metasymbolic." But "categories of religious thinking" are already, as such, a step beyond the "awareness of something that can be neither conceptualized nor symbolized." "Religious thinking is in perpetual danger of giving primacy to concepts and dogmas and to forfeit the immediacy of insights," Heschel writes. Yet "insights" are not themselves immediate, even though they are derived more directly from the awareness of the ineffable than concepts. The fact that he is referring to a metasymbolic reality leads Heschel, like Huxley and Stace, to regard the images which he uses to point toward that reality as themselves beyond the symbolic.

The symbol stands in twofold relation to the direct relationship that gives rise to it. As long as it is recognized as symbol, it may point back to the nonsymbolic religious reality. But when "the finger pointing at the moon is taken for the moon itself," as it says in a Zen Buddhist text, then it may stand in the way of our meeting with God.

This attitude toward religious symbolism implies a radical reversal of the idealist and mystical view that sees the symbol as the concrete manifestation of some universal, if not directly knowable, reality. The meaning of the symbol is found not in its universality but in the fact that it points to a concrete event which witnesses just as it is, in all its concreteness, transitoriness, and uniqueness, to the relation with the Absolute. The symbol does, of course, become abstract when it is detached from a concrete event. But this is a metamorphosis that deprives the symbol of its real meaning just by giving it the all-meaning of the "universal" and the "spiritual." This all-meaning is always only a substitute for the meaning apprehended in the concrete. Any symbol is, of course, itself a step toward the more general. If we speak of Adam and Eve and the myth of the Garden of Eden, this is certainly universal, but only in the sense that it happens with every individual anew, not in the sense that it arises from something beyond space and time and concrete human existence. If we speak of the legend of the parting of the Red Sea, we are talking of a particular moment in history. As soon as we say that the Passover is a symbol of freedom, however, we have lost the immediacy of the historical moment—its uniqueness and concreteness—and have gone over into the realm of vague abstractions. Actually it is the other way around. Freedom is a symbol of the Passover. It comes from that moment of history, and others like it, and it becomes alive again in all concreteness in the Negro spiritual, "Go down, Moses," arising, as it does, out of the slavery of the black in America. At a "Dialogue of Underground Churches and Communes" at Pendle Hill, a well-known Protestant leader of "The Submarine Church" stated that "at Auschwitz Christ was a Jew." "Was he not always a Jew?" one of those present asked in bewilderment. "I am speaking of him as a symbol," the underground theologian replied and added, "Christ died six million times at Auschwitz." When it came my turn, I insisted that it was not a symbolic Christ who died in Auschwitz but six million actual persons, each of whom died his or her individual death! Quite apart from the fact that he appropriated the extermination of the Jews for Christian purposes, it is precisely this "universal" approach to symbols that enabled the Nazis to see the Jews not as unique human beings but as so many manifestations of the hated universal, "Jew." For Adolf Eichmann six million murders of persons like himself was transmuted into the abstract symbol of "the final solution"!

We do not have to put aside particularity and the reality of time. On the contrary, they have to do with the full seriousness of the moment. The fact that this moment will not come again does not mean it is an unreal or illusory moment. It is the only moment that is given us now to make real. Because the symbol means the covenant between the Absolute and the concrete, its meaning is not independent of lived human life in all its concreteness. Not only does this lived concreteness originally produce the symbol, but only this can renew its meaning for those who have inherited it and save it from becoming merely spiritual and not truly existential. When the prophet Hosea takes as his wife a whore and then she betrays him, it is not what he says to Israel but the actual event of her turning away, as Israel turns away and goes whoring after strange gods, that is the symbol.

If the religious symbol is grounded in such a concrete and particular event, how then does it carry over from that moment of history to this? It can only do that if it is renewed again in all concreteness in another moment of lived history to which it speaks. William Blake bases his poem-preface to "Milton" on the historical fact of Jesus walking in Jerusalem: "And did those feet in ancient time," but he transposes the setting immediately to contemporary England: "Walk upon England's mountains green?" And he ends by demanding that that ancient event be real in the present, "Among these dark Satanic Mills":

> I will not cease from Mental Fight,
> Nor shall my Sword sleep in my hand
> Till we have built Jerusalem
> In England's green & pleasant Land.

Blake ends his preface to "Milton," after his poem, by quoting a statement about the Hebrew prophets from the Hebrew Bible: "Would to God that all the Lord's people were Prophets" (Num. 11:29).

"All symbols are ever in danger of becoming spiritual and not binding images," writes Buber. "Only through the man who devotes himself is the original power saved for further present existence. Buber does not mean the one who devotes oneself to the symbol the way a theologian might. He means the one who devotes oneself to the hour, who involves one's whole being in one's response to its claim. The life of such a person, her nonsymbolic meeting with the people and things that confront her, may ultimately, indeed, be the truest and most meaningful symbol of our relation to the divine. For the modern person, too, the highest manifestation of the religious symbol is a human life lived in relation to the Absolute, and this relationship is possible even when there is neither image nor symbol of God but only the address which we perceive and the demand to which we respond in our meeting with the everyday. Those who have tried to safeguard religion by reverting to tradition and those who have tried to safeguard it by seeking some universal essence of religion, not to mention the "God is dead" theologians who wish to preserve all the icing of religion without the cake, have alike fallen into the dualism of our age in which people live in one world and have their ideals and symbols in another.

In an age in which our alternatives seem increasingly to be reality divested of symbols or symbols divested of reality, the prerequisite to an image of God may be the rediscovery in our lives of an image of authentic human existence such as that which Albert Camus has provided us in Dr. Rieux, the atheistic helper who stands his ground and faithfully encounters the plague that comes again and again "for the bane and the enlightening of men."

9

Legend, Myth, and Tale

A rabbi, whose grandfather had been a disciple of the Baal Shem, was asked to tell a story. "A story," he said, "must be told in such a way that it constitutes help in itself." And he told: "My grandfather was lame. Once they asked him to tell a story about his teacher. And he related how the holy Baal Shem used to hop and dance while he prayed. My grandfather rose as he spoke, and he was so swept away by his story that he himself began to hop and dance to show how the master had done. From that hour on he was cured of his lameness. That's the way to tell a story!"[1]

If the matrix of religion is the event that gives rise to the touchstone of reality, then we may expect to find in legend, myth, and tale as faithful and full an expression of religious reality as in creed, ritual, and social group. This presupposes, of course, that legends, myths, and tales are not illustrations of preexisting abstract ideas but that ideas, on the contrary, are monological and static abstractions from the dramatic, dialogical reality of the event, some part of which is still preserved in legend, myth, and tale.

The most concrete and dramatic form of the religious symbol is the myth. Or perhaps it would be more accurate to say that one of the first abstractions from myth is the symbol. C. G. Jung and Ananda K. Coomaraswamy tend to see the myth as an embodiment in different forms and cultures of a perennial reality, the psychological process whereby integration of the personality is achieved and the divine Self realized within the personal unconscious or the spiritual process whereby the one becomes the many and the many returns unto the one. Ernst Cassirer's understanding of myth, in contrast, leaves room for the concrete, particular event and the dialogue with it; and his distinction between *discursive* and *mythical thinking* offers us an important insight into the place of the myth in the dialogue of touchstones that constitutes much of religious tradition.

Discursive thinking denotes what has already been noticed. It classifies into groups and synthesizes parts into a whole. It does not contemplate a particular case but instead gives it a fixed intellectual meaning and definite character by linking it with other cases into a general framework of knowledge. The particular is never important in itself but only in terms of its relation to this framework. An even, gray light illumines the whole series of linked happenings. Mythical thinking, in contrast, is not concerned with relating data but with a sudden intuition, an immediate experience in which it comes to rest. It is like a strong white light that focuses on a single event in such a way that everything else is left in darkness. "The immediate content... so fills his consciousness that nothing else can exist beside and apart from it." This content "is not merely viewed and contemplated, but overcomes a man in sheer immediacy."[2] For all this, there is a telltale residue of German philosophical idealism in Cassirer that leads him to see the historical fact as meaningful only as a member of a course of events or a teleological nexus and not in its particularity and uniqueness, as one would suppose from the rest of his thought on myth.

Henri Frankfort's treatment of myth builds on that of Cassirer but is more dialogical than is Cassirer's. Making use of Buber's distinction between the I-Thou and I-It relations, in itself quite close to Cassirer's contrast between mythical and discursive thinking, Frankfort identifies myth with the dynamically reciprocal I-Thou relationship in which every faculty of the human being is involved. He recognizes, moreover, the unique and unpredictable character of the Thou—"a presence known only insofar as it reveals itself."

> "Thou" is not contemplated with intellectual detachment; it is experienced as life confronting life....The whole man confronts a living "Thou" in nature; and the whole man—emotional and imaginative as well as intellectual—gives expression to the experience.

Frankfort recognizes that myth arises not only in connection with humanity's relation to nature, the cosmos, and the change of the seasons, but also in our relation to a transcendent God in the course of history. But when he speaks of the will of God, the chosen people, and the Kingdom of God as "myths," he tends to remove from history the concreteness that is of its very essence.

> The doctrine of a single, unconditioned, transcendent God... postulated a metaphysical significance for history and for man's actions....In transcending the Near Eastern myths of immanent godhead, they [the Hebrews] created...the new myth of the will of God. It remained for the Greeks, with their peculiar *intellectual* courage, to discover a form of speculative thought in which myth was entirely overcome.[3]

It appears that, even for Frankfort, myth is primarily important as a form of thought rather than as an embodiment of concrete events.

We must turn to Martin Buber for a thoroughly dialogical and consistently concrete understanding of myth. Although in his early thinking Buber also saw myth as a particular manifestation of a universal mystical reality, by 1907 he already distinguished between the *pure myth* in which there is variety without differentiation and the *legend* in which the subject is divided and God and the hero or saint stand opposed to one another as I and Thou. In 1921 Buber elaborated this concept into a distinction between myth, saga, and legend. *Myth* is the expression of a world in which the divine and the human live next to and in one another; *saga* is the expression of a world in which they are no longer intertwined and the human being already begins to sense with a shudder what is over against one; *legend* expresses a world in which the separation is completed, but now a dialogue and interchange takes place from sphere to sphere and it is of this that the myth tells. True history must include just that concreteness and uniqueness that Cassirer attributes to mythical thinking; for real history contains at its core the memory of the concrete and particular meeting between I and Thou. "I hold myth to be indispensable," writes Buber, "but I do not hold it to be central....Myth must verify itself in man and not man in myth. What is wrong is not the mythicization of reality which brings the inexpressible to speech, but the gnosticizing of myth which tears it out of the ground of history and biography in which it took root." Buber refuses the alternatives of factual history or universal and timeless myth and proclaims the history that gives rise to myth, the myth that remembers history:

> What is preserved for us here is to be regarded not as the "historization" of a myth or a cult drama, nor is it to be explained as the transposition of something originally beyond time into

historical time: a great history-faith does not come into the world
through interpretation of the extrahistorical as historical, but by
receiving an occurrence experienced as a "wonder," that is as an
event which cannot be grasped except as an act of God.[4]

The *saga* is the direct and unique expression of the reporter's
knowledge of an event. Rather, this knowledge is itself a legendary one,
representing (through the organic work of mythicizing memory) the
believed-in action of God in dialogue with a person or people. It is not
fantasy which is active here but memory—that believing memory of
the souls and generations of early times which arises without arbitrary
action from the impulse of an extraordinary event. Even the myth that
seems most fantastic of all is created around the kernel of the organically
shaping memory. "Here, unlike the concept familiar in the science of
religion, myth is nothing other than the report by ardent enthusiasts
of that which has befallen them. Here history cannot be discovered from
the historical wonder; but the experience which has been transmitted
to us, the experience of event as wonder, is itself great history and must
be understood out of the element of history."

This same combination of history, event, and wonder recurs in
Buber's mature retelling of Hasidic tales in which he reconstructed the
pure event in the form of the legendary anecdote.

They are called anecdotes because each of them communicates
an event complete in itself, and legendary because at the base of
them lies the stammering of inspired witnesses who witnessed
to what befell them, to what they comprehended as well as to
what was incomprehensible to them; for the legitimately inspired
has an honest memory that can nonetheless outstrip all
imagination.[5]

This approach to event does not dismiss the comparative aspects
of the history of religion, but leaves room for uniqueness. "Irrespective
of the importance of the typological view of phenomena in the history
of the spirit, the latter, just because it is history, also contains the
atypical, the unique in the most precise sense." This concern with
uniqueness is a natural corollary of the bond between the Absolute and
the concrete, the particular. From this standpoint, legend, myth, and
tale point us back to the concrete, unique event from which they took
their rise. The mythical element may also, of course, become so strong
that the kernel of historical memory tends to be obscured. Then, where
event and memory cease to rule, myth replaces them by a timeless
image.

Some myths contain within themselves the nexus of a historical event experienced by a group or by an individual; many have lost their historical character and contain only the symbolic expression of a universal human experience. Even in the latter case, countless concrete meetings of I and Thou have attained symbolic expression in the relatively abstract form. The universality and profundity of these myths lie in the fact that they are products of actual human experience and tell us something about the structure of human reality that nothing else can. The myth of the Garden of Eden is universal, not as a timeless truth arising from somewhere beyond concrete human existence, but rather as something that happens anew to every human being.

"The point of mythology," writes Harry M. Buck, "is that man does not act objectively toward the world; he encounters it and participates in it. Myth is not merely a story told, but a reality lived, a sanction for a way of life and a pattern for worship." The type of myth that Buck has in mind is what we have called universal—one in which the universality grows out of the existential·

> The myth is not meaningful or true because it contains elements of history, but because it places certain events—whether or not items of chronological history—into a scheme which possesses an existential character. That scheme is an expression of man's view of himself.[6]

The first criterion for a religious myth, according to Buck, is its involvement with metahistorical time. In this he follows Mircea Eliade, who succeeded his and my teacher Joachim Wach to the chair of history of religion at the University of Chicago. Like Eliade, Buck sees the myth as paradigmatic, "an expression of a classical archetype and itself the archetype for future thought and action." Though this emphasis on archetypes has a Jungian slant that Eliade shares, for Eliade and Buck the importance of true myth is that it points us back to the primordial time that Eliade calls *in illo tempore*. From this perspective "the Passover is not a true myth, because it does have a points of origin in historical time and not *in illo tempore*; but it fulfills many of the same functions as a myth." The Passover, indeed is what Buber calls a saga, the product of the organically shaping memory that is still faithful to a kernel of historical event.

In *Cosmos and History* Mircea Eliade sets in opposition the archetypal, cyclical approach to time of "archaic man," which in the last analysis nullifies history and with it any uniqueness of event, with the modern historical, linear approach that he sees as abandoning us in the end to the terror of history. Archaic humanity defended itself with all the weapons at its disposal against that very novelty and irreversability that make up the essence of historical time. The archaic, or "primitive," human being, like the mystic and the religious person in general, lives in a continual present in which he relives and repeats the gestures of another and, through this repetition, lives always in an atemporal present:

> What is of chief importance to us in these archaic systems is the abolition of concrete time, and hence their antihistorical intent. This refusal to preserve the memory of the past, even of the immediate past, seems to us to betoken...archaic man's refusal to accept himself as a historical being,...the will to devaluate time.[7]

In biblical Judaism, and hence in Judaism, Christianity, and Islam, there is affirmed for the first time "the idea that historical events have a value in themselves, insofar as they are determined by the will of God":

> Without finally renouncing the traditional concept of archetypes and repetitions, Israel attempts to "save" historical events by regarding them as active presences of Yahweh....History no longer appears as a cycle that repeats itself *ad infinitum*, as the primitive peoples represented it....Directly ordered by the will of Yahweh, history appears as a series of theophanies, negative or positive, each of which has its intrinsic value.[8]

Having set forth this contrast, Eliade advances numerous arguments against the historical view of time and in favor of the antihistorical, archaic view, which is also his own: the great majority of Jews and Christians have never accepted the historical view anyway; even the elite who accepted it looked forward to its abrogation. In a Messianic age that places *illud tempore* at the end of time instead of the beginning; in the myth of the eternal return, even history is taken up into archetypal time; even the three great history religions—the Iranian, Judaic, and Christian—"affirm that history will finally cease *in illo tempore,*" thus reviving the ancient doctrine of the periodic regeneration of history; Marxism implies the overcoming of history in the "true" history that follows it, whereas various doctrines of historical immanentism, such as Nietzsche's and Heidegger's, have no relief to offer in the face of the terror of history. Eliade also contrasts the doctrines of progress and historical linearism of the modern world with the recrudescence of cyclical views of time in Spengler, Toynbee, and Sorokin and the longing for the return to the "golden age" in Joyce and T. S. Eliot.

Eliade, to be sure, sees Christianity as transcending, once for all, the old themes of eternal repetition and other archaic approaches to time by revealing the importance of the religious experience of faith, the value of the human personality, and the uniqueness of the fact of the Incarnation. Nonetheless, and by the same token, he sees Christianity as the religion of "fallen man"; for history and progress are both, in his view, a fall, "both implying the final abandonment of the paradise of archetypes and repetition." Lest we think this is simply a detached academic exposition, we must note Eliade's judgment on modern history. Though historical humans might reproach archaic humans with having sacrificed creativity through remaining imprisoned within the mythical horizon of archetypes and repetition, archaic humans (speaking through Eliade) see modern humans as without defenses against the terror of history and, so far from being able to *make* history, as totally compelled and controlled by it:

> For history either makes itself . .or it tends to be made by an increasingly smaller number of men who not only prohibit the mass of their contemporaries from directly or indirectly intervening in the history they are making. . ., but in addition have at their disposal means sufficient to force each individual to endure, for his own part, the consequences of this history, that is, to live immediately and continuously in dread of history. Modern man's boasted freedom to make history is illusory for nearly the whole of the human race.[9]

In contrast to this sorry fate of the modern "historical" human, the archaic human "can be proud of his mode of existence, which allows him to be free and to create. He is free to be no longer what he was, free to annul his own history through periodic abolition of time and collective regeneration." Christianity stands somewhere in between, because its new category of faith that sees all things possible to the human as well as the divine, emancipates humanity from any kind of natural "law" and constitutes the only new formula for human collaboration with the creation since the traditional horizon of archetype and repetition was transcended.

> It is only by presupposing the existence of God that he conquers, on the one hand, freedom (which grants him autonomy in a universe governed by laws or, in other words, the "inauguration" of a mode of being that is new and unique in the universe) and, on the other hand, the certainty that historical tragedies have a transhistorical meaning, even if that meaning is not always visible

for humanity in its present condition. Any other situation of
modern man leads, in the end, to despair. It is a despair provoked
not by his own human existentiality, but by his presence in a
historical universe in which almost the whole of mankind lives
prey to a continual terror (even if not always conscious of it).[10]

In the light of this situation, Christianity as the "religion of the 'fallen
man,' " is, at most, the best of a very bad bargain!

Because of Eliade's eminence, because of his growing influence,
because of the vast array of facts from the historical and archaic religions
that he marshals in support of his point of views and because, on the
face of it, his point of view seems the opposite of the approach that
we are here taking toward history and myths we must make some
response to the thesis that he has so compellingly set forth.

One must distinguish, to begin with, between the validity of
Eliade's thesis as the description of many archaic and not-so-archaic
religious doctrines and the overall point of view to which he wishes
to elevate it. As he himself recognizes, what is in question here is a
matter of interpretation, i.e., each set of facts may be interpreted from
the standpoint of the other:

> The crucial difference between the man of the archaic civilizations
> and modern, historical man lies in the increasing value the latter
> gives to historical events, that is, to the "novelties" that, for
> traditional man, represented either meaningless conjunctures or
> infraction of norms (hence "faults," "sins," and so on) and that,
> as such required to be expelled (abolished) periodically. The man
> who adopts the historical viewpoint would be justified in
> regarding the traditional conception of archetypes and repetition
> as an aberrant reidentification of history (that is, of "freedom" and
> "novelty") with nature (in which everything repeats itself). For,
> as modern man can observe, archetypes themselves constitute a
> "history" insofar as they are made up of gestures, acts, and decrees
> that, although supposed to have been manifested *in illo tempore*,
> were nevertheless manifested, that is, came to birth in time, "took
> place," like any other historical event.[11]

This recognition that archetypes are themselves born of historical events
in no way invalidates those religions and myths that do rest upon an
archetypal point of view in which all history is removed to sacred space
and sacred time. But it does invalidate any general claim that *all* religious
myth must be of this nature, and it supports what we have earlier
observed concerning the historical and/or existential kernel even of
universal myths.

The second response that we can make is that Eliade nowhere discusses faith as existential trust but sees it basically as a world view that posits the existence of God and deduces from this the transhistorical meaning of history. In his book *Two Types of Faith*, which he subtitled *A Study in the Interpenetration of Judaism and Christianity*, Martin Buber identified faith as trust in relationship (*emunah*) with biblical and Pharisaic Judaism and with the teachings of Jesus; faith in the truth of a proposition (*pistis*) he identified with Greek thought and Paulinism. The faith which Jesus preached was the Jewish *emunah*—"that unconditional trust in the grace which makes a person no longer afraid even of death because death is also of grace." Paul and John, in contrast, made faith in Christ (*pistis*) the one door to salvation. This meant the abolition of the immediacy between God and man that had been the essence of the biblical Covenant and the kingship of God. " 'I am the door' it now runs (John 10:9): it avails nothing, as Jesus taught, to knock where one stands (before the 'narrow door' it avails nothing, as the Pharisees thought, to step into the open door, entrance is only for those who believe in the door.' "[12]

In his discussion of *tasdig* in *On Understanding Islam*, Wilfred Cantwell Smith makes a closely similar distinction between faith as existential trust and involvement and faith as mere knowledge or belief:

> If I give *tasdig* to some statement, I not merely recognize its truth in the world outside me, and subscribe to it, but also incorporate it into my own moral integrity as a person.... *Tasdig* is to recognize a truth, to appropriate it, to affirm it, to confirm it, to actualize it. And the truth, in each case, is personalist and sincere.... Faith is then the *recognition* of divine truth at the personal level. Faith is the ability to recognize truth as true for oneself, and to trust it.... More mystically, it is the *discovery* of truth (the personal truth) of the Islamic injunctions: the process of personal verification of them, whereby, by living them out, one proves them and finds that they do indeed become true, both for oneself and for the society and world in which one lives.
>
> Tasdig is the inner appropriation and outward implementation of truth. It is the process of making or finding true in actual human life, in one's own personal spirit and overt behaviour, what God—or reality—intends for man.... *Tasdig* means not 'to believe' a proposition but rather to recognize a truth and to existentialize it.... The question is not what one believes, but what one does about what one believes or recognizes as true. At issue, in the matter of faith, is what kind of person one is.[13]

A corollary of Eliade's approach to faith is the fact that he regards historical and linear time only from the "apocalyptic" standpoint and not at all from the "prophetic":

> Since the days of Isaiah, a series of military defeats and political collapses had been anxiously awaited as an ineluctable syndrome of the Messianic *illud tempus* that was to regenerate the world.[14]

To appreciate the significance of this limitation in Eliade's understanding of the biblical approach to history, we must look, however briefly, at the two ideal types—prophetic and apocalyptic—that Martin Buber sets forth.

The Hebrew prophets sought God to "know" him, to be in direct contact with him, and not in order to hear future things. Even their predictions of the future were for the sake of the present, that the people might turn again to the way of God. Those who were pure prophets (as opposed to Ezekiel, Daniel, and Deutero-Isaiah, in whom various degrees of the apocalyptic were admixed) are distinguished from the apocalyptic ones, as from the seers and diviners of other religions, by the fact that they did not wish to peep into an already certain and immutable future but were concerned only with the full grasping of the present, both actual and potential. Their prophecy was altogether bound up with the situation of the historical hour and with God's direct speaking in it. They recognized the importance of human decision in determining the future and therefore rejected any attempts to treat the future as if it were simply a fixed past that had not yet unfolded. Their attitude corresponds to the basic biblical view that we are set in real freedom in order that we may enter the dialogue with God and through this dialogue take part in the redemption of the world.

> The time the prophetic voice calls us to take part in is the time of the actual decision; to this the prophet summons his hearers. . .
> In the world of the apocalyptic this present historical-biographical hour hardly ever exists, precisely because a decision by men constituting a factor in the historical-suprahistorical decision is not in question here. . . .The apocalyptic writer. . .does not really speak, he only writes.[15]

The time of the true prophet is not *illud tempore* but the experienced hour and its possibility. That of the apocalyptic writer is an inevitable future in which history is overcome. The prophetic approach to history "promises a consummation of creation," the apocalyptic "its abrogation and supersession by another world completely different in nature."

The prophetic allows "the evil" to find the direction that leads toward God, and to enter into the good; the apocalyptic sees good and evil severed forever at the end of days, the good redeemed, the evil unredeemable for all eternity; the prophetic believes that the earth shall be hallowed, the apocalyptic despairs of an earth which it considers to be hopelessly doomed.[16]

Eliade's understanding of biblical Judaism and Christianity is essentially apocalyptic not prophetic, which is not surprising considering that his own view of the "terror of history" is essentially an apocalyptic one. Furthermore, though he recognizes a difference between the archaic and antihistorical religions and the historical ones, in the end he takes the antihistorical as the normative approach to all religions. He offers us as the objective conclusions of the historian of religion what is, in fact, the passionate choice of a "live forced option," in William James' phrase. Nowhere is this clearer than in his discussion of "the East," by which he apparently means Hinduism and early Buddhism:

The East unanimously rejects the idea of the ontological irreducibility of the existent, even though it too sets out from a sort of "existentialism" (i.e., from acknowledging suffering as the situation of any possible cosmic condition). Only, the East does not accept the destiny of the human being as final and irreducible. Oriental techniques attempt above all to annul or transcend the human condition. In this respect, it is justifiable to speak not only of freedom (in the positive sense) or deliverance (in the negative sense) but actually of creation; for what is involved is creating a new man and creating him on a suprahuman plane, a man-god, such as the imagination of historical man has never dreamed it possible to create.[17]

If we recognize this passionate statement for what it is—a touchstone of reality representative of Eliade's own view—and not as the necessary conclusion of the phenomenological study of the history of religions, we can make it a part of our own dialogue of touchstones. Then, too, we can avoid the equal and opposite error of imposing a biblical view of history on nonhistory religions. In the face of this, what general statements can we make about myths? First, the one we have already made—that some myths do, in fact, have a historical kernel and other, universal ones, an existential kernel, one that is repeated over and over in the history of the human race. Second, that there are, indeed, myths that have come loose from both the historical and the existential kernels that gave rise to them. This latter type of myth, in its regular recurrence, gives rise to the perennial philosophies and theories of archetypes. But even here, "myth must verify itself in man and not man in myth." The archetypes too have a human base and arise out of the loam of earthly, human existence. This in no way denies the archetypes, but it roots them in the lived concrete rather than in some Platonic universal or some mystical sphere floating above time and history. In this sense, we may echo Buber's words: "What is wrong is not the mythicization of reality which brings the inexpressible to speech, but the gnosticizing of myth which tears it out of the ground of history and biography in which it took root." What is inexpressible is that betweenness that lies at the heart of the life of dialogue. Myth is the pure form of the meeting. It points us back to immediacy as no concepts could.

10

Religion and Literature

The Bretons believe in the demonic book.

It has different names, one in each region. In that of Quimper it is called Ar Vif, that is, The Living.

It is a gigantic book. When it stands upright, it has the height of a man.

The pages are red, the letters are black.

But he who goes up to it and opens it sees nothing except red. The black signs only become visible when one has fought with the Vif and overpowered it.

For this book lives. And it will not let itself be questioned. Only he who conquers it tears from it its mystery.

He must labor with it hours at a time as with a headstrong horse, until covered with sweat he stands in front of it and reads this book that he has tamed.

It is a dangeraus book. One fastens it up with a thick padlock and hangs it on a chain which is attached to the strongest beam. The beam must be warped.

He who has subdued the Vif knows the secret names of the demons and knows how to summon them.

He does not walk like all the world. He hesitates at every step, for he fears to tread on a soul. He has experienced something.

I think that every real book is Ar Vif.

The real reader knows this, but far better still the real writer—for only the writing of a real book is actual danger, battle, and overpowering. Many a one loses his courage midway, and the work that he began in the reading of the signs of the mystery, he completes in the vain letters of his arbitrariness. There exists only a little reality of the spirit in this book-rich world.[1]

Just before the publication of my book *To Deny Our Nothingness* in 1967, I lectured at a California state college on some of the contemporary images of the human discussed in it, many of which are illustrated through the interpretation of literature. The professor of English who squired me around that day was unusually silent. Finally at dinner, he looked at me and said, "Do you consider literature to be merely an illustration of philosophy?" "No, I don't," I replied. Then he explained to me, gently but firmly, that the latest thing in literature was the New Criticism, or form analysis, and that was quite enough for literature and that the latest thing in philosophy was linguistic analysis and that was quite enough for philosophy. "I understand that," I said, "but don't you think there is room for someone like myself who knows both philosophy and literature to go a step further and find where the two meet?" "Well, it is rather messy!" he exclaimed.

There are times, indeed, when the meeting between literature and philosophy, religion, or theology is "rather messy." But these are for the most part special instances of the general mismeeting between literature and the interpretation of literature. The most frequent form which this mismeeting takes is that of reducing a literary work to specific categories outside it. The great quarrels among schools of literary interpretation are often quarrels about how best we can reduce a great work of literature that should speak to us as a whole into one or another separate aspect. This is all too often common to all the contending schools.

Whether in *Moby Dick*, for example, you say the harpoons are phallic symbols or falling into the whale's head a return to the womb, or you deal with it as the "hero journey," or see the whole thing in Jungian terms as a descending into the archetypal unconscious and working through to the individuation of the self, what you tend to do is to reduce the actual novel to the set of meanings that you have brought to it and prevent *its* saying what it is. This also means reducing the dynamic moving event of what takes place between you and the book to something that can be put into a static category. Precisely the same thing happens if you approach literature looking for illustrations of a given philosophy or theology. Once more you destroy the concreteness of your encounter with the literature and make it subservient to already fixed patterns of thought. When Queequeg's coffin comes up at the end of *Moby Dick*, it is a resurrection symbol, just as in Dostoevsky's novel *Crime and Punishment* there is a whole symbolism of Lazarus risen from the dead. Yet you dare not go from the symbol to the meaning of the book unless that symbol has become dramatically real in the book itself as it has not in either *Moby Dick* or *Crime and Punishment*.

What is true of symbol mongering is also true of myth mongering. Both lie at the heart of the mismeeting between literature and religion. The collector's urge of the modern leads us to seek a universal myth in the myths of all peoples, whether it be that of the flood, of creation, or of the dragon and the dragon slayer. These myths were human being's first way of thinking—dramatic events rather than discursive reasoning. We try instead to derive a secondary meaning by identifying resemblances among myths. We extract a perennial myth and feel we are very close to the heart of reality when in fact we are freezing on the doorstep. No myth catches us up as it did the ancients so that for that moment all that is real and important is the heightened reality of the mythic event. The myth monger asks us to accept a rich sense of everything having significant relation to everything else in place of any immediate insight into any particular event or reality.

Both the symbol monger and the myth monger tend to see particular literary works as endlessly reproducing universal themes and in so doing lose the very heart of religion, literature, and myth. They find the meaning of literature in the static symbol or concept and not in the concrete unique event and its dramatic, dynamic unfolding in time. A similar distortion is introduced by those who reduce a work to a single point of view—*Moby Dick* as "Melville's quarrel with God" or Billy Budd as a Christ symbol—or who identify the author's conscious intention with the intention that is implicit in the book. Dostoevsky wrote a letter to his niece in which he said, "I want Prince Myshkin to be a Christ figure, a really good man, a Don Quixote." But the intention that becomes manifest in *The Idiot* is very different from this conscious intention. Prince Myshkin is not in the least like Christ. He does not say to the woman caught in adultery, "Go and sin no more," but seeks instead to marry her and destroys both her and himself in the process.

When Dostoevsky wrote book V of *The Brothers Karamazov*—Ivan and the Grand Inquisitor—he described it in a letter as the real center of the book. But when he wrote book VI, he said the same thing. We cannot regard Ivan as identical with the Grand Inquisitor. We have to take into account his thwarted relationship with Smerdyakov and the extent to which he was a semiconscious accomplice in his father's murder. Neither can we take Father Zossima as the answer to the questions so agonizingly raised by Ivan, despite Dostoevsky's assertion that he is; for he is only the other half. Ivan has the alienation from, Father Zossima the closeness to, nature and the spirit, and there is nothing that unites them.

It is equally inadmissible to reduce Kafka's novels to a single point of view, whether it be nihilism, the insurance bureaucracy, the anticipation of the totalitarian state, waiting for grace, or God seen through the wrong end of the telescope. In a religious play such as T. S. Eliot's *Murder in the Cathedral*, we have to recognize that the Thomas à Becket whom Eliot presents in the first act as a complex modern person, tempted by motives of pride to be lowest on earth in order to be highest in heaven, cannot be dramatically squared with the pre-destined martyr, the "Blessed Thomas," of the second act. The dramatic effectiveness of the play is vitiated by an intention that is not worked through.

The very effort of the more sophisticated to avoid the mismeetings between religion and literature that we have discussed often leads to another, equally serious mismeeting, that is, the attempt to preserve the separateness of theology and literature as disciplines, language, or modes of consciousness while searching for a metatheory that underlies them or a formal meeting after each has attained a reflective distance from the literature itself. Whether this metatheory takes the form of a philosophy of symbolism, a phenomenology of linguistic compre-hensions, a psychology of unconscious archetypes, or an ontology of the disclosure of the meaning of being, it has the same effect of relating religion and literature in terms of concepts and world view rather than in terms of the work itself. If religion and literature are not already united in the piece of literature before us, no aesthetic or theory of symbolism will bring about their meeting. What is more, to consign literature to separate, established disciplines means to approach it with fixed methods and to neglect the all-important task of discovering new methods in relation to each work.

Some seek to avoid all mismeetings by restricting the intercourse between religion and literature to an examination of literature for its explicitly religious contents. Comparing literary expressions of doctrines, cults, and social groupings is valuable, of course. But still more valuable is comparing the basic attitudes toward reality reflected in literary images of the human. This means taking seriously the full address of literature to the wholeness of the human. The most fruitful approach to the meeting of religion and literature, therefore, is not to treat literature as if it were covert theology but to discover in our meeting with it that image of authentic human existence that is implicit in the very style of most great literature.

In its very particularity, the image of the human in literature gives us the wholeness of the human as more abstract disciplines cannot. Next to the lives of actual persons, literature comes closest to retaining the concrete uniqueness of individuals while at the same time enabling us to enter into a sufficiently close relationship with these persons that they can speak to us as bearers of the human, exemplifications of what it does and can mean to be a human being. It is for this reason that I claim in *To Deny Our Nothingness* that literature is the real homeland of the human image. But I also point out that it is the dialogue between author and character and between character and reader that produces the image of the human.

> No novel can present an image of man if its author merely stands in objective relation to his character; none can present such an image if the author merely identifies with his character in a subjective way that destroys the aesthetic and personal distance between author and character. It is the dialogue between author and character that produces the image of man; this image is never a direct expression of the author's views, but a genuine product of dialogue. Conversely, the image produced never takes on the fixed quality of a visual image, but retains the open, unfinished quality of living dialogue. The dialogue between author and character also makes possible a dialogue between character and reader—the personal response of reader that is, in the end, the most important element of any character's becoming an image of man for him. He does not take over this character as an image through some sort of visual impression, but through a personal, even, in a sense, reciprocal relationship with him.[2]

The image of the human, understood as a basic attitude toward reality, is a ground that is not identifiable in the first instance as literature, theology, religion, or philosophy, though having implications for all of them. Religion and literature do not meet in the once- or twice-remove of theology and literary criticism but in a matrix deeper and older than both of them. If we go back before the time of the rise of a secular literature, generally seen as a worldly distraction to be kept away from young girls and from the religious, we find that originally literature was one of the basic expressions of numinous awe or wonder, as in the Vedic hymns and the Psalms. The Book of Job was not "the Bible as living literature"; it was living literature that was later taken into the Bible. We cannot recover those depths out of which the Book of Job came unless we can come with a rare openness and readiness to respond and even to be disturbed.

The meeting of religion and literature is not achieved by starting with the finished ideas of religion and then trying to find literature to illustrate them. We must, rather, dig deeper into both religion and literature in order that we may recover and discover for ourselves that ground where they are one: those basic human attitudes which arise in our response to ultimate life-realities and to the daily life-situations that confront us. The notion that so many people have today that meaning in literature is to be found most directly in the novel of ideas or the drama of ideas is exactly backward. On the contrary, we only reach the level of abstraction and timeless ideas after hundreds of thousands of years of dealing with the more concrete in legend and in myth. Even drama began as a religious celebration; only much later did it acquire fixed roles and parts and become the detached drama of our stage. Religion and literature have a common matrix, and that matrix still informs their meeting, when it takes place. Literature, indeed, is often far closer to original religious reality than any of its later objectifications in creed, doctrine, theology, and metaphysics.

To approach the meeting of literature and religion in terms of the image of the human means to understand literary interpretation as essentially dialogical, as the English literary critic Walter Stein has recognized in his book *Criticism as Dialogue*. Despite his falling into such monological patterns of thinking as his exclusivist insistence that Christian radical humanism is the *only* adequate orientation open to the literary critic, his search for cosmic order, his concern with "metaphysical" adequacy, and his confusion of "dialogue" and "dialectic," Stein recognizes in all explicitness that a proper seriousness" toward the literature which "confronts us *exacts*" the author's confrontation of works of literature as "images of existence, a weighing of their ultimate 'adequacy to reality.' " Dialogue means real meeting with otherness in contrast to dialectic, which usually takes place as the unfolding of a single consciousness through contrasting "points of view." Stein understands this too when he sees the task of the dialogical critic as being set for him by the problematic but essential demand that he reach out, through the most adequate confrontation and self-exposure he can achieve, toward the visions of reality which confront him. What makes this dialogue a real meeting with otherness rather than a reading *in* of theological or metaphysical assumptions is that "readiness to confront ultimate questions" which enables the critic's judgment to emerge from his "innermost grasp of, and response to, the work in its complex uniqueness; so that it will be informed by his antecedently organized responses to life, and at the same time be found irreducible to any terms other than itself."

> The critic, if he is doing his job, cannot operate from the outside, with the help of a series of theological norms: if he does not sit down humbly in front of his poem or novel, prepared to receive it first of all on its own terms, and allow his response to develop from the centre of his personality, he will have nothing relevant to contribute.

In judging great literature, he is himself judged in his fundamental convictions.[3]

A still more radical dialogical approach to literature is that of the American literary critic and philosopher of speech Walter J. Ong. Ong recognizes, as more and more contemporary critics are doing, that the chronological approach to literature of the traditional literary and intellectual historian must be complemented by a synchronic approach which not only keeps in view the fact that the literature of the past is read in and from the standpoint of the present but also accepts the way in which contemporary literature modifies our relationship to antiquity.[4] Still more important, he sets the appreciation and interpretation of literature within the dialectic of objective and aural correlatives, of literature as "a well wrought urn" and of the jinni within the urn that cannot be expelled. This jinni is the personal voice that no amount of form criticism can permanently banish, the voice of the I addressing the Thou that breaks through even the thickest of masks and the most remote of objective forms to reestablish the reality of the Word that is spoken and the word that is heard. "A literary work can never get itself entirely dissociated from this I-thou situation and the personal involvement which it implies." "Poetry is often involved and mysterious, but by its very existence within our ken it is destined to communicate." Indeed, drawing upon the two basic movements of distancing and relating that Martin Buber puts forward in his philosophical anthropology, Ong asserts that the greater the remoteness between the voice of the writer that creates the poem and those who hear or read it, the more evocative the work becomes. "All communication," says Ong, "is an attempt to crash through...the barriers which bar the ultimate compenetration of the 'I' and the 'thou.'" Thus for Ong the voice in literature is already a summons to faith in the sense of "trust in" rather than in the sense of "belief that." Faith in the possibility of communication is faith in someone with whom we can communicate.

> Our belief in a play or a poem is thus an invitation to the persons involved in composing it and presenting it to us either to say something worth our while or to betray our trust in them as persons. It involves a kind of openness to them and to their meaning at all levels, to what Professor Philip Wheelwright in *The Burning Fountain* styles "depth experience."[5]

This openness to meaning at all levels implies an openness to being changed by our encounter with literature. That faith to which Ong prints is really existential and interhuman trust. This interhuman trust, this readiness to be open and respond without any prior commitment to assent, accounts for the possibility of an image of the human coming alive for us in our meeting with literature as Coleridge's "willing suspension of disbelief" could never do. It is only this personal involvement, combined with obedient listening and faithful response to the voice of the other which addresses us in the novel, poem, or play, that enables us to take literature out of the brackets of the purely aesthetic or the merely didactic so that our own image of the human, or basic attitude, may enter into dialogue with the human image, or basic attitude, underlying the work which confronts us.

This brings to light a further religious dimension of our wrestling with literature than the one Ong referred to. If religion means bringing the whole of one's existence into dialogue with the "nameless Meeter," then literature as genuine personal dialogue must be an integral part of religious reality as we know it. Religion and literature, then, would not be thought of as different modes or languages, however much theology and literary criticism may be properly spoken of in that way, but as differing degrees of fullness of a single dialogical reality. If this means in one sense subsuming our dialogue with literature under our meeting with ultimate reality, it means in a still deeper sense that our meeting with ultimate reality takes place only within the very structures and events of our concrete daily existence, no unimportant part of which is our dialogue with literature.

The life of dialogue, as Martin Buber points out in *I and Thou*, "teaches you to meet others and to hold your ground when you meet them." Applied to the dialogue with literature, this means the combination of faithfulness to literature in its concrete uniqueness and otherness, including the whole fullness of style and form, with response to that literature from the ground of one's own uniqueness. Reversing the emphasis, we can say that approaching the meeting of religion and literature in terms of the image of the human implies not only bringing ourselves to the dialogue but the most faithful possible listening to the implicit intention, the underlying attitude, the point of view of the work of literature. Since every work of literature, even a poem, is a frozen speaking in which the voice must be liberated from the objective form, a really faithful listening will make it impossible to reduce the work to a single directly expressed point of view. From this it follows that it is not the symbol, myth, or metaphor, still less the theological concept or metaphysical idea, but the tension of points of view that discloses the truly religious depth-dimension of a novel, play, or poem.

It is in the problem of point of view more than any other that the metaphysical dimension of Herman Melville's great novel *Moby Dick* is found. This metaphysical dimension is not the picture of what reality *is*, but of our relation to that reality. The changing, ever-shifting point of view in *Moby Dick* corresponds with our ever-changing, ever-shifting attitude toward the reality that confronts us. *Moby Dick* is a gigantic poem in which each stanza, each image, is of significance in itself, and which at the same time moves along from image to image and from chapter to chapter in such a way that the meaning of each particular image must be found within the dynamic, dramatic progression of the whole. *Moby Dick* is a metaphysical novel, but we must distinguish between the explicitly metaphysical passages that Melville so liberally strews throughout for poetic and symbolic purposes and the implicit metaphysics which we touch on only when we have gone through the dramatic situation and the characters into the basic attitude toward existence that we glean from the interplay of symbolic suggestion, action, and point of view. We can neither say that the evil associated with the White Whale is simply Melville's picture of the universe and forget about "crazy Ahab," pitted "all mutilated" against it, nor can we say that Moby Dick's "intangible malignity" is merely a projection of Ahab's madness and forget about the hostile reality confronting Ahab. It was necessary for Melville to go imaginatively to the uttermost extreme with Captain Ahab and not just stop short in his imagination with Ishmael and turn back home.

> By going all the way with Ahab and at the same time turning back with Ishmael and by holding the tension of these two opposing points of view within the form of *Moby Dick* itself, Melville creates an artistic meaning and balance great enough to contain his question, great enough, too, not to attempt an answer. Melville's point of view comprehends both Ishmael's point of view and Ahab's without being identical with either, or being a moderate balance between them. . . .The greatness of *Moby Dick* does not lie in its providing us with an image of man but in its refusing to do so—in the honesty, the intensity of concern, the breadth of scope.[6]

The most impressive and most positive example of the disclosure of a religious dimension of reality through point of view is the work of Franz Kafka. Those who seek to understand and interpret Kafka through some allegorical key, whether religious, psychoanalytic, or sociological, miss the simple fact that, paradoxical as it is, Kafka's world is not a transparent one through which we can glimpse some other, more familiar reality. It is just what it is in its irreducible opaqueness and absurdity, the product of an altogether unique and concrete way of seeing human existence. "The only really difficult and insoluble problems are those which we cannot formulate," writes Kafka, "because they have the difficulties of life itself as their content."

Kafka rigorously presents his novels to us only through Joseph K.'s or K.'s perspective. Kafka's hero stands face to face with a reality which transcends him but which he sees only from his own point of view. As a result, we too are denied any overall, objective vantage point on K.'s relation to the world. Kafka gives up the position of the all-knowing metaphysician in favor of the limited knowledge that arises only in personal involvement—in facing and contending. Kafka's hero does not encounter some theological Transcendent; he confronts a world that cannot be removed into himself.

> Kafka offers us an image of modern man confronting a transcendent reality which can neither be dismissed as unreal nor rationalized as anything less than absurd. Kafka's hero is neither able to affirm meaning *despite* what confronts him as do Nietzsche's Zarathustra, Sartre's Orestes, and Camus' Sisyphus, nor to fix meaning *in* what confronts him, as do Plato's philosopher or Kierkegaard's "knight of faith." Unable to believe any longer in an objective absolute or order through which his personal destiny is determined or in a Biblical God who calls him, he nonetheless knows himself as a person face to face with a reality which transcends him. This reality demands from him response and punishes a failure to respond even while it offers neither confirmation nor meaning in return for response nor any guidance as to which response is "right" and which "wrong."[7]

What is said above also applies to that popular form of contemporary literature that we call biography. Much contemporary biography is really fiction, a deliberately novelized version of a life to lend connections and meanings where none may be. But even where the biographer has greater faithfulness to his subject than to the mass audience for which he writes, there is, of course, an element of selection, of art, and even of legend and mythicization that enters in. We do not need to ask that a biography be true to the "facts," for life itself is something more than a collection of facts. Yet we may fairly ask for an honest faithfulness that tries to bring before us a unique human reality which otherwise we might not be able to enter into dialogue with.

A letter of gratitude that Martin Buber wrote in 1953 for an essay on the life of his old friend Oskar Loerke expresses this relation between biography, dialogue, and the human image in a classic manner. "Your essay not only enriched Loerke's image in my memory," wrote Buber, "but made it truly an image for the first time. For the image of a dear departed is not, in fact, a fixed one but a shape that changes through real time."[8] This observation takes on particular poignancy in light of the fact that Loerke is one of the three friends who Buber believed died of guilt for their participation in the cultural activities of Nazi Germany!

In the course of seventeen years of work on the three volumes of *Martin Buber's Life and Work,* I became convinced of the fundamental falsification that is often introduced by the evolutionary or developmental approach to biography. This struck me particularly vividly when I read Dag Hammarskjöld's *Markings* in preparation for my chapter on Buber and Hammarskjöld. To understand the meeting and the continuing dialogue between these two great men, I would need to understand what most biographers necessarily leave out of account: the uniqueness of each person taken in himself and the unique, present meeting between them that can never be grasped as merely a sum of their two uniquenesses. In any case, I could never regard Hammarskjöld as merely a part of Buber's environment or as merely an event within the flow of Buber's personal becoming. Biography leads us to see events as clustered about a life—as if the event were contained in the life rather than, as is actually the case, the *life* in the events. To see the event—a meeting with other persons and situations—as merely part of a life process or development is necessarily to see it one-sidedly. To see the life in the event, in contrast, is to begin to glimpse the profound two-sidedness of every event.

The Sufis and Muslim culture in general use the rhyming pair of Arabic words, *gal* (talk) and *hal* (state), to convey the distinction between talking about an experience or state of being and actually encompassing that in one's person. The title that Buber placed above the Hasidic tale in which Rabbi Leib comes to see the maggid of Mezritch to watch him lace and unlace his felt shoes, "Not to Say Torah but to Be Torah," is not, as it might seem, a contrast between what a person is and what a person says. Rather, it is the basic way in which we speak to one another—through what we are. The whole person, who has brought his or her inner contradiction into some meaningful personal direction, communicates "Torah"—instruction and guidance on the way—even by his or her most casual and unintentional acts. All a person's gestures, utterances, and actions bear the stamp of the unique person that he or she is. This person will also teach in words, but what he or she *is* is the guarantor of what he or she *says.* In another tale the same Rabbi Leib contrasts apparent speaking, mere words, and real speaking, with or without words: "What does it amount to—that they expound the Torah! A man should see to it that all his actions are a Torah and that he himself becomes so entirely a Torah that one can learn from his habits and his motions and his motionless clinging to God." If this is so, not only can a unique, concrete event underlie a legend, myth, or tale but the telling of a tale may itself be an event, as when

the lame disciple was healed while showing how the Baal Shem danced!
The maggid of Mezritch once said to his disciples:

> I shall teach you the best way to say Torah. You must cease to be
> aware of yourselves. You must be nothing but an ear which hears
> what the universe of the word is constantly saying within you.
> The moment you start hearing what you yourself are saying, you
> must stop.[9]

11

Solitude and Community

If a person were in such a rapturous state as St. Paul once entered, and he knew of a sick man who wanted a cup of soup, it would be far better to withdraw from the rapture for love's sake and serve him who is in need.

A long time ago in China there were two friends, one who played the harp skillfully and one who listened skillfully.

When the one played or sang about a mountain, the other would say: "I can see the mountain before us."

When the one played about water, the listener would exclaim: "Here is the running stream!"

But the listener fell sick and died. The first friend cut the strings of his harp and never played again.

When a man is singing and cannot lift his voice, and another comes and sings with him, another who can lift his voice, then the first will be able to lift his voice too. That is the secret of the bond between spirit and spirit.

The motto of life is "Give and take." Everyone must be both a giver and a receiver. He who is not both is as a barren tree.[1]

The Hindu search for superconsciousness and for enlightenment raises the question of whether the essence of the true person is to be found in consciousness or in the whole person. Is it found by leaving the world that is given to us—the social world, the world of nature, the world of the senses? Or is it found by remaining in relation to the life of the senses and to other people? Is the goal of life enlightenment and individual spiritual salvation or is it a way of life that does not attain individual perfection yet affirms and redeems the human world? When inwardness and inner spiritual development are seen as the goal of life, external actions tend to become relativized. As a result, the problem of ethics is never a problem of "What ought I do in this situation?" but of "What is the spiritual stage I have reached and what is the right way for me to act in terms of this spiritual stage?"

Many religions confront us with the question of whether the highest and most authentic existence is not that in which not only lust but also the total post-Freudian attitude toward sex as a wholesome and natural thing must be overcome in favor of the use of this energy for spiritual enlightenment. Gandhi suggests that the highest stage is the stage of chastity. But one finds the same in Saint Paul who says, "I wish you could be chaste, even as I, but if you cannot contain, it is better to marry than to burn." All over the world, in fact, there are mystics who suggest that the highest way is the way that overcomes the "vulgar sexual act" and directs its energy toward God. They believe that the goal of spiritual perfection demands all of your energies—not just on the level they now are, but transformed and elevated through concentration and devotion—to become the basis of a whole new state of spiritual being. One cannot leave aside any part of one to do this.

On the other hand, there is an implied dualism here, not only between spirit and flesh, but also between individual consciousness and the social world, which is considered, if not an evil world, at least a lesser world. The two of these factors work together to induce us to concentrate attention on the inner, on inward spiritual perfection, the realization of our spiritual essence. This constitutes a great issue in the history of religions, one that excludes the possibility of any common "essence" that could be extracted from all religions. Does one hold that the true goal of spiritual existence is this sort of inner perfection in which one relates to the world either as a hindrance or as a steppingstone to this perfection? Or does one believe that what is asked of one is a completion of the world that will forever leave oneself imperfect? Hasidism holds that there is a third alternative to giving oneself over to the phantasmagoric play of the satisfaction of the senses and of lust, on the one hand, or leaving that behind and trying to move altogether into an individual sphere of chastity, on the other—namely, serving God with the "evil" urge.

The great modern philosopher, Alfred North Whitehead, defined religion as what one does with one's solitariness. My teacher, Joachim Wach, in his book *Sociology of Religion*, says that, world-over, religion is a phenomenon of groups, whether it be the original disciples clustered around the master, the brotherhood, the sect, the denomination, the church, or the *Imam*, the wider Islamic brotherhood. The history of most religions confirms this. Early Buddhism was intensely concerned with the career of the Arhat—the individual seeking release from an existence of suffering through attaining Nirvana. Yet, even so, early Buddhism was centrally concerned with the *Sangha*, the brotherhood of monks, and each individual monk was obliged not only to seek for his own salvation but to follow the Buddha in going out to "turn the wheel of the doctrine."

Even the early Christian anchorites who lived in the desert, often a great many miles from anyone else, had a real sense of brotherhood and an intense concern with one another.

This does not get us to the heart of the issue, however. Most of those today who are concerned with attaining one or another type of "altered consciousness" are *not* concerned with getting away from the company of other human beings entirely. In his famous Naylor Sonnets, the well-known economist Kenneth Boulding, who was a mystic before it became a contemporary fad to be one, asks:

> Can I have fellowship with them
> Who fed on locusts
> And on husks of swine,
> Slept without tent,
> Went naked as a sign,
> And made the unforgiving
> Earth their bed,
> When I with gentle raiment
> Have been clothed,
> And have sat down to dine
> And slept comforted?[2]

Boulding concludes that he *can* join the Christian anchorites only in the "fellowship in the deserts of the mind." Since Boulding wrote those sonnets, "inner space," as we like to call it, has become a notoriously *group* phenomenon, whether in the communes and drug experiments of the 1960s, the flowering of growth groups and the Human Potential movement, or the various neo-Oriental cults that have arisen.

If religion *were* what one does with one's solitariness alone, as Whitehead says, then an all-important part of our existence would be cut off from religion, and religion would necessarily be an expression of the exception or fragmentation of life rather than its wholeness. Yet much that we have identified with religion down through the ages—prayer, mystic ecstasy, contemplation, *samadhi*, nirvana—*seems* to be just what Whitehead claimed. But it seems to be this way because the modern mystic, in contrast to the mystics of the ages, tends to isolate the mystical experience from its full communal, social, and traditional context and just thereby misses its essence. In searching for the mystic experience, we may lose the concrete uniqueness and the social significance of the mystical life. The ancient Hindu took the social orders with its castes and caste duties, for granted; it was as much a part of the *dharma* as the individual himself. The modern neo-Hindu leaves out that order in favor of the individual aspect of the experience alone.

The familiar metaphor of life as a dream is illuminating if we examine it in depth. The Hindu concept of existence as *maya* is often translated as "illusion." But we are in no position to understand this concept if we imagine that somehow the world of the senses, *nama-rupa* name and form, good and evil, are all relative, while we remain in our individual selves absolute. The fact is that our consciousness of self is just as relative as the world. What is more, we cannot even grasp this notion of relativity except in relation to some higher consciousness to which we are awakened. Therefore, enlightenment is always compared in one form or another to an awakening from a dream. Our dreams are not unreal but, relative to our waking lives, they are, or seem to be, less real. Similarly, our waking lives are not unreal; yet relative to *samadhi*, a higher mystical consciousness that we can attain, they may seem relatively unreal.

None of this implies that for the ancient Hindu the social is any less real than the individual; quite the contrary. Yet the perspective that this metaphor of the dream lends us may, nonetheless, be misleading. It takes for granted consciousness, whether it be individual consciousness as for Descartes ("I think, therefore I am.") or the fuller consciousness of Brahman is Atman and Thou Art That, as *the* touchstone of reality. What we are comparing is the relative reality of levels of consciousness. But the full existence of the person in community is not a matter of consciousness alone. The contact with others through which our touchstones of reality come into existence can give us no knowledge of those others as they are minus our relation to them. Yet it is, for all that, a contact with real otherness that communicates the limitedness of the very consciousness which in our world views and mystic ecstasies seems to us unlimited. In our human life together we build a common reality that comes from just this meeting with otherness, this transcendence of consciousness. Hence this reality can never properly be grasped from the analogy of the greater reality of the dreamer than the dream, focusing as it does on consciousness alone and leaving out the limits of consciousness that are vouchsafed us in our contacts with other existing beings.

The self in its integrity, its uniqueness, and its individuality is indispensable to religious experience, not, however, as the subject and center of that experience but as the sharer and participant in a religious reality that transcends it. There are depths within the self that largely lie unexplored, and it is for this reason that an emphasis upon the need of centering and inwardness, or what the Quakers call "the inward light," is not amiss. Yet it is not simply by voyaging inward—to the archetypal depths that unfold to us when we attain individuation or even to the nondualistic, nonindividual Self of the Upanishads, that the self becomes a sharer in religious reality. For to do this leads to that other paradox that is the counterpart of Lao-tzu's "By never being an end in himself, he endlessly becomes himself," namely, that in transcending and denying the self and going inward, one ends up in absolutely affirming the Self. At this point the dangers of [self] "inflation" against which Jung warned are real indeed. Nor is the ground that the self has thereby attained as shoreless and infinite as it first appears. Without the life of dialogue, without the genuine meeting with otherness that cannot be removed into the self (or even the Self), some part of the wholeness of human existence, and with it the address to us of the divine in the particular, will deny itself to us.

"Husband is not dear because of husband but because of Self within the husband. Wife is not dear because of wife but because of Self within the wife," says the Brihadaranyaka Upanishad. In the nondualistic (*advaitin*) interpretation of the Hindu Vedanta, this approach to the interpersonal certainly does not exclude furthering the self-realization of the other as well as one's own. But the unity of the two is in the depths of identity, not in the "betweenness" of the relationship. One goes inward to find the Self; one does not find it, except through analogy, in meeting. Uncurtailed personal existence, Buber asserts, is found not in "You over there am I," but in "I accept you as you are":

> When taken seriously in the factual, waking continuity of intercourse with one another, the ancient Hindu "That art thou" becomes the postulate of an annihilation of the human person, one's own person as well as the other; for the person is through and through nothing other than uniqueness and thus essentially other than all that is over against it. And even if that supposed universal Self should remain in the ground of the I, it could no longer have intercourse with anyone.

Buber recognizes, of course, that the saying "That art thou" is solely intended in the original teaching for the relation between Brahman and Atman, the Self of being and the self of the human person. Later ages, however, have extended it to the relation between person and person. When this is done, the love between husband and wife serves as a parable of unification but is no longer in itself a touchstone of reality.

> The man who adheres to the teaching of identity may, of course, when he says "Thou" to a fellow man, say to himself in reference to the other, "There are you yourself," for he believes the self of the other to be identical with his. But what the genuine saying of "Thou" to the other in the reality of the common existence basically means—namely, the affirmation of the primally deep otherness of the other, the affirmation of his otherness which is accepted and loved by me—this is devalued and destroyed in spirit through just that identification. The teaching of identity...contradicts the arch reality of that out of which all community stems— human meeting.[3]

We are confronted here with basic differences in the understanding of reality, meaning, and value that are, in the last instance, religious in nature. Buber makes the above critique in the context of his philosophical anthropology with its teaching that one should, in the words of Heraclitus, "follow the common." No nondualist Vedantist would concern himself with Buber's criticism because for him true personal existence and the true *We* of community are found precisely on the road that Buber holds annihilates them. To say this is not to reduce everything to the merely relative but to recognize a fundamental issue in our understanding of the human.

Early Buddhism held to the teaching of *anatta*, or no self, yet also taught the necessity of the path of the Arhat, the disciple who escapes from the suffering of existence by entering Nirvana. Later Buddhism, especially in the metaphysical doctrines of the Mahayana, denied that there is any individual self to be liberated through entrance into Nirvana while in the popular Mahayana religious ideal, the Bodhisattva takes the vow not to enter into Nirvana until *all* sentient beings are delivered from the sufferings of existence. The most awesome exemplar of this vow is the Buddhist monk Santideva. He has been called the Thomas à Kempis of Buddhism, but his goal is actually far broader than his medieval Christian counterpart. While Thomas à Kempis aimed at individual salvation and mystic peace through the imitation of Christ, Santideva aimed at a total practical (not metaphysical) selflessness that has never been surpassed:

In reward for all this righteousness that I have won by my works, I would fain become a soother of all the sorrows of all creatures. May I be a balm to the sick, their healer and servitor, until sickness come never again; may I quench with rains of food and drink the anguish of hunger and thirst; may I be in the famine of the ages end their drink and meat; may I become an unfailing store for the poor, and serve them with manifold things for their need. My own being and my pleasures, all my righteousness in the past, present, and future, I surrender indifferently, that all creatures may win through to their end. The stillness lies in surrender of all things, and my spirit is fain for the stillness; if I must surrender all, it is best to give it for fellow-creatures. I yield myself to all living things to deal with me as they list; they may smite or revile me for ever, bestrew me with dust, play with my body, laugh and wanton; I have given them my body, why shall I care? Let them make me do whatever works bring them pleasure; but may never mishap befall any of them by reason of me.[4]

The nearest Christian equivalent to this is Saint Francis's prayer:

> O Lord, make me an instrument of Thy peace.
> Where there is hatred, let me sow love
> Where there is injury, pardon
> Where there is doubt, faith
> Where there is despair, hope
> Where there is darkness, light
> Where there is sadness, joy.
>
> O Divine Master
> Grant not so much that I seek
> To be consoled, as to console
> To be understood, as to understand
> To be loved, as to love.

The last three lines of the prayer, however, fall short of the spirit of Santideva. In the sublimest sense of the term they are still self-regarding:

> For its is in giving that we receive,
> It is in pardoning that we are pardoned,
> It is in dying that we are born to Eternal
> Life.

Lao-tzu too comes surprisingly close to Santideva: "Only he who is willing to give his body for the sake of the world is fit to be entrusted with the world. Only he who can do it with love is worthy of being the steward of the world." Both Lao-tzu and his much later disciple, Chuang-tzu, understood that "in all human relations, if the two parties are living close to each other, they may form a bond through personal trust." They also understood how words cannot take the place of such personal closeness and trust: "What starts out being sincere usually ends up being deceitful.... Anger arises from no other cause than clever words and one-sided speeches."⁵ Lao-tzu, as we have seen, teaches openness to the heart of the other, the flowing interaction of the Tao that leads to what I call "the partnership of existence."

Confucius, too, for all his contrasts with Lao-tzu, pointed to "reciprocity" as the cardinal virtue in the relations between person and person. "Do not do to others what you would not like yourself." He did not, to be sure, understand this as flowing spontaneity but rather as courtesy, consideration, loyalty, respect. Lao-tzu said:

> If I keep from meddling with people, they take care of themselves,
> If I keep from commanding people, they behave themselves,
> If I keep from preaching at people, they improve themselves,
> If I keep from imposing on people, they become themselves.

Confucius, in contrast, teaches that real love entails placing a demand on the other for the sake of the relationship: "How can he be said truly to love, who exacts no effort from the objects of his love? How can he be said to be truly loyal, who refrains from admonishing the objects of his loyalty?" Confucius was not a stranger to the Tao, but he also taught the importance of structure and propriety, justice, and filial loyalty:

> Someone said, What about the saying "Meet resentment with inner power [te]"? The Master said, In that case, how is one to meet inner power? Rather meet resentment with upright dealing and meet inner power with inner power.⁶

PART FOUR

The Tension Between Past and Present

12

Peter Pan's Shadow:
Tradition and Modernity

"To make for the good life, the God of Israel is assumed to have revealed to His people the Torah....To hold out hope for the future, God is conceived as certain to send the Messiah for Israel's redemption."

Mordecai Kaplan, *Questions Jews Ask*

"God is a symbol of man's own powers..."

Erich Fromm, *Psychoanalysis and Religion*

The place of the deity seems to be taken by the wholeness of man....self-realization amounts to God's incarnation."

C. G. Jung, *Psychology and Religion: East and West*

We cannot find touchstones of reality by going back to tradition. We can only find them through renewing tradition, through making it living again in the present. "Not our fathers, but we here the living, stand on Mount Sinai to receive the Covenant." This does not mean that there is no difference or tension between our fathers and us. "Over an abyss of sixteen hundred years I speak to you," says Saint Nicholas at the beginning of Benjamin Britten's *St. Nicholas Cantata*. If we attempt to continue tradition without the awareness of this abyss, without holding the tension between the traditional and the contemporary, we lose the tension that makes such handing down, the original meaning of *tradition*, fruitful. Only when we have three elements—our personal uniqueness, the will to be open, and holding the tension with tradition—is there a meaningful dynamic.

In his discussion of renewal and reform in Islamic history, John Voll offers us an illuminating insight into the relation of tradition and modernity in Islam, particularly in relation to what today is called Islamic "fundamentalism":

> *Tajdid* is usually translated as "renewal" and *islah* as "reform." Together they reflect a continuing tradition of revitalization of Islamic faith and practice within the historic communities of Muslims. It provided a basis for the conviction that movements of renewal are an authentic part of the working out of the Islamic revelation in history. . . . In changing circumstances and with different implications, *islah* and *tajdid* have always involved a call for a return to the basic fundamentals of Islam as presented in the Quran and Sunna of the Prophets. . . . Although the era of the prophets and their *islah* efforts is over, the work of *islah* . . . continues as a part of the responsibility of believers. . . to increase the righteousness of the people. . . .
>
> The long term continuity of this mode of Islam can be seen by examining three themes which appear in the manifestations of *tajdid-islah* in the major eras of Islamic history, both pre-modern and modern. They are: 1) the call for a return to, or a strict application of the Quran and the Sunna of the Prophet; 2) the assertion of the right of independent analysis (*ijtihad*) of the Quran and the Sunna in this application, rather than having to rely upon and imitate the opinions of the preceeding generations of the learned men of Islam. . . and, 3) the reaffirmation of the authenticity and uniqueness of the Quranic experience, in contrast to other Islamic modes of synthesis and openness. . . .
>
> Basing his view directly on the Quran and the sunna, he feels free to challenge the communal consensus and institutional tradition. . . . These two dimensions of *tajdid* provide the basis for a potentially revolutionary type of thought or movement that, at the same time, remains rooted within the Islamic perspective rather than attempting to "go beyond" the fundamental sources of Muslim inspiration. . . . the *tajdid-islah* mode can be distinguished from other great modes of Islamic expression by the degree of willingness to accept or engage in great cultural syntheses in a conscious way. . . . *taidid-islah* efforts have opposed syntheses that risked undermining the special Quranic foundation of Islamic society. This is in contrast, for example, to the more contemplative mystic mode of Islam in which there is a greater conscious

willingness to recognize the universality of authentic religious experience. The mystic mode thus tends to create rather than oppose syntheses.

. . .One of the great and continuing dialogues within Islamic historical experience has been between the authenticity-emphasizing renewalist and the more universalist representatives of Islamic mysticism. . . .There are two different sides to the post-modern mood that often clash or represent contradictory elements in various societies. These two sides are the desire to create institutions and modes of action that have authenticity and firm foundation in meaningful identities, and also the unwillingness to accept existing formulations or traditional ones without radical questioning. Usually the striving for authenticity involves a reacceptance of some traditional expression while the critical mood rejects such acceptance.

In this context, . . .the search for authenticity becomes a form of rigid neo-conservatism that rejects, in its extreme form, any critical scientific thought, or it may become a punitive ritualism in support of the state and in opposition to modernist liberal elements.[1]

If cutting ourselves off from tradition is one danger, there is an equal danger in retaining the time-hallowed symbols yet reading into them new meaning so freely that, like Peter Pan's shadow, it is sewed onto the old. "Forms in themselves are nothing," Martin Buber has said, once they have been cut off from their origin, that which pervaded them as the soul pervades the body. "Once they have grown empty, one cannot fill them with a new, timely content; they will not hold it. Once they have decayed, they cannot be resuscitated by infusion with a spirit other than their own."

The most glaring example I know of this arbitrary transvaluation of religious symbols is the Reconstructionist philosophy of Mordecai Kaplan, one of the most significant and influential of contemporary Jewish theologians. Basing his own thought on the evolutionary naturalism of John Dewey and others, Kaplan offers a conscious reevaluation of Judaism in place of the unconscious ones that have been effectuated in the past to resolve the tension between tradition and the thought of the time (Aristotle, Plato, Kant, or the universalism of the Enlightenment, to name a few). Kaplan's strength lies in the honesty with which he has set the problem of how to bring the Jewish tradition into vital relation with the modern world; in his recognition of the importance of the Jewish people, civilization, and culture; in his opening the way to fuller identification with Judaism for the modern American

Jew; and in his rejection of the unduly abstract, universalist tendencies of nineteenth-century Reform Judaism. Kaplan defines Judaism as "a religious civilization"—

> the ensemble of the following organically interrelated elements of culture: a feeling of belonging to a historic and indivisible people, rootage in a common land, a continuing history, a living language and literature, and common mores, laws and arts, with religion as the integrating and soul-giving factor of all these elements.[2]

That religion really is the "integrating and soul-giving factor" in Kaplan's view is called into question, however, by his further statement that "the 'Torah' or Israel's way of life, represents culture" whereas " 'the Holy One' represents religion," which must itself be reinterpreted "so that it can be rendered compatible with a reasonable conception of naturalism."

In Kaplan's basic theological work, *The Meaning of God in Modern Jewish Religion* (1936), God becomes either identical with the aspirations and values of human, or Jewish, civilization, or he becomes the instrumentality through which they are fulfilled—a type of creative cosmic force which guarantees that nature is so constituted that this fulfillment is inevitable. In his reevaluation of Judaism in *The Meaning of God*, Kaplan retains a series of terms, each of which, *by its very meaning* quite as much as by its traditional usage, implies relation to *otherness* and to *transcendence*, and makes them all immanent. Holiness, Judgment, Atonement, Sovereignty, Kingship, Covenant, Salvation— each in turn is arbitrarily converted into self-realization, significance, values, creative force, organic growth, evolution. What we are left with is an impossible dualism in which the outer form is provided by tradition, the inner meaning by modern culture. To "love the Lord thy God with all thy heart, soul, and might" becomes seeking God in all of life, and seeking God Kaplan defines in modern Platonic as investigating "truth, beauty, goodness" to their utmost reaches. This dualism of outer form and inner meaning is perhaps more of a threat to the survival of Judaism or any other religion than an aid. The traditional structures and shapes of all religions have developed out of the religious reality of that religion as it has been imprinted in cultural and social forms and cannot be separated from that origin without destroying the vital relationship of the worshiper to the primordial religious reality that again and again gives rise to the form. To preserve them with an entirely new, so-called modern meaning, pinned on like Peter Pan's shadow, is to preserve them in name only. In fact, not only the relationship to the form and hence its meaning, but the form itself will change in accordance with the actual meaning it has for the modern worshiper.

In *The Future of an American Jew* (1948), Kaplan equates faith in God with a striving for self-fulfillment in conformity with the conditions inherent in the nature of the universe. Yet on the next page he defines "the religious element in a people's civilization as institutions, places, historic events, popular heroes and other objects of popular reverence to which superlative importance or sanctity is ascribed." Not only is the fact of the people's holding these important sufficient to make them *sancta*, but there is no difference between the *sancta* of Judaism, such as the Sabbath and the Prophets, and the *sancta* of the American nation, such as the Fourth of July and the Stars and Stripes. These latter "represent American religion" to which the American Jew presumably owes equal reverence along with the God of Judaism! Where in all this is there still a discernible religious element or room for a prophetic protest against the idolatry of nationalism? "Whatever a civilization values highly it views as, in some measure, a manifestation of God in human life." The revelation of God becomes identical with the prospering of human affairs: "Even where God is not consciously felt or identified, He nevertheless functions through those aspects of man's environment and inner life which make for man's security, welfare and spiritual growth."

Most baffling of all is Kaplan's combination of Jewish peoplehood as the core of Judaism with universal values in terms of which Judaism is to be reinterpreted. "Ritual and religious symbolism are the main technique for effecting 'consciousness of kind' among Jews," writes Kaplan. A rite or symbol has value for Judaism quite as much "if it makes us Israel-conscious" as if it makes us "God-conscious." Yet "one of the main tasks of Jewish religion of the future" is "to reinterpret the classic cultural heritage of the Jewish past from the viewpoint of our modern this-worldly and universal concept of salvation." "The distinctiveness of Jewish religion must not appear in any difference of aim between it and other ethical religions." "Any ideal that is of universal significance, that belongs not to the worship of Power but of Spirit, is capable of adoption by, and adaptation to, any and all religious traditions." Here again we have an impossible dualism—between a particular religious tradition and universal values which exist independently of that tradition and are applied to it!

In the end, like ethical humanism, Kaplan takes for granted both the source and the resources of moral values, defining religion pragmatically as "a dynamic response to man's need to give meaning to his life" and the "Torah of the Lord" functionally as "whatever is perfect and restores the soul" (*A New Zionism* 1955). *Questions Jews Ask* (1956) is replete with this same pragmatic inversion of biblical Judaism: "To make for the good life, the God of Israel is assumed to have revealed to His people the Torah....To hold out hope for the future, God is conceived as certain to send the Messiah for Israel's redemption." Though we cannot demonstrate the correctness of the assumption that the universe is congenial or favorable to human fulfillment, "we hold to it, because it is indispensable to mental health and the sense of moral responsibility." "Without faith in God, in this sense, there can be no valid ethics, because without it, one can find no rationale for that measure of self-sacrifice and self-transcendence which is indispensable for ethical living."

In other words, we do not know that God exists—*even in Kaplan's sense* of Cosmic Process, a "Power not ourselves that makes for righteousness"—yet we must act *as if* he exists in order that we may have a rationale for ethical living. But the person who rejects self-sacrifice and self-transcendence will hardly be moved by Kaplan's appeal to retain them for the sake of "ethical living," for that person will reject "ethical living" too! William James to the contrary, one cannot will to believe *just in order to attain* beneficial results. Either there *is* meaning in life that can be discovered in our meeting with reality, or there is not. There is no meaning "As If."

Evolutionary naturalism is not the only form in which contemporary thinkers have tried to sew Peter Pan's shadow onto traditional religious values and institutions in our day. While Freud may have dismissed religion as the "illusion" of our ignorant ancestors, many of our contemporaries have followed Erich Fromm, C. G. Jung, and others in reinstating religion with a whole new set of immanentistic psychological values in which religion, instead of becoming a function of natural process or ethical living, becomes a function of humanist psychology or the individuation of the person.

Erich Fromm represents a halfway point between Mordecai Kaplan and Carl Jung because his universalist approach to religion is deeply rooted, like Kaplan's, in traditional Judaism and because he, too, espouses a humanistic naturalism, albeit a psychological and somewhat mystical one. The nature of an individual's love for God corresponds to the nature of his love for man, states Fromm. But this is hardly true for Fromm himself, whose usual recognition of the otherness of the other party in the healthy mature relationship between person and person entirely disappears in his various discussions of religion. In human relations, Fromm affirms the self *and* the other and denies that one must choose between self-love and love of others. In religion Fromm posits the self *or* the other, denying *a priori* the possibility that the

human person may "fulfill himself" in relation to what transcends him.
In both spheres, however, he allows a pragmatic motif to dominate in
a spirit very similar to that of Mordecai Kaplan. He defines ethics in
terms of what produces a mature, integrated personality, and he defines
religion in the same extrinsic way. *Good* and *bad* in religion, as in ethics,
are functions of the psychological effect of a type of relationship rather
than of any intrinsic value or disvalue in the relationship itself. What
matters to the psychologist, writes Fromm in *Psychoanalysis and Religion*,
is what human attitude a religion expresses and what kind of effect
it has, whether it is good or bad for the development of human powers.

"Authoritarian religion," according to this formula, is bad, and
therefore presumably untrue, because in it one projects one's own
powers on a transcendent God and crushes oneself under a burden
of guilt and sin. One's only access to oneself is through God, whom
one must beg to return some of what was originally one's own.
Completely at God's mercy, one feels oneself a sinner, without faith
in one's fellows or in oneself. Incapable of love, one tries in vain to
recover some of one's lost humanity by being in touch with God. "The
more he praises God, the emptier he becomes. The emptier he becomes,
the more sinful he feels. The more sinful he feels, the more he praises
God—and the less able is he to regain himself."

Fromm's category of *authoritarian religion* is somewhat more
recognizable, even in his caricature of it, than his category of *humanistic
religion*. Like Aldous Huxley, Fromm presents us with a perennial
philosophy—"a core of ideas and norms" common to the teachings of
Lao-tzu, Buddha, the Prophets, Socrates, Jesus, Spinoza, and the
philosophers of the Enlightenment. This common core Fromm describes
as striving to recognize the truth, being independent and free, relating
to one's fellow men lovingly, knowing the difference between good and
evil, and learning to listen to the voice of one's conscience. The
variegated assortment of religions and philosophies Fromm lists as
humanistic may all affirm the human, but they do so in such contrasting
ways as to make their similarities less important than their differences.

One need only contrast biblical Judaism and Hasidism with
Spinoza and the Enlightenment to see immediately that Fromm's
either/or of transcendent versus immanent religion is entirely
inadequate. A third category of transcendence-immanence, of the
human in dialogue with God, of the self *and* the reality over against
it, is necessary to do justice to biblical and Hasidic Judaism; much of
Christian and Sufi mysticism; Hindu Bhakti, or devotional religion; and
a large part of Mahayana Buddhism. Fromm characterizes humanistic
religion as "centered around man and his strength," developing the
power of reason, experiencing the solidarity of all living beings,

experiencing "oneness with the All," achieving the greatest strength
and realizing the self "Inasmuch as humanistic religions are theistic,
God is a symbol of *man's own powers* which he tries to realize in his
life." But Job did not look on the God with whom he contended as "a
symbol of man's own powers," nor did St. Francis or the Baal-Shem-
Tov remove their God from a reality over-against them to a potentiality
within them. To interpret them in this way is fundamentally to distort
them.

   In contrast to Freud and even Fromm, Carl G. Jung is open to
every variety and manifestation of religion. So far from considering
religion an illusion, Jung finds in the religions of mankind the golden
ore that, when it is extracted and refined, becomes the alchemist's stone
not only of healing but of personal integration and spiritual fulfillment.
Jung's approach to religion and psychology is gnostic in its concern for
saving knowledge, in its attitude toward the unification of good and
evil, and in its pointing toward an elite of those who have attained
individuation and got beyond the relativity of good and evil. It is *modern*
in the fact that none of the Gnostic symbols Jung uses have the
transcendent value that they originally possessed but all stand for
transformations and processes within the psyche, shading as that does,
for Jung, into a vast, collective, and essentially autonomous area that
is reached through, but is not dependent upon, the individual conscious
ego or even the personal unconscious.

   If to Jung the Christian symbol is *gnosis* and the compensation
of the unconscious still more so, his gnosis is rooted in the psyche, and
it is psychic experience that is expressed in Jung's *gnostic* myth. In
Psychology and Alchemy, Jung sees Christ as not only *not condemning* the
sinner but also as *espousing* him. The medieval alchemists preferred to
"seek through knowledge rather than to find through faith," and in this
"they were in much the same position as modern man, who prefers
immediate personal experience to belief in traditional ideas." If Jung
here again equates knowledge with personal experience, he is still more
modern in asserting that "the central ideas of Christianity are rooted
in Gnostic philosophy, which, in accordance with psychological laws,
simply *had* to grow up at a time when the classical religions had become
obsolete." Jesus becomes the great prototype of the Modern Gnostic:

> There have always been people who, not satisfied with the
> dominants of conscious life, set forth. . .to seek direct experience
> of the eternal roots, and, following the lure of the restless
> unconscious psyche, find themselves in the wilderness where,
> like Jesus, they come up against the son of darkness.[3]

In *Aion* Jung asserts that the totality of the self is indistinguishable from the God image. Jung substitutes for Christ's teaching of *perfection* the archetypal teaching of *completeness*, which he identifies with Paul's confession, "I find then a law, that, when I would do good, evil is present within me." What Paul lamented, Jung affirms, namely, the experiencing of evil within oneself:

> Only the "complete" person knows how unbearable man is to himself. So far as I can see, no relevant objection could be raised from the Christian point of view against one accepting the task of individuation imposed on us by nature, and the recognition of our wholeness or completeness, as a binding personal commitment.[4]

Gnostic salvation of the soul in relation to the transcendent God is now equated with bringing the warring opposites of the conscious and unconscious into "a healthier and quieter state (salvation)." Though the history of the Gnostic symbol of the *anima mundi* or original Man "shows that it was always used as a God-image," we may assume, says Jung, "that some kind of psychic wholeness is meant (for instance, conscious + unconscious)." "I have not done violence to anything," Jung finds it necessary to explain. Psychology establishes "that the symbolism of psychic wholeness coincides with the God-image." The Gnostics possessed the idea of an unconscious—the same knowledge as Jung's—"formulated differently to suit the age they lived in." To say that "each new image is simply another aspect of the divine mystery immanent in all creatures" is absolutely synonymous to Jung with saying that "all these images are found empirically to be expressions for the unified wholeness of man."

Instead of seeing the Gnostics as they for the most part were—enormously abstruse system-builders and mythicizers—Jung turns them into modern thinkers, "theologians who, unlike the more orthodox ones, allowed themselves to be influenced in large measure by natural inner experience." The Gnostic dissolution of Christ's personality into symbols for the kingdom of God is praised by Jung as representing "an assimilation and integration of Christ into the human psyche" through which human personality grows and consciousness develops. "By making the person of Christ the object of his devotions," claims Jung, man "gradually came to acquire Christ's position as mediator."

Here Jung seems to identify God with individuated man, and the new mystery that he proclaims is the mystery of God become man.

> A modern mandala is an involuntary confession of a peculiar mental condition. There is no deity in the mandala, nor is there any submission or reconciliation to a deity. *The place of the deity seems to be taken by the wholeness of man.*

If we want to know what happens when the idea of God
is no longer projected as an autonomous entity, this is the answer
of the unconscious psyche. *The unconscious produces the idea of a
deified man.*

The goal of psychological, as of biological, development is
self-realization, or individuation. But since man knows himself
only as an ego, and the self, as a totality, is indescribable and
indistinguishable from a God-image, *self-realization*—to put it in
religious or metaphysical terms—*amounts to God's incarnation*.[5]

The remarkable thing about these statements is that Jung sees no
essential difference between the modern person's relation to the inner
self and the ancient person's relation to the divine other. Jung ascribes
certain qualities of otherness to the archetypal unconscious, to be sure,
in particular that sense of numinous awe of which Rudolph Otto has
spoken. But he has robbed his commanding voice of the essential
otherness by identifying it with one's own destiny, one's law, one's
daimon, one's creativity, one's true self, one's life-will. For this "voice"
never comes from the other that one meets (other people are seen by
Jung as projections of one's own anima or animus) but from within.
While Jung may retain a certain amount of inverted divine transcendence
or wholly otherness in his view of the transpersonal objective psyche,
he rules out of *primary* consideration as revelation and command the
life between person and person. Jung's ineffable and unconscious
"objective psyche" is other than one's conscious ego and even one's
personal unconscious, but it is not other than the self in the larger and
more complete sense in which Jung uses that term. Nor is it other in
the sense in which I am really other than you, however overwhelming
the universal psyche may be. Therefore, it seems to me a misuse of terms
when some of Jung's followers suggest that one relates to the objective
psyche as Thou. The mutuality of the I-Thou relationship that enabled
Abraham and Job to contend with God seems to be entirely lacking
in Jung's understanding of the relation between the personal ego and
personal unconscious, on the one hand, and the objective psyche, on
the other.

If anything, the collective unconscious, or objective psyche, is a
more basic and all-inclusive reality to Jung than is God. God too is a
"psychic reality like the unconscious," an archetype which already has
its place in that part of the psyche that is preexistent to the consciousness. This gives God, and the other archetypes, an autonomy from the
conscious mind, but they are nonetheless psychic. Although Jung dares
not claim that a God which cannot be known in the psyche does not

exist, he says that for all practical purposes such a God does not exist because we can know the existence of only what is psychic.

> The conception of God as an autonomous psychic content makes God into a moral problem—and that, admittedly, is very uncomfortable. But if this problem does not exist, God is not real, for nowhere can he touch our lives. He is then either an historical and intellectual bogey or a philosophical sentimentality.[6]

In *Answer to Job*, Jung's psychologism goes to the absurd length of psychoanalyzing God. "From the human point of view Yahweh's behavior is so revolting," he writes, "that one has to ask oneself whether there is not a deeper motive hidden behind it. Has Yahweh some secret resistance against Job?" According to Jung, "he pays so little attention to Job's real situation that one suspects him of having an ulterior motive which is more important to him." Jung sees God, indeed, as projecting his shadow side "with brazen countenance" and "remaining unconscious at man's expense." Even Freud never took so literally the unmasking of motives characteristic of psychological man! In *Answer to Job* Jung rejects the charge of psychologism on the curious grounds that he regards the psyche as *real*—and then offers abundant evidence that the charge is justly made. That he falls into the logical error of seeing reality as *either* physical or psychic is clear from such statements as "God is an obvious psychic and non-physical fact, i.e, a fact that can be established psychically but not physically" and "Religious statements without exception have to do with the reality of the psyche and not with the reality of physis."

The only action that Jung recognizes as real is from the unconscious and never from any independently other person or reality. Hence he states, "God acts out of the unconscious of man"; "It is only through the psyche that we can establish that God acts upon us"; and "Only that which acts upon me do I recognize as real and actual." Even the Holy Scriptures are "utterances of the soul," and God is indistinguishable from the unconscious, or more exactly from the archetype of the self within the unconscious. Like many ancient Gnostics, Jung begins by distorting the imageless God of the Old Testament into the evil Creator God. Only a *modern* Gnostic, however, could hold this god to be a projection of the collective unconscious of mankind, as Jung does, and yet rant at it in a highly personal manner. "Yahweh displays no compunction, remorse, or compassion, but only ruthlessness and brutality. The plea of unconsciousness is invalid, seeing that he flagrantly violates at least three of the commandments he himself gave out on Mount Sinai." God, to Jung, is not conscious and is therefore

not human. Yet he is seen by Jung as conscious enough to be aware
that he is inferior to the human and at the same time human enough
to be personally jealous!

God, for Jung, is the "loving Father" who is unmasked as
dangerous, unpredictable, unreliable, unjust, and cruel, in short "an
insufferable incongruity which modern man can no longer swallow."
The essential content of the unconscious, writes Jung, is *the idea of
the higher man* by whom Yahweh is morally defeated and whom he was
later to become." Man not only judges God, in Jung's reading; he
ultimately replaces him. The apocalyptic writers such as Ezekiel foresee
"what is going to happen through the transformation and humanization
of God, not only to God's son as foreseen from all eternity, but to man
as such." The incarnation of God in Christ is not enough; for Christ
is perfect man but not complete, i.e., sinful man. The new incarnation
will be that of God in sinful man. *"God will be begotten in creaturely man."*

This, Jung quite rightly remarks, "implies a tremendous change
in man's status, for he is now raised to sonship and almost to the
position of a man-god." The deification of man as "man-god" that
Dostoevsky foresaw as the abysmal consequence of "the death of God"
is now openly hailed by Jung. *"God wanted to become man and still wants
to."*

> From the promise of the Paraclete we may conclude that God
> wants to become *wholly* man; in other words, to reproduce himself
> in his own dark creature (man not redeemed from original sin).
> God. . .wants to become man, and for that purpose he has chosen,
> through the Holy Ghost, the creaturely man filled with darkness—
> the natural man who is tainted with original sin and who learnt
> the divine arts and sciences from the fallen angels. The guilty man
> is eminently suitable and is therefore chosen to become the vessel
> for the continuing incarnation, not the guiltless one who holds
> aloof from the world and refuses to pay his tribute to life, for in
> him the dark God would find no room.[7]

Man now unites the light and dark, the good and evil of the divine
in himself. Man "has been granted an almost godlike power": he must
know God's nature "if he is to understand himself and thereby achieve
gnosis of the Divine."

Jung sees no middle ground between sinless and sinful, no
possibility of the sinful person transforming and hallowing the instincts
rather than simply celebrating and integrating them. By identifying the
real self with the autonomous center in the unconscious, Jung is in
danger of taking his own inner knowledge for the will of God and

imposing it upon others. That Jung may not entirely have escaped from this danger is suggested by his celebration in *Answer to Job* of the new Roman Catholic dogma of the Assumption of Mary. He considers this dogma "to be the most important religious event since the Reformation"—not because of any of the reasons that the Catholic Church would hold to be important but because it gives the feminine principle the place in the deity that Jung's psychology calls for![8]

Freud has retained of religion the superstitious terror and the propitiation of the angry father. Fromm has retained of religion all this *plus* the very real humanistic values he finds in a variety of religions and philosophies. Jung has retained the uncanny, numinous dread of religion, its overwhelming power, the human sense of creatureliness and its possibilities of ecstasy. But none of the three has been able to allow religion to speak with its own voice and in its own terms. All three have transformed it, each according to his own notion of the psyche, claiming thereby to have arrived at the true essence beneath the surface appearance. Religion that is not taken at face value but reduced to what it "really is" is no more truly met than the person whose stated words and conscious intentions one entirely dismisses in favor of one's own "insight" into the workings of the other's unconscious.

I am not suggesting that Freud, Fromm, or Jung failed to develop touchstones of their own based on the immediate encounters and events of their lives. I am speaking, rather, of the authority with which psychology has been invested in our age, as theology and philosophy were in other ages. There has *always* been a problem of tradition and modernity; for tradition is an organically growing and changing phenomenon, and all great religions have witnessed the passing on of religious insights and teachings to people whose land, culture, language, and life-conditions were vastly different from those among whom the religion originally arose. What is different about our contemporary problem of tradition and modernity is, first, that for many psychology has taken the place that philosophy, theology, or the physical and biological sciences held in other ages. Second, contemporary thinkers and seekers are exposed to a vast array of conflicting and interacting cultures, philosophies, psychologies, and religious traditions, which often leads to universalist formulations rather than to that mutually confirming pluralism for which I call. Third, the tension between religion and science and the triumph of secularism have led many to a *conscious* reevaluation that accomplishes the transvaluation of meaning which in past ages took place unconsciously.

The object of my critique of Kaplan, Fromm, and Jung has not been to disparage their thought in itself but to show how each illustrates, in a quite different way, the problem of "Peter Pan's shadow"—the attempt to sew modern meanings onto ancient tradition in a fairly arbitrary way that leaves us with an impossible dualism between form and content. None of this implies that it is illegitimate for a psychologist to express his or her views on religion. What we are focusing on here, rather, is the tendency to bolster these new insights by recasting them in old forms, putting new wine into old skins. Kaplan does this through holding onto the rituals and traditions of Judaism while reinterpreting them in terms of naturalist, evolutionary, and universalist meanings. Fromm and Jung, in contrast, wed their thinking to no one religion, though Fromm originally stems from Judaism and Jung consistently applies his thought to a radical reinterpretation of Christianity.

Do not other theologians and philosophers of religion reinterpret and reevaluate? Of course. For tradition is a dialogue, and there is no way that we can bring ourselves into identity with the founders of a tradition. Yet the necessity of responding from where we are can be done with full consciousness of the tension between the present and the past and of the difficulty of making the past living again in the present. Or it can be done without faithfulness to the original tradition in such a way that the tensions are covered over and sleight-of-hand reinterpretations are introduced in the name of harmonizing ancient religion and modern thought. I once went to a Reform Jewish Seder service on the first night of Passover during which I noticed that on one page in the *Haggadah* (the book of prescribed prayers and rituals), it said in English, "May next year be a year of peace and prosperity," whereas on the facing page in Hebrew it read, "Next year may Messiah, the son of David, come." Those who could still read the Hebrew had their choice of the older or the newer meaning. Those who knew only English had the smooth, modern meaning, without any tension.

Much liberal Judaism in America and elsewhere has developed along similar lines. Liberal Judaism has often contented itself with the affirmation of universal values, seeing biblical and Jewish history as the mere occasion for the manifestation of those values. It has tended to substitute for the biblical covenant "ethical humanism" and for the prophetic demand in the specific historical situation the "progressive revelation" of ideal moral values to be realized in some future "Messianic age." Although I do not hold with those Christians who claim that Unitarians and Universalists are not really Christians and still less with those "born again" Christians who reserve for themselves alone the title of Christian, I suspect that something similar has happened in liberal Christianity.

Our problem is in no way confined to liberalism versus traditionalism. I once read a book on Conservative Judaism that criticized the Orthodox as clinging too much to the past and the Reform as giving in too easily to the present. Actually each of these interpretations of Judaism claims to be what the author held for Conservative Judaism: the *right* tension between past and present, tradition and modernity. And the same is true with all the varied interpretations and reinterpretations of Christianity, Islam, Hinduism, and Buddhism, to name a few.

I do not criticize Fromm and Jung because they cannot accept traditional religion as they understand it, and I respect Kaplan's honesty in trying to accomplish consciously those reevaluations that he feels will be made unconsciously anyway. What I am asking is that we hold the tension, that we not make the problem easier for ourselves than it is. If we do, our traditions will die while our modernity will soon cease to be modern, as is already evident in Kaplan's philosophy of religion.

How many of the American followers of the "universal" teaching of Bahai really understand the origin of Bahai as an Islamic religion and political sect and hold the tension with it? How many practitioners of Transcendental Meditation take seriously the Hindu teaching that is implicit, though regularly denied, in their mantras and meditations? How many of the beat and hippie Zen following in the fifties and sixties took seriously the roots of Zen in Buddhism? For that matter how many Catholics face squarely the anachronism that is involved in the authority of the pope being based on Jesus' saying, "On this rock [*Petra*/Peter] I found my church," when no church even remotely resembling the vast hierarchical structure of the Catholic Church existed in the time of Jesus?

An Orthodox Jewish friend and scholar criticized my chapter on "Jesus: Image of the Human or Image of God?" on the ground that my understanding of Jesus' teachings does not conform to that of orthodox Christianity. In so doing, he was following a religious formalism that I must reject in favor of that dialogue of touchstones that in turn deeply affects our own touchstones of reality. Every person has the right to a personal dialogue with the teachings of Jesus, the Buddha, Ramakrishna, Lao-tzu, Black Elk, or the Third Zen Patriarch. But we must not forget that it *is* a dialogue—that we are bringing our own quite unique ground into tension with the great religious teachers. Insofar as I was able, I listened obediently and responded wholeheartedly to what Jesus has to say through the admittedly opaque lenses of the Gospels and of the various translations of those Gospels into English. In so doing I do not claim to be a scholar of the New Testament. But neither am I simply reading into Jesus' teachings my own philosophy. I am listening and responding, entering into dialogue, and bringing the results of that dialogue into my dialogue with others.

13

The Dialectic Between Spirit and Form

There were three friends
Discussing life.
One said:
"Can men live together
And know nothing of it?
Work together
And produce nothing?
Can they fly around in space
And forget to exist
World without end?"
The three friends looked at each other
And burst out laughing.
They had no explanation.
Then they were better friends than before.

Then one friend died.
Confucius
Sent a disciple to help the other two
Chant his obsequies.

The disciple found that one friend
Had composed a song.
While the other played a lute,
They sang:
    "Hey, Sung Hu!
    Where'd you go?
    Hey, Sung Hu!

Where'd you go?
You have gone
Where you really were.
And we are here—
Damn it! We are here!"

Then the disciple of Confucius burst in on them and exclaimed:
"May I inquire where you found this in the Rubrics for obsequies,
This frivolous carolling in the presence of the departed?"

The two friends looked at each other and laughed:
"Poor fellow," they said, "he doesn't know the new liturgy!"[1]

To have laid bare the fine or coarse threads with which the shadow
of modernity has been stitched onto the Peter Pan of the religious
tradition has not, of course, solved the problem of the tension between
the two. But it may perhaps warn us against making our already difficult
problem worse through seeking to manipulate old symbols or fabricate
new ones in order to meet the need of the time. We have pointed to
the necessity of combining personal uniqueness, the will to be open,
and holding the tension with tradition in order for there to be a
meaningful dynamic, and we have stressed the need to contend with
the tradition in order to make an honest witness to our own uniqueness
and to the Dialogue with the Absurd that has characterized our lives.
    Even if all these warnings and admonitions were heeded, it would
not guarantee any smooth continuity of tradition. Quite the contrary.
If, as Buber says, one cannot fill forms that have grown empty with
a new, timely content in a spirit other than their own, then we may
be faced with a period of waiting in the darkness in order that we may,
as Gabriel Vahanian has put it, "wait without idols." If the philosopher
has destroyed the images of God that swell up and block the way to
God, if the finger pointing to the moon has been taken for the moon
itself and then has been discarded altogether, then what else is there
except for the religious person to "proceed across the darkness to a new
meeting with the nameless Meeter"? If, as Buber says at the end of "The
Dialogue of Heaven and Earth," we await in whatever form it comes
the new appearance of our cruel and kind Lord, then we cannot predict,
much less prescribe, what that form will be. In this wilderness night,
Buber also says, no way can be pointed out. All we can do is to wait
with ready soul until the morning dawns and a way becomes visible
where no one could have foreseen. If this is so, then we cannot demand

for pragmatic reasons that tradition be taken over intact from the past as if there were no problem at all.

It was several times suggested to Buber that he should liberate Hasidism from its "confessional limitations," i.e., its integral relationship to the stream of Judaism in which it arose, and make of it a universal religion of mankind. "To take such a 'universal' path would have been pure arbitrariness on my part," Buber replied. It was not necessary for him to leave his ancestral house in order to speak a word to those outside the Jewish tradition, Buber asserted. He could stand in the doorway and utter a word into the street, and the word that was uttered thus, from one "house of exile" to another, would not go astray. In his Foreword to *For the Sake of Heaven*, Buber states that he has no teaching but only wishes to point to realities such as he has made visible in that Hasidic chronicle-novel and in *The Tales of the Hasidim*. Buber undertook this great lifework not for the sake of renewing Judaism alone but also for that of Western man—in order to point to a meaningful image of human existence in the face of the absence of any in our time. Or put in his own language, he saw this time as one of the "eclipse of God"; he pointed out the human contribution to this eclipse; and he pointed to a way that might help us to make ready for a new historical situation in which the finger of God might again be present and discernible in history.

Our most significant insight into the relation of Buber as a modern interpreter and man of faith to the Hasidic tradition is his reply to Rivka Schatz-Uffenheimer, and by implication to her teacher, Gershom Scholem, concerning the charge that the tapestry with which he has portrayed Hasidic teaching is one-sided, insufficiently historical and objective, and "woven of selective strands." Buber did not see or wish others to see his task as an objective, historical one, any more than he saw it as a merely subjective one. It was, rather, a dialogue—between a scholar and a man of faith, on the one hand, and a rich religious tradition, on the other—that he brought to the Western world against its own will, because of the need of the hour.

No one, including Scholem, denies Buber a comprehensive and exact knowledge of all the literature of Hasidism, tales and formal teachings alike. But in this historical hour, Buber did not feel that he had the luxury of presenting this tradition simply as an objective historian and scholar. Precisely because of the degeneration of both forms and spirit in the modern world, he felt it necessary to stress one tradition of Hasidism—that which originated with the Baal Shem and focused on the hallowing of the everyday—over the other—that which originated with his successor the Maggid of Mezritch and focused on the nullification of the worldly and the particular for the sake of spiritualization. He was quite ready in his replies to show why he took up the strands that he did and why he let the others lie. But the assumption of his critics, namely that the only valid task was that of full historical exposition, he could not accept.

Instead, Buber put forward a dialogical approach to religion and human experience and to the history of religion that dared to see the interpreter himself as a "filter" for the needs of faith of modern man!

> Since the time in my preoccupation with this subject when I reached a basic study of the sources, i.e., since about 1910 (the early works were not sufficiently based), I have not aimed at presenting a historically or hermeneutically comprehensive presentation of Hasidism. Already at that time there grew in me the consciousness that my task by its nature was a selective one. But at the same time there grew in me an ever firmer certainty that the principle of selection that ruled here did not originate in a subjective preference. In this respect this task of mine is essentially of the same nature as my work on Judaism in general. I have dealt with that in the life and teaching of Judaism which, according to my insight, is its proper truth and is decisive for its function in the previous and future history of the human spirit. This attitude of mine includes valuation, of course, from its base up; but this valuation is one—on this point no doubt has touched me during the whole time—which has its origin in the immovable central existence of values. Since I have attained to the maturity of this insight, I have not made use of a filter; I became a filter.[2]

Buber's understanding of the dialectic between spirit and form is made even clearer in his reply to Scholem himself. This reply began with a long section on "the two different ways in which a great tradition of religious faith can be rescued form the rubble of time and brought back into the light"—that of historical scholarship and that of faithfully and adequately communicating the vitality and power of this faith. The latter "approach derives from the desire to convey to our own time the force of a former life of faith and to help our age renew its ruptured bond with the Absolute." For this approach it is necessary to have an adequate knowledge of the tradition in all its spiritual and historical connections, but it is not necessary to present all of them but only a selection of those elements in which its vitalizing element was embodied, a selection based not upon objective scholarship but "upon the reliability of the person making the selection in the face of criteria; for what may appear to be mere 'subjectivity' to the detached scholar can sooner or later prove to be necessary to the process of renewal."

Second, this person "should not be expected to turn away from the traditional reports concerning the life of the pious in order to give primary emphasis to the theoretical doctrine to which the founder and his disciples appealed for their authority. Even in the founding of the great world religions, what was essential was not a comprehensible doctrine but an event which was at once life and word. And when, as in Hasidism, religious life reaches back to a much earlier doctrine in order to establish its legitimacy, it is not the old teaching as such which engenders the new life of faith in a later age but rather the context of personal and community existence in a which a far-reaching transformation of the earlier teachings takes place.[3]

For Buber to say that he became a filter by no means implies that he was able to take over all the forms of Hasidism and make them his own. In *Philosophical Interrogations* he begged his readers not to identify his own teachings with his interpretations of Hasidism; for the latter used language that he could not himself responsibly employ. "If I had lived in the days when people fought over the word of God and not its caricature," Buber once said, "I too would have left my father's home and become a Hasid." But he also said, "It would have been an unpermissible masquerade for me, who has such a different relationship to the Jewish law, to have become a Hasid." This does not mean that Buber saw his task as purely an intellectual or an interpretative one. On the contrary, he wrote in 1924:

> Since I began my work on Hasidic literature, I have done this work for the sake of the teaching and the way. But at that time I believed that one might relate to them merely as an observer. Since then I have realized that the teaching is there that one may learn it and the way that one may walk on it. The deeper I realized this, so much the more this work, against which my life measured and ventured itself, became for me question, suffering, and also even consolation.[4]

A number of years ago an American rabbi writing in Mordecai Kaplan's journal *The Reconstructionist* pronounced "the contemporary revival of interest in Hasidism" a romantic idealization oftentimes to the point of extravagance. He blamed this "neo-mystical orientation" on "the influence of Martin Buber's literary work in this field during the past half century," a blame in which I myself must share to some degree because I have translated and edited four of Buber's books on Hasidism. The antidote for this neo-Hasidic sickness, said the author, is "an examination of the elements of irrationality and fantasy in Hasidic doctrine." Such a reexamination "may have a sobering effect upon those who have been overly influenced by the current romanticist conception of Hasidism." After depicting the ignorant and superstitious intellectual climate in which Hasidism grew and spread, he presented an attack on the nonsensical claims for supernatural powers advanced on behalf of the Baal Shem both by the "Besht" himself and his followers.

One of the sources he listed for his material on the Besht is the stories in Buber's *The Legend of the Baal-Shem*, the first of my own translations of Buber's Hasidic works. Nothing could have been more obvious, one would have thought, than that these legends make no claim to historical accuracy. Yet he takes them as reliable historical documents on which to base his criticism. After all this and much more, he comes out with the remarkable conclusion that, whatever Hasidism may have contributed to the Jewish people of the eighteenth century by way of warmth, enthusiasm, joy, and sense of fellowship, Hasidism is an anachronism in our day. "The deep chasm that separates us intellectually from Hasidism," the radical difference in their universe of discourse and ours, make any attempt to revive Hasidism "as a religious philosophy and movement for our contemporaries" a "confusion of nostalgia and sentimentalism with the imperatives and requirements of a modern man's faith." If there are among our contemporaries some "whose religious backgrounds and mental framework enable them to believe in and practice the Hasidic way of life," then these are persons who may be dwelling physically in twentieth-century America, "but they are living intellectually in 18th century Poland."[5]

The "logic" of this testimony in the name of modern "rationalism" amounts to saying that if there are some elements in a religious tradition that appear quite foreign to the contemporary American or European, therefore the movement as a whole has nothing to say to us. By the same logic one would have to dismiss the Bible and most of the other world scriptures and myths as utterly irrelevant for "modern man" because there is ample evidence in them of beliefs concerning the supernatural, the demonic, and the miraculous that "modern man" must consider the products of ignorance and superstition or of an outmoded world view.

Nonetheless, this reexamination helps us clarify the problem of the relation between tradition and modernity and with it the dialectic between spirit and form. That Hasidism can be revived as an element in a modern religious philosophy is not only imaginable but undeniably actual in a number of important contemporary philosophies of Judaism, such as those of Martin Buber, Abraham J. Heschel, Mische Maisels, Elie Wiesel, my own, and even, to a lesser extent, Leo Baeck, the great representative of liberal Judaism. What is more, the Hasidic emphases on community, fervor, and the overcoming of the dualism between spirit and life are all of the greatest possible significance for contemporary religious life.

But I would be less than candid if I did not add that while it is possible to take over some of the forms of Hasidic life, such as the *niggunim* or wordless melodies, the dance called the hora, fervor in prayer, the use of the Hasidic tale, and the sense of living community, it is all but impossible for *most* persons of modern western consciousness to take over others. Those who can—and in our day there is an impressive revival of Hasidism not only among the Lubavitcher Hasidim but many others—often carry over the trappings of eighteenth-century Poland in an understandable effort not to see the rich tradition of Hasidism dissolve entirely into the secular life of the modern world. In so doing, in my opinion, they impede the living dialectic between spirit and form by confining the spirit within the fixed forms of earlier times. This opinion is obviously not shared by the many *baal-teshuvim* and *baal-teshuvoth* who have found their way "back" to Hasidism, often from secular or very watered-down Jewish backgrounds or even from forays into Oriental religions.

The American counterpart of the Mea Shearim district of Jerusalem is the Williamsburg district of Brooklyn. Many years ago I spent Shabbat at the home of a Williamsburg Hasid and stood from ten till two in the morning in a tiny *shtuebl* packed with more than a hundred disciples of the Satmor Rebbe, good-naturedly fighting and shoving for the *shirayim,* food that the Rebbe gives from his thirteen-course meal. I was deeply impressed, particularly at one point when, after wishing the Rebbe would pass me a drumstick and then thinking that, dressed as I was, I was the last person he would thus honor, some one handed me a drumstick and said, "The Rebbe sent this for you!" Nevertheless, I took away with me the sense of a childlike devotion of the Hasidim to the Rebbe quite foreign to the individualized consciousness of the modern Jew.

When I next visited Williamsburg to witness the dancing on Simhas Torah, I naively went into the synagogue of the Klausenberger Rebbe with a non-Jewish friend to inquire as to the time of their services. I was confronted by a young man with a bright red beard who, instead of answering my question, asked me, "Are you a Jew?" "Yes," I replied. "Do you speak Yiddish?" "No," I said. "You are a Jew and you don't speak Yiddish!" he snorted contemptuously. Then he turned to my friend, whose bowtie and cap marked him as a smart Greenwich Villager, and, pointing to him as a Hasid of the time of the Maccabees might have pointed to a swine that had been brought into the Temple, exclaimed indignantly, "And you brought *him* into the Synagogue!" My friend shrank out of the door, and I began to wonder whether my years of devotion to Hasidism had been misplaced.

I have used the illustration of Martin Buber's interpretation of Hasidism because it is a subject that I know enough about that I can make the fine distinctions necessary for an understanding of the subtle dialectic between spirit and form. The same focus can be applied to the interaction of spirit and form within any religious tradition. Take, for example, the reformations that have occurred periodically in all great traditional religions—sometimes within them, like the Brethren of the Common Life in fifteenth-century Europe, and sometimes as a disruption that creates new religions, like the Protestant Reformation of Luther, Calvin, Zwingli, and Knox. The root meaning of *reformation* is, of course, re-formation. The claim of every reformation is that it is necessary to break with traditional forms because, although these forms have developed directly and organically from the original events and impulses that gave rise to the religion, somehow along the way they have lost the unique spirit that lay at the heart of the religion.

The reformer, therefore, is one who creates the new in the name of the old. Luther, for example, went back to the tradition of St. Paul and emphasized justification by faith over justification by works. Yet his re-formation did not literally take over the forms of the Church in Paul's day. Rather it created new forms that were held to carry on the original teachings of Christianity more faithfully than the encrustations of the Catholic Church during Luther's time. The Counter-Reformation, in turn, tried to preserve the intactness of the Church through attacking Protestantism, on the one hand, but also through reforming the Church from within, on the other. Similarly, modern Orthodox Judaism arose not, as it claims, as a direct continuation of the tradition of Rabbinical Judaism but as a conscious response to the challenge of Reform Judaism.

Our Dialogue with the Absurd offers us no guarantee of a smooth continuity of religious tradition or, in an age when both religious forms and religious spirit have fallen into question, any sureness of finding the right dialectic between spirit and form. We can speak in general of the traditions and forms of particular religions. No description of Christianity would be complete without mentioning Easter, Good Friday, Christmas, and the Mass, and no description of Judaism would be complete without mentioning the various holidays and sabbath observances that have characterized religious Jews for millennia. But when it comes to our own task of finding the right tension between religious tradition, our personal uniqueness, and the contradictions and absurdities of the world in which we live, no general description any longer has any meaning. Rather there are a thousand particulars that give form in a life and express its basic attitudes, a thousand ways in which one can *be* Torah rather than merely say it.

We are constantly creating new religious forms as we respond to the spirit and are permeated by it, and we do so in a faithful dialogue and tension with the spirit and form of tradition. "To be a spiritual heir, one must be a pioneer," writes Abraham Joshua Heschel. But he also writes, "To be worthy of being a pioneer, one must be a spiritual heir"!

14

The Paradox of Religious Leadership

The Grand Augur, who sacrificed the swine and read omens in the sacrifice, came dressed in his long dark robes, to the pig pen, and spoke to the pigs as follows: "Here is my counsel to you. Do not complain about having to die. Set your objections aside, please. Realize that I shall feed you on choice grain for three months. I myself will have to observe strict discipline for ten days and fast for three. Then I will lay out grass mats and offer your hams and shoulders upon delicately carved platters with great ceremony. What more do you want?"

Then, reflecting, he considered the question from the pigs' point of view: "Of course, I suppose you would prefer to be fed with ordinary coarse feed and be left alone in your pen."

But again, seeing it once more from his own viewpoint, he replied: "No, definitely there is a nobler kind of existence! To live in honor, to receive the best treatment, to ride in a carriage with fine clothes, even though at any moment one may be disgraced and executed, that is the noble, through uncertain, destiny that I have chosen for myself."

So he decided against the pigs' point of view, and adopted his own point of view, both for himself and for the pigs also.

How fortunate those swine, whose existence was thus ennobled by one who was at once an officer of state and a minister of religion.

People think that a Sheikh should show miracles and manifest illumination. The requirement in a teacher,

167

however, is only that he should possess all that the disciple needs.

The teacher and the taught together produce the teaching.

No matter where the truth is in your case, your teacher can help you find it. If he applies only one series of method to everyone, he is not a teacher, let alone yours.

Once upon a time there was a dervish. As he was sitting in contemplation, he noticed that there was a sort of devil near him.

The dervish said: "Why are you sitting there, making no mischief?"

The demon raised his head wearily. "Since the theoreticians and would-be teachers of the Path have appeared in such numbers, there is nothing left for me to do."

The Baal-Shem said:
"We say: 'God of Abraham, God of Isaac, and God of Jacob,' and not: 'God of Abraham, Isaac, and Jacob,' for Isaac and Jacob did not base their work on the searching and service of Abraham; they themselves searched for the unity of the Maker and his service."[1]

The religious leader is a central concern in any phenomenological study of religion. Appoached dialogically, this concern necessarily deepens into the contemplation of a phenomenon that is *by its very nature* problematic and even paradoxical. This phenomenon is not that of the inauthentic religious leaders who through all time have usurped divine authority for very human ends of power, wealth, fame, or repression. It is, rather, that of the authentic religious leader. This latter person genuinely wants to lead his or her charges to greater immediacy in their dialogue with the divine. Yet he or she tends to take the place of that immediacy by his very function as leader. What is more, the followers often foist upon the leader the task of vicariously representing them before God with or without his consent and even to the point of idolatry! Again and again in the history of the world's religions, someone who has come to show others an image of the human, a meaningful way of personal and social existence in dialogue with God, has been transformed by those who come after into an image of God, a human image to be worshiped in place of the imageless God, someone to relieve one of the task of being a lamp unto oneself, as the Buddha put it.

This is particularly evident today when, with the growing interest in Oriental religions and their second-, third-, and fourth-hand derivatives, enthusiasts of all ages are being offered a rich and variegated assortment of gurus to choose among. A paperback entitled *The Guru Supermarket* shows someone pushing a shopping basket with a pair of spindly brown legs sticking out from below. One might think that young people would be hopelessly confused, if it were not for the fact that there is a striking resemblance to a supermarket in which one manages to choose among a great variety of brands, variously packaged and priced, and somehow trusts that one has made the right choice!

The past decades have seen the phenomenon of many young people forsaking their homes *and* their cultures to become members of any number of handy cults. Accusations of brainwashing on the part of confused parents have been equaled by accusations of counter-brainwashing when these parents call in self-styled experts to deprogram their children and try to get them back. The courts are understandably confused about when the absolute allegiance of a young person to this or that religious leader is to be understood as an act of faith and when it is to be understood as the consequence of manipulation! Meanwhile, the alternative religions have become big business, presented with all the media techniques of what used to be called "Madison Avenue," salting away millions in Swiss banks, building up powerful organizations and churches that claim exemption from taxes and public scrutiny. Others come along and present a smoothly packaged, sophisticated, expensive, synthetic amalgam of many of these trends. Such cults and churches train teachers all over the world, raise ever higher the prices of what the leaders impart, and establish international universities and centers of research. They sponsor prestigious conferences on the unity of science and religion replete with Nobel Prize laureates. The seemingly primitive displays of their followers with their robes, drums, and copies of books to be sold at airports and train stations, are matched by ever-slicker magazines and research foundations. Nor are the pentecostal movements in Protestant and Catholic churches today one whit behind with their powerful apparatus of radio and television programs, publications, armies of young workers, students set to monitor their professors' teaching of religion, and arrays of charismatic personalities, to follow whose teachings and dictates is itself counted a religious act!

Because of the complexity of modern society and the sophistication of the media, the problem of religious leadership is greatly aggravated, but it is by no means new. When T. S. Eliot's Thomas à Becket identifies his own will with the will of God and sees himself as nothing but a selfless instrument in God's hands, the greatest humility becomes, unconsciously, the greatest arrogance. Thomas's opening speech in Eliot's poem-play *Murder in the Cathedral* already sets the whole of the dramatic action within the framework of an objective heavenly hierarchy in which each of the saints and martyrs has a destined place to which he is called:

> They know and do not know, that action is suffering
> And suffering is action. Neither does the actor suffer
> Nor the patient act. But both are fixed
> In an eternal action, an eternal patience
> To which all must consent that it may be willed
> And which all must suffer that they may will it,
> That the pattern may subsist, for the pattern is the action
> And the suffering, that the wheel may turn and still
> Be forever still.

Thomas's sense of his destined place in this heavenly hierarchy is expressed with utmost clarity in his Christmas Sermon in the Interlude between part I and part II. A Christian martyr is no accident, he says, and still less is it "the effect of a man's will to become a Saint."

> A martyr, a saint, is always made by the design of God, for His love to men, to warn them and to lead them, to bring them back to His ways. A martyrdom is never the design of man; for the true martyr is he who has become the instrument of God, who has lost his will in the will of God, not lost it but found it, for he has found freedom in submission to God. The martyr no longer desires anything for himself, not even the glory of martyrdom.... So in Heaven the Saints are most high, having made themselves most low.

Thomas's statement that the martyr does not even desire the glory of martyrdom is unconvincing in Thomas's case because the sermon is centered on Thomas's own expectation of becoming a martyr: "I do not think I shall ever preach to you again;...it is possible that in a short time you may have yet another martyr." Four days later Thomas insists, against the protests of the priests, that the knights who have come to kill him be admitted to the cathedral. In so doing, he puts his action once again within a heavenly framework and one, moreover, that neither priests nor knights nor any common person can understand:

> It is not in time that my death shall be known;
> It is out of time that my decision is taken
> If you call that decision

To which my whole being gives entire consent.
I give my life
To the Law of God above the Law of Man.
Those who do not the same
How should they know what I do?
How should you know what I do?...

Thomas's pride and his sense of superiority to all the other actors in this drama is as clear in these final speeches as it was at the beginning.

The inescapable corollary of this view is that the common person is someone who must blindly follow the charismatic leader and thank God at the same time for bestowing such undeserved grace on the totally unworthy, all of which is expressed again and again by the chorus of the women of Canterbury. Their final chorus, the last lines of the play itself, is an acknowledgment by them of their essential, almost natural inferiority to the saints and martyrs through whom they find salvation:

Forgive us, O Lord, we acknowledge ourselves as type of the common man,
Of the men and women who shut the door and sit by the fire;
Who fear the blessing of God, the loneliness of the night of God,
the surrender required, the deprivation inflicted;
Who fear the injustice of men less than the justice of God;
Who fear the hand at the window, the fire in the thatch, the fist in the tavern, the push into the canal,
Less than we fear the love of God.
We acknowledge our trespass, our weakness, our fault; we acknowledge
That the sin of the world is upon our heads; that the blood of the martyrs and the agony of the saints
Is upon our heads....
Blessed Thomas, pray for us.[2]

The prototype of this hierarchical view of religious leadership is not to be found in the teachings of Jesus or even of St. Paul but in the *Republic* of Plato, the fountainhead of Greek and all of western philosophy. Deeply embittered by the martyrdom that the Athenian democracy forced upon his teacher Socrates, Plato envisaged an authoritarian state in which the various castes are governed by the royal myth, or lie, and in which the Philosopher-King, the highest representative of the Guardian Class, does not just know the Good but is seen as identical with it!

It is striking that Islam, concerned as it was not just with religious insight but with social and political governance, took over Plato's idea of the philosopher king and combined it with their image of Mohammed as the true prophet, preserving the hierarchical sense that only the prophet knows the truth and that others must, therefore, follow the prophet unquestioningly:

> A real law-giver must, therefore, be a prophet philosopher. But, conversely, every true prophet-philosopher must be a law-giver. A true prophet or a genuine philosoher, merely by virtue of being this, cannot remain within the confines of his own personality but must go forth to humanity, or to a nation, both with a divinely revealed religion and with a law based upon it. He must be able to formulate his religious consciousness into a definite pattern of religio-political life for people to follow. From this, again, it would be obvious how the ordinary or 'imperfect' mystics and philosophers are to be distinguished from the prophet or the true philosopher.[3]

This notion of unquestioning obedience also carried over to the Sheikh/*murid* (master-disciple) relation among the Sufis. Jelaluddin Rumi compares the disciple to a parrot who "sees himself mirrored in a teacher's body and doesn't see or hear what's behind the mirror of discourse." Many repeat what dervishes say as a formality; but only rarely "a great mercy has shown them a Truth."

> If you want dervishood, spiritual poverty, and emptiness, you must be Friends with a Sheikh. Talking about it, reading books, and doing practises don't help. Soul receives from soul that Knowing.[4]

In her discussion of the Sufi path and the master/disciple relationship, Annemarie Schimmel brings out so beautifully the paradox of religious leadership to which we have pointed—in which what is good and essential seems to issue almost inevitably into historical degeneration, that I shall cite her at great length:

> The master who had to teach the method and the exercises had first to test the adept to determine whether he was willing and able to undergo the hardships that awaited him on the Path.... Usually three years of service were required before the adept could be formally accepted in a master's group—one year in the service of the people, one in the service of God, and one year in watching

over his own heart....The disciple would probably not have undergone these trials had he not had absolute trust in his master. It was, and still is, a rule that a preformed affinity has to exist between master and disciple. Many Sufis wandered for years throughout the Islamic world in search of a *pir* to whom they could surrender completely....

The novice who has entered the master's group becomes "like the son of the sheikh"...The sheikh helps him to give birth to a true "heart" and nourishes him with milk like a mother...The Sufis have always been well aware of the dangers of the spiritual path and therefore attribute to the sheikh almost unlimited authority....One might read all the books of instruction for a thousand years, but without a guide nothing would be achieved.

The master watches every moment of the disciple's spiritual growth...The sheikh interprets the *murid's* dreams and visions, reads his thoughts, and thus follows every movement of his conscious and subconscious life...in the hands of the master the murid should be as passive as a corpse in the hands of an undertaker. Ghazaali, the main representative of moderate Sufism in the late eleventh century, also maintained that complete and absolute obedience is necessary, even if the sheikh should be wrong...This attitude in later times lent itself to dangerous consequences...But the original intent was genuine: the master should act like a physician, diagnosing and healing the illnesses and defects of the human soul...the sheikh would teach him how to behave in each mental state...the methods could not be alike for everybody, and the genuine mystical leader had to have a great deal of psychological understanding in order to recognize the different talents and characters of his *murids* and treat them accordingly.[5]

Something of the danger of this adulation of the Sufi master is indicated when we are told that the disciple "has to honor and obey his sheikh, even if the sheikh is a veritable satan" or that "the good deeds of the pious are the bad deeds of those who are brought near," so that the "saint" felt free to abolish religiously prescribed norms in favor of a union with the divine will such that those dwelling on lower levels of the path—let alone the common people—were incapable of understanding and appreciating his actions. The common people ascribed to the Sufi leader the ability to work miracles, an ability which the great Sufi masters did not question but which they considered snares on the way toward God that keep the adept from further progress on the Path. The miracle mongering of the "shopkeeper sheikhs" was

described in one saying as "the menstruation of men," for they come
between man and God just as the days of impurity cut the husband
off from intercourse with his wife.[6]

Like the institution of the zaddik in Hasidism, the office of *khalifa*
in the main convent often became hereditary, leading "to a deterioration
of the office and to an accumulation of power and wealth in the hands
of certain *pir* families, in whom, in the course of time, not too many
traces of true spirituality were left." In the course of time, excessive
importance was attributed to the sheikh or *pir*, who was seen as the
master of spiritual alchemy, the sea of wisdom, the ladder toward
heaven, and the mirror whom God puts before the adept. True
mysticism was replaced by magic, and many who preached poverty
as their pride became wealthy landlords at the expense of their poor
ignorant followers. Although a great admirer of the spiritual philosophy
of Sufis, the modernist poet Muhammad Iqbal repeatedly deplored the
commercialization and blind obedience that marked the Sufis of South
Asia. Amulets and shrines of dead masters abounded, leading Iqbal
to accuse the sheikhs of selling the bones of their dead ancestors![7]

The problematic phenomenon of religious leadership is found no
less in the biblical tradition, which fused with the Greek in creating
traditional Christianity. We need only think of the profound irony in
the speech attributed to the Lord in which he tells the reluctant prophet
Samuel to go ahead and crown Saul king as the people demand:

> But the thing displeased Samuel when they said, "Give us
> a king to govern us." And Samuel prayed to the Lord. And the
> Lord said to Samuel, "Hearken to the voice of the people in all
> that they say to you; for they have not rejected you, but they have
> rejected me from being king over them. According to all the deeds
> which they have done to me, from the day I brought them up
> out of Egypt even to this day, forsaking me and serving other gods,
> so they are also doing to you. Now then, hearken to their voice;
> only, you shall solemnly warn them, and show them the ways
> of the king who shall reign over them."
> So Samuel told all the words of the Lord to the people who
> were asking a king from him. He said, "These will be the ways
> of the king who will reign over you: he will take your sons and
> appoint them to his chariots and to be his horsemen, and to run
> before his chariots; and he will appoint for himself commanders
> of thousands and commanders of fifties, and some to plow his
> ground and to reap his harvest, and to make his implements of
> war and the equipment of his chariots. He will take your daughters
> to be perfumers and cooks and bakers. He will take the best of

your fields and vineyards and olive orchards and give them to his servants. He will take the tenth of your grain and of your vineyards and give it to his officers and to his servants. He will take your menservants and maidservants, and the best of your cattle and your asses, and put them to his work. He will take the tenth of your flocks, and you shall be his slaves. And in that day you will cry out because of your king, whom you have chosen for yourselves; but the Lord will not answer you in that day."
—RSV, Sam. 8:4–18

The relevance of this passage to the problematic of religious leadership does not arise simply from the fact that Samuel is the prophet and judge who rules the people in the name of God and who anoints Saul king in God's name. It also arises from the fact that the king too is seen as religious leader, one whose task it is to continue the Covenant, to make real the kingship of god in every aspect of community life. It is out of the failure of the kings in this task that the Hebrew prophets arise, bringing to the king the demand of the covenant, saying like Amos to the priest at Beth-El, "I am no prophet, nor son of a prophet. . . . But when the lion roars, who can but tremble? When the Lord God speaks, who can but prophesy?" And it is out of the repeated failure of the prophets that the messianic vision of the *true* king arises in the Immanuel of Isaiah and the "suffering servant of the Lord" of Deutero-Isaiah. The word *Messiah*, indeed, is nothing other than the Anglicization of the Hebrew *Meschiach*, which means "anointed." Yet with what profound irony and misgiving is the first king of Israel anointed by Samuel!

In a penetrating essay, "Biblical Leadership," Buber points out that before the advent of the kings, it is the weak and humble, rather than the strong, who are chosen to lead, and that they carry out their leadership not through historical success and power but through failure. "The Bible knows nothing of this intrinsic value of success." The failures of both Moses and David are given in detail, and "this glorification of failure culminates in the long line of prophets whose existence is failure through and through." The *servant of the Lord*, likewise, is one who sees his strength and readiness as all in vain. His mouth is like a sharp sword, but the Lord has hid him in the shadow of his hand. God has made him into a polished shaft, an arrow that is ready to fly, and then has concealed him in his quiver (Isa. 49:2). Yet this failure does not mean that the biblical leader does no work. His work is done not in the heights of power but in the depths of history; his truth is hidden in obscurity.

This existence in the shadow, in the quiver, is the final word of
the leaders in the biblical world, this enclosure in failure, in
obscurity, even when one stands in the blaze of public life, in the
presence of the whole national life.[8]

What Buber writes here can only be understood within the context
of a dialogical approach not only to religion but to history. Within this
context the problematic of religious leadership deepens into a paradox.
Biblical history, Buber suggests, is the history of God's disappointments
in the dialogue with the people who continually fail to answer and
continually rise up and try to answer. The way of this history leads from
disappointment to disappointment and beyond them to the messianic.

Biblical leadership, correspondingly, falls into five types according
to the great stages in the history of the people. First, there is that of
the Patriarchs—Abraham, Isaac, and Jacob—who beget the people.
Second there is that of the Leader—Moses—who leads the people in
their wandering. Third, there is that of the Judges, who rise up on
special occasions to set the people right, who refuse, like Gideon, to
be crowned king because God alone is King, and who repeatedly fail
in their task of establishing a direct kingship of God. Fourth, there is
that of the Kings, who are anointed to make real the kingship of God
and on whom the Bible lays the blame for the failure in the dialogue
with God. Fifth, there is that of the Prophets, who call King and people
to account for their failure in the dialogue, who cut themselves off from
the natural instincts that bind them to community, and whose reward
is to be treated by the people as their enemy.

All these types of religious leadership lead to the idea of the
messianic leader through whom at last an answer will be spoken with
man's whole being that will answer the word of God, an answer that
is, thus, an earthly consummation in and with humankind.

This is what the messianic belief means, the belief in the real
leader, in the setting right of the dialogue, in God's disappointment being at an end. And when a fragment of an apocoyphal
gospel has God say to Jesus; "In all the prophets have I awaited
thee, that thou wouldst come and I rest in thee, for thou art My
rest," this is the late elaboration of a truly Jewish conception.[9]

In the chapter, "Jesus: Image of the Human or Image of God?",
we will recall, I ask whether Jesus does not stand in this messianic
succession. When Jesus asks his disciples, "what do men say that I am"
And what do you think that I am?" is he asking a real question as
someone with a unique place in the messianic history of Judaism that

cannot be understood by any already existing category? Or is he speaking out of the sure knowledge of his divinity, the Messiah Come, or even, as in Byzantine times, the Pantocrator?

The history of the great religions is bound up, Buber suggests, with the problem: How do human beings stand the test of anointing? This is not a test of them as individuals in isolation but precisely as leaders looked to by the people, often looked to for success or at the very least to take the place of the people in the dialogue with God. The history of the kings is the history of the failure of the anointed to realize the promise of his anointing, and the rise of messianism correspondingly is the belief in the anointed king who realizes the promise of his anointing.

But the significance of the biblical leader is not limited to the context of the biblical Covenant and biblical messianism. "The biblical leaders are the foreshadowings of the dialogical man, of the man who commits his whole being to God's dialogue with the world, and who stands firm throughout this dialogue." These are persons who are leaders precisely insofar as they allow themselves to be led, "insofar as they take upon themselves the responsibility for that which is entrusted to them," and make it real. What we are accustomed to call history is from the biblical standpoint only the great failure, the refusal to enter into the dialogue, not the failure in the dialogue, as exemplified by the biblical leader. By the same token, the significance of the failure of the latter is not limited to the history of biblical messianism but casts light on the paradox of religious leadership in general:

> The way, the real way, from the Creation to the Kingdom is trod not on the surface of success, but in the deep of failure. The real work, from the biblical point of view, is the late-recorded, the unrecorded, the anonymous work. The real work is done in the shadow, in the quiver. Official leadership fails more and more, leadership devolves more and more upon the secret.[10]

What is in question here is not the familiar contrast between the personal charisma of Francis of Assisi and official charisma—"the divinity that doth hedge round the head of a king," that atrocious caricature of biblical leadership that the monarchs of France arrogated to themselves by "the divine right of kings." It is rather the contrast between the charisma of the genuine leader and the "dark charisma" of those whose work in history remains anonymous. The genuine charismatic leader is a man like Theodor Herzl, who identified himself so totally with the cause of the Zionist movement which he founded that questioning him was, to him, tantamount to disloyalty to the cause.

The "dark charisma" is that of persons like Martin Buber and his friends in the "Democratic Fraction" who represented, if anything only the "negative charisma" of the unsuccessful. In his autobiographical fragment, "The Cause and the Person," Buber asks whether there might not be yet another reality, different from that of obvious world history:

> a reality hidden and powerless because it has not come into power; whether there might not be, therefore, men with a mission who have not been called to power and yet are, in essence, men who have been summoned; whether excessive significance has not perhaps been ascribed to the circumstances that separate the one class of men from the other; whether success is the only criterion; whether the unsuccessful man is not destined at times to gain a belated, perhaps posthumous, perhaps even anonymous victory which even history refuses to record; whether, indeed, when even this does not happen, a blessing is not spoken, nonetheless, to these abandoned ones, a word that confirms them; whether there does not exist a "dark" charisma.[11]

The history of Hasidism is an especially poignant exemplification of the contrast between these two types of leadership. Originally, to be sure, the Baal Shem and those who followed him were recognized leaders of the community who saw it as their task to bring their followers into greater immediacy in their dialogue with God. After several generations, however, dynasties of *zaddikim* developed in which it was no longer personal spiritual qualities but, like the Kings of the Bible, the succession of birth that determined on whom the leadership of the communities of the Hasidim would devolve. The *zaddik*, or rebbe, was not just a priest with a priestly function, but a leader responsible for the total life of his community and of each family and each individual in it. Therefore, his power for healing and help could equally easily become a power for domination and exploitation.

Some zaddikim had sufficient wholeness that they could descend into the whirlpool and help the afflicted and troubled souls without getting stuck themselves. Others found themselves sucked down into the whirlpool. Still others were like the "wicked," of whom the Seer of Lublin spoke, who did not turn even on the threshold of hell; "for they thought they were being sent to hell to redeem the souls of others"! And some dark and enigmatic figures like Menahem Mendel of Kotzk abjured the task of leadership in the last years of their lives and compared themselves to the "Sacred Goat." Originally the Sacred Goat walked up and down on the earth and the tips of his black horns touched the stars. But then he gave of his horns to countless suffering and demanding persons. Now he still walks up and down on the earth, but he no longer has horns with which to touch the stars!

Buber's great Hasidic chronicle-novel *For the Sake of Heaven* is a profound study of the paradox of religious leadership within Hasidism but also, by implication, in the modern world where a false messianic on every side leads people to seek the goal of justice by the ways of injustice. This novel is based on the tragic tension between two actual historical figures—the Seer of Lublin and his disciple, the Yehudi, or "the Holy Jew." The Seer of Lublin wishes to hasten the coming of redemption through magical, mystical intentions and prayers that will strengthen Napoleon, whom he identifies with the apocryphal Gog of the land of Magog, and thus force God to send the Messiah. The holy Yehudi, in contrast, stays clear of magic and teaches that redemption can come only through our turning back to God with the whole of our individual and communal existence. The Seer's religious leadership rests, correspondingly, on that "miracle' mystery, and authority" that Dostoevsky's Grand Inquisitor espoused whereas the Yehudi's rests on the call to the turning that respects the power of response of every individual person.

At the Seer's suggestion, the Yehudi leaves him and founds a congregation of his own, even while remaining a loyal disciple of the Seer. Through the Seer's emphasis on the divine power of the zaddik and through the awe of his disciples, the Seer holds the place of an oriental potentate in his congregation. The Yehudi, in contrast, preserves an informal and democratic relation with his disciples. The Seer uses his disciples for magic purposes; the Yehudi helps his disciples find the path they seek to pursue of and for themselves. He teaches his disciples that man's turning is not for the sake of individual salvation alone but for the redemption of the whole of creation—for the sake of the Shekinah, God's indwelling glory, which is in exile. Redemption takes place not in isolation, moreover, but in a communal life of justice, love, and consecration.[12]

The death of the Yehudi, who deliberately enters into a fatal ecstasy in order to bring back a message from Heaven for the Seer, shares with Jesus the paradigm of the suffering servant. The moments before his death are given up entirely to the thought of the Shekinah, for whom he has suffered and endeavored during his life. Repeating the words of Deutero-Isaiah about the servant of the Lord, the lamb who is led to slaughter, the Yehudi dies with the phrase on his lips, "The only one to declare Thy oneness." Of all the religious leaders who work "for the sake of heaven" in this novel, only the Yehudi has refused to work for redemption with external means or to accept a division of the world between God and the devil or a redemption that is anything less than the redemption of all evil. His struggle with the Seer is a part of this affirmation of the oneness of God. It prevents us from seeing the conflict of the story as one between good and evil. Rather it is, like the conflict between Herzl and Buber, a tragedy in that special sense in which Buber defines it, the "cruel antitheticalness" of existence itself, the fact that each is as he or she is and there are not sufficient resources in the relationship to bring the opposition into genuine dialogue and to prevent it from crystallizing into oppositeness.

The Yehudi is a charismatic figure, like Thomas à Becket; he too is the center of a religious community. But he is not so through appointment, like Thomas, but because he is the person that he is. His charisma is personal and not official. Thomas stands closer to the Seer, who receives a special reverence and credence from his disciples and stands at the head of a structured, authoritarian community. From the Seer's point of view, the Yehudi's martyrdom might resemble that of Thomas à Becket because the Seer hopes that it will help in his magical-apocalyptic actions to bring about the coming of the Messiah. But from the point of view of the Yehudi, his dying is not part of any predestined design or any spiritual hierarchy, and he accomplishes no purpose by his death in the sense of a means that can lead to some end. He is simply an image of a human being who takes suffering on himself. He stands, Buber suggests, in the succession of figures who, in every generation, become Deutero-Isaiah's "suffering servant of the Lord." But he is also and equally the image of a person who refuses to allow the tragic contradiction of existence to cut him off from faithful relationship with the teacher whom he acknowledges even while he opposes him. The Yehudi does not speak of his enemies as beasts and madmen, as does Eliot's Thomas. "You are not to think that those who persecute me do so out of an evil heart," he says to a disciple. "The fundamental motive of their persecution of me is to serve Heaven." He does not leave the evil of the world unredeemed; he brings the tragic contradiction into his relationship with God.[13]

In Western Europe and America, the traditional *rav* of Eastern Europe and the *zaddik*, or rebbe, of Hasidism, was succeeded by the "rabbi," who is supposed to combine the functions of both—teacher, interpreter of the law, spiritual inspirer, and counselor to the troubled and the needy. Sometimes this leads to being all things to all people and very little to any, which is also true of the Protestant minister and the Catholic priest. When I was visiting professor at Hebrew Union College in Cincinnati in 1956, I came to know one of the first-year students, an exceptionally fine man who at the age of forty-five had given up a thriving music business in Honolulu to undertake five years of arduous training that would lead to his becoming a Reform rabbi at the age of fifty! One night when he and I were having peanut butter sandwiches in the kitchen, he asked me, "Doctor, how is it you never thought of becoming a rabbi?" "I have enough difficulty maintaining my integrity as a teacher," I replied.

I did not mean by this that either teachers or rabbis are persons without integrity. What I meant was that the greater the demand placed upon one by one's students or one's congregants, the more difficult it is to maintain one's integrity—to hold in authentic tension one's uniqueness as a person and one's function in one's social role and to reject the pseudo confirmation that comes from being elevated above the people. It goes without saying that the religious leader is in far greater danger in this regard than the teacher, who is (occasionally) respected in this society but hardly venerated and certainly not asked to be a spiritual stand-in for the student. Nor was I thinking of my questioner when I replied, but of his fellow seminarians, mostly far younger men who were being taught to intone and do casework but had not had the time to work through to a personal religious position of their own or to personal maturity. When these young men became rabbis, they would be turned into "father figures" and "spiritual guides" by their congregants!

Just how central this problem is today, even among the most traditional of religions, is shown by the controversies surrounding whether priests must be celibate and cannot marry, whether women can become rabbis, ministers, and priests, whether avowed homosexuals may properly serve as religious leaders. These issues would not be nearly so bitterly fought if it were not for the investment that parishioners have in their religious leaders being fathers, guides, moral exemplars, and spiritual substitutes for them.

The *paradox* of religious leadership is only plumbed if we recognize that in a dialogical approach to religion the ultimate touchstone is the immediacy of contact with ultimate reality, whether that contact be made in prayer, cult, creed, or the countless concrete happenings of the everyday. We must recognize equally that all religious tradition is carried on by a dialectic between immediacy and mediacy, directness and indirectness, dialogue and intellectual dialectic, spirit and form. God, according to Hasidic teaching, is like a father who brings himself to the level of the child in order progressively to lead him upward until he can stand on his own feet as an equal. The same, but much more so, could be said of the religious leader, an excellent example of which is the Zen master Bankei:

> When Bankei held his seclusion-weeks of meditation, pupils from many parts of Japan came to attend. During one of these

gatherings a pupil was caught stealing. The matter was reported
to Bankei with the request that the culprit be expelled. Bankei
ignored the case.

Later the pupil was caught in a similar act, and again Bankei
disregarded the matter. This angered the other pupils, who drew
up a petition asking for the dismissal of the thief, stating that
otherwise they would leave in a body.

When Bankei had read the petition he called everyone before
him. "You are wise brothers," he told them. "You know what is
right and what is not right. You may go somewhere else to study
if you wish, but this poor brother does not even know right from
wrong. Who will teach him if I do not? I am going to keep him
here even if all the rest of you leave."

A torrent of tears cleansed the face of the brother who had
stolen. All desire to steal had vanished.[14]

How can the religious leader stand the test of "anointing," i.e.,
of the responsibility of religious leadership, if his or her followers desire
to find security in him or her, long for a symbiotic union in which they
are dominated by him or her, or even magically desire to possess what
the other one has and they feel they lack? Idolatry is not just a matter
of wooden idols, or of silver and gold ones, but of giving up
responsibility for oneself to another.

One sabbath Rabbi Zevi Hirsh interrupted his teachings at the
third meal and said:

"There are hasidim who travel to their rabbi and say that
save for him there is no rabbi in all the world. That is idol worship.
What should they say? They should say: 'Every rabbi is good for
his people, but our rabbi is best for what concerns us.' "[15]

Imitation can also be a form of idolatry:

The gatekeeper in the capital city of Sung became such an expert
mourner after his father's death, and so emaciated himself with
fasts and austerities, that he was promoted to high rank in order
that he might serve as a model of ritual observance.

As a result of this, his imitators so deprived themselves that
half of them died. The others were not promoted.[16]

Just as children need parents and pupils teachers, so we need
religious leaders. Yet we need ones who do not put themselves in the
place of God, ones who know, as Lao-tzu enjoined, how to stay in the

front of people without their knowing. By this latter I do not mean facilitators, who reject the name of teacher but are often more authoritarian than any teacher. I mean rather those who understand in their very beings the difference between *imposing upon others* through eloquent sermons, superior mediamanship, manipulation, and propaganda, and *helping others unfold*, each in his or her own way and according to his or her unique relation to the truth.

On the eve of the New Year Rabbi Mendel entered the House of Prayer. He surveyed the many people who had come together from near and far. "A fine crowd!" he called out to them. "But I want you to know that I cannot carry you all on my shoulders. Every one of you must work for himself."

In modern times a great deal of nonsense is talked about masters and disciples, and about the inheritance of a master's teaching by favorite pupils, entitling them to pass the truth on to their adherents. Of course Zen should be imparted in this way, from heart to heart, and in the past it was really accomplished. Silence and humility reigned rather than profession and assertion. The one who received such a teaching kept the matter hidden even after twenty years. Not until another discovered through his own need that a real master was at hand was it learned that the teaching had been imparted, and even then the occasion arrose quite naturally and the teaching made its way in its own right. Under no circumstance did the teacher even claim "I am the successor of So-and-so." Such a claim would prove quite the contrary.

The Zen master Mu-nan had only one successor. His name was Shoju. After Shoju had completed his study of Zen, Mu-nan called him into his room. "I am getting old," he said, "and as far as I know, Shoju, you are the only one who will carry on this teaching. Here is a book. It has been passed down from master to master for seven generations. I also have added many points according to my understanding. The book is very valuable and I am giving it to you to represent your successorship."

"If the book is such an important thing, you had better keep it," Shoju replied. "I received your Zen without writing and am satisfied with it as it is."

"I know that," said Mu-nan. "Even so, this work has been carried from master to master for seven generations, so you may keep it as a symbol of having received the teaching. Here."

The two happened to be talking in front of a brazier. The instant Shoju felt the book in his hands he thrust it into the flaming coals. He had no lust for possessions.

Mu-nan, who never had been angry before, yelled: "What are you doing!"

Shoju shouted back: "What are you saying!"[17]

In the end what is decisive in religious leadership is not *expounding* the Torah but *being* the Torah, not performing miracles but the way in which one lives one's daily life.

When Bankei was preaching at Ryumon temple, a Shinshu priest, who believed in salvation through the repetition of the name of the Buddha of Love, was jealous of his large audience and wanted to debate with him.

Bankei was in the midst of a talk when the priest appeared, but the fellow made such a disturbance that Bankei stopped his discourse and asked about the noise.

"The founder of our sect," boasted the priest, "had such miraculous powers that he held a brush in his hand on one bank of the river, his attendant held up a paper on the other bank, and the teacher wrote the holy name of Amida through the air. Can you do such a wonderful thing?"

Bankei replied lightly: "Perhaps your fox can perform that trick, but that is not the manner of Zen. My miracle is that when I feel hungry I eat, and when I feel thirsty I drink."[18]

A similar story comes to us from Sufi sources. A theme in popular biography is the encounter of the learned scholar and his initiator into higher truth, the God-intoxicated dervish. In this motif the scholar, often Jelaluddin Rumi, is returning home after a successful lecture with an armload of his own writings and other scholarly treatises. The wild dervish, Shams of Tabriz, suddenly appears and, grabbing the books, throws them into a nearby well. "My knowledge has been destroyed," gasps the scholar. To which the dervish replies, "If it could be so easily removed—of what use is it?"!

This distinction also applies to those who impose their views in good faith because they sincerely believe the word they speak is not their own but God's. A young graduate student at the Humanistic Psychology Institute at Sonoma State College accused me of tearing the covers off the Bible, of starting with the Buddha rather than with where the Bible starts, with Jesus Christ. Asked by one of his fellow students, "What would you feel if we said, 'That is your bag and this is ours'?" he replied, "Your bag is false because you speak with the pride of men. But mine is true because I speak with the words of God."

What gives us enough ground to stand on so that we can find our own uniqueness, our inmost passion that stirs our hearts and calls us most deeply, and yet be open to others? "This is *my* way, what is yours?" says Nietzsche's Zarathustra when asked about *the* way, and adds: "As for *the* way it does not exist." For me, the ultimate test of religious leadership is twofold: First, does it help those who are led to find their own ground rather than coasting along forever in depen-dence upon guru, zaddik, minister, or priest? Second, does it lead to greater openness to dialogue with the world, toward building a "community of otherness," or does it lead to ever greater closedness in which one takes refuge in the cult or church of the like-minded, the community of affinity? These two questions necessarily belong together, for the heart of the community of otherness lies in the dialogue of touchstones among the members of the community. In this dialogue the religious leader needs his or her followers as much as the followers need the leader if religious reality is to arise between them.

It is told:

Once, on the evening after the Day of Atonement, the moon was hidden behind the clouds and the Baal Shem could not go out to say the blessing of the New Moon. This weighed heavily on his spirit, for now, as often before, he felt that destiny too great to be gauged depended on the work of his lips. In vain he concentrated his intrinsic power on the light of the wandering star, to help it throw off the heavy sheath: whenever he sent some one out, he was told that the clouds had grown even more lowering. Finally he gave up hope.

In the meantime, the hasidim who knew nothing of the Baal Shem's grief, had gathered in the front room of the house and begun to dance, for on this evening that was their way of celebrating with festal joy the atonement for the year, brought about by the zaddik's priestly service. When their holy delight mounted higher and higher, they invaded the Baal Shem's chamber, still dancing. Overwhelmed by their own frenzy of happiness they took him by the hands, as he sat there sunk in gloom, and drew him into the round. At this moment, someone called outside. The night had suddenly grown light; in greater radiance than ever before, the moon curved on a flawless sky.[19]

PART FIVE

Religion and Human Wholeness

15

Spontaneity, Decision, and Personal Wholeness

In the age when life on earth was full, no one paid any special attention to worthy men, nor did they single out the man of ability. Rulers were simply the highest branches on the tree, and the people were like deer in the woods. They were honest and righteous without realizing that they were "doing their duty." They loved each other and did not know that this was "love of neighbor." They deceived no one yet they did not know that they were "men to be trusted." They were reliable and did not know that this was "good faith." They lived freely together giving and taking, and did not know that they were generous. For this reason their deeds have not been narrated. They made no history.

Rabbi Yudel, a man known for his fear of God and the harsh penances he imposed on himself, once came to visit the maggid of Zlotchov. Rabbi Mikhal said to him: "Yudel, you are wearing a hair shirt against your flesh. If you were not given to sudden anger, you would not need it, and since you are given to sudden anger, it will not help you."

The Seer of Lublin said: "I prefer a passionate opponent to a lukewarm adherent. For the passionate opponent might still turn to you with all of his passion. But from a lukewarm adherent there is nothing more to be hoped."[1]

If religion were pure dialogue and pure immediacy, there would be no need for a philosophy of religion, but neither would there be

189

any such things as religious forms and structures, traditions, and organizations. Actually religion is made up of a complex interaction between immediacy and form, flowing and structure, and the real issues are not the choice between the one side and the other but the nature of the blend, which often adds up to the emphasis that is needed at any given historical juncture. Lao-tzu's respect for spontaneity and Confucius's respect for propriety both have their place in an understanding approach to religion, whatever its nature and manifestation. Thus an adequate philosophy of religion must be concerned with both dialogue and dialectic, meaning by the latter the swinging interaction between the immediacy of dialogue and the mediacy of structure and form.

This dialectic must be understood on many different levels. It takes place even within the individual person who cannot persist in immediacy of dialogue and who uses touchstones of reality, insights, symbols, and concepts both as residues of earlier moments of dialogue and helpers to enter into new dialogue. For the master and disciple, the brotherhood, the tribe, the church, synagogue, denomination, and sect, this dialectic is multifaceted and multileveled. What is more, the concern for continuance—or the preservation and perseverance of the religious tradition—regularly makes the emphasis upon form and structure so great that the dialectic itself is endangered and what is passed down is a set of structures and forms which no longer move back to that immediacy which gave rise to them.

A dynamic, as opposed to a static and merely descriptive, approach, must seek to plumb some of the problems to which this swinging interaction and the encrustations that prevent it give rise. To examine them all would be an encyclopedic task. What we can do is to try to fathom some representative problems from the side of the religious person, having dealt, however briefly, with the side of the religious tradition in part four.

The problem for the religious person is not unlike that of the alternation between the I-Thou and the I-It in general. Our passion needs direction; our excitement needs containment; our moments of ecstasy must alternate with moments of simple calm. The right rhythm of alternation between one and the other differs from person to person and situation to situation. Therefore, it cannot be specified by any technique but only apprehended by moment-by-moment awareness, "a heart of wisdom." Both within tradition itself and in any given living generation, there are books and persons that act as purveyors of wisdom. Yet few are the religious persons fortunate enough to have gurus, rebbes, priests, or roshis sufficiently attuned to their uniqueness that they can give them what they need at that moment. That is why the Seer of Lublin said: "It is impossible to tell men what way they should take. For one way to serve God is through the teachings, another through prayer, another through fasting, and still another eating." Although he himself was a *zaddik*, a Hasidic rebbe, in this saying, at least, he referred his disciples not to the superior wisdom of the *zaddik* but to that of their own heart: "Everyone should carefully observe what way his heart draws him to, and then choose this way with all his strength."

Unfortunately, many substitute social awareness for the awareness of their most central wish—that calling and drawing of the heart which, if anything, gives us our profoundest glimpse into the meaning of the "I." But even where one does not turn away from oneself to the oldest tradition or the latest fad for guidance, the heart itself often seems to offer promptings that are confused and contradictory. Some hold with Genesis 6 and 8 that it is only the *imaginings* of the heart, and not the heart itself, that are evil from youth onward. Others hold with Jeremiah, "The heart is deceitful and infinitely corrupt. Who can understand, it?" Still others follows the Zen text on "Trusting in the Heart." In all three cases it is clear that the subjective world to which we refer ourselves is not seldom as perplexing and misleading as the objective. One answer to this perplexity is implicit in the Seer's statement, namely, the distinction between the many impulses that throng and crowd one another, each calling for attention and gratification, and the powerful innermost wish that calls the heart itself.

What we mean by the *heart* is the wholeness of the person, and here too one can be mistaken. Human history is littered with sad exemplars of mistaking intensity, logic, emotion, or inspiration for human wholeness. One of the reasons such a mistake is made is that we tend to trust one of our faculties more than another and wish to identify the *I* with that faculty preeminently. For many persons, this expresses itself as a trust in reason as objective and a mistrust of emotions or feelings as subjective. In our day, on the other hand, some correctives to this tendency have swung us so far in the other direction that intuitions and feelings are given our sole confidence, and reason and logic are depreciated and looked down upon. The contemporary emphasis upon feeling leads many today to confuse the reciprocal release of pent-up emotions and deeply repressed feelings with genuine relationship, as if real mutuality must automatically emerge from self-expression. It is understandable that many people who are intellectually detached or in some other way cut off from their emotions hope to break through their blocks and get back to what they really feel. Unfortunately, many such people are as cut off from the feelings of others as their own, in addition to which they are programmed to listen for cues and to put other people on pegs rather than to really hear them. This situation is made still worse when they fall into labeling, identifying feeling with reality and declaring that *their* words are really feelings while the words of others are intellectual abstractions or "merely words."

Our feelings are important, of course. We must go back to them and start there. But there are many people today who seem to want to end there, and in so doing, they miss the path to human wholeness. When we have a deep and perhaps violent emotional breakthrough, it is a revelation of something hidden in the depths of our souls, something heretofore perhaps entirely unsuspected. If this emotion that has been brought to the light is intense and if it is associated with religious symbols or cults, we can easily be misled into seeing it as the only reality and into depreciating what before was accessible to the conscious mind. An equal and corollary danger to our wholeness as persons is to see the breakthrough as complete in itself, instead of seeing it as a little light lighting up a long, dark road up a mountain and down into a canyon—a road that we must walk in our everyday life before this breakthrough can be made lasting and meaningful.

The concentration on feeling means the concentration on individual feeling, the feelings experienced within us and expressed to others. This dualism between inner feelings and outer facade may lead us to overlook the social matrix and the social nature of feelings, especially as they are connected with religious symbols and with cultic activities, such as praying, communion, and individual or group worship. The temper of the religious tradition and the religious group and the emphases of the religious leader inevitably affect our attitude toward our own emotions so that what we express is not the raw emotion but the emotion shaped by our attitude as a member of this religious group. This is nowhere more strongly demonstrated, perhaps, than in a revival meeting or in the Pentecostal phenomenon of speaking in tongues. The social matrix of feeling is seldom recognized. Instead, feeling is sometimes regarded as a substantive reality that is in us and only needs to be brought out.

We cannot avoid the route of feeling, yet expecting and demanding feeling can get in the way of true spontaneity and may lead, instead, to that supreme contradiction in terms—*planned spontaneity*. It takes a great deal of listening to allow what happens to come forth spontaneously—not inhibited by an image of oneself that tells one in advance what one's strengths and weaknesses are supposed to be, but also not inhibited by the group pressure to express the emotions approved of, expected, and even demanded by the group. We would like to live more intensely, more vitally, more fully. We would like to share love and joy. Often in religious groups this is exactly what happens. But the more we aim at this goal, the more one part of us will be looking on from the sidelines, anticipating and measuring results, and for that very reason not living fully in the present, not being whole.

The same applies to our concern with our own sinfulness and our desire for repentance. "Rake the muck this way, rake the muck that way, it is still muck," said the Rabbi of Ger. "What does Heaven get out of it? While I am brooding over my sins, I could be stringing pearls for the delight of Heaven!" Our problem is that we are divided within ourselves, that we are not in genuine dialogue with one another, and that we live immersed in a deep existential mistrust. These sicknesses of our human condition cannot be overcome simply by the will to wholeness, openness, and trust or by the magic of technique.

In the years since the mystical experiences of which I tell in *Touchstones of Reality*, I have again and again been troubled by the question of how I can put together the overwhelming intensity and certainty of those experiences and the shattering of occulty that followed. Reflecting on these experiences many years later, I wrote that I carried with me back into the world a deep confusion as my "touchstones of reality broke up or gave way to another until finally they all ceased to be lifeways for me.

> I was left with unanswerable questions as to what in all that I had experienced was real and what was self-deception, or even delusion, in which intensity and the release of repressed forces masqueraded as personal wholeness and irresistible compulsion masqueraded as the "will of God." Intensity, I soon recognized, often seems to be wholeness because it helps us look away from those anxieties in ourselves that we are afraid to face.[2]

I have often delighted in George Santayana's definition of a fanatic as a person who redoubles his efforts as he loses sight of his goal!

I have been helped in these confusions as I have gradually reached a personal wholeness that, if never sure or complete, nonetheless can grow from one moment of meeting to the next so that we can live with what Buber in *The Way of Man* calls a "relaxed vigilance." I have been helped too by Buber's understanding of genuine decision, not as the clenched fist and the set jaw that imposes one part of the person on the other but as the "rapture" that gives all of our passions direction in response to situation and event.

Leslie H. Farber, the distinguished psychoanalyst, has elaborated this distinction in his writings in the form of a contrast between *will* and *willfulness*. True *will* he defines as an appropriate alternation between the unconscious will of the first realm, the will of the whole being, and the conscious will of the second realm, the will of deliberate decision. *Willfulness*, in contrast, is the attempt of the will of the second realm to do the work of the first—to ape spontaneity, wholeness, strength.[3] Seen from both Buber's and Farber's points of view, there need be no conflict between spontaneity and genuine decision because genuine decision means decision of the whole being and as such includes our spontaneity. When will and spontaneity are in conflict, it is always really willfulness that is in question, the willfulness that wants to handle both sides of the dialogue. The will that helps us grow, religiously and otherwise, is that of the person whose trust is grounded in the partnership of existence. But the will that sees everything as depending on it alone, easily falls into despair when it cannot "master" the situation.

The same is true of our awareness of ourselves. True self-awareness does not turn us into objects through reflection and analysis. Rather, it is an intuitive awareness of ourselves that grows in listening and responding if we use ourselves as a radar screen: hearing not just how the other responds but also how we ourselves respond to the other.

If there is a danger of mistaking intensity for personal wholeness, there is also a danger of mistaking personal wholeness, at those rare moments when we attain it, for the "will of God." This danger is intensified if we begin with a philosophy of religion that makes us seek totally to lose or annihilate the self and to become either one with God or an instrument of his will. A striking example of this is Eliot's *Murder in the Cathedral*. In this work, as we have seen, Eliot imposes on his audience an objective, universal, and sacred design that it must accept, and he makes of his central figure the main spokesman for that design. In his long speeches toward the end, Thomas claims that he now has no will of his own, that he has became entirely an instrument of God to carry out God's objective design. Identifying himself with objective reality, he thinks he is acting in complete humility precisely at the point where he has projected his own point of view onto the universe at large. To do this is to deny the self-evident ground on which one stands—the inescapable reality of one's own particular existence and one's own point of view.

This pseudo objectivity stands in marked contrast to the great religious figures of the world's history—Job contending with God, St. Francis receiving the stigmata in passionate love for Christ, the Buddha stubbornly persevering until he attains his own enlightenment in his own way, Arjuna wrestling with Krishna over what he should do in battle, and Jesus in the Garden of Gethsemane praying, "Father, if it be Thy will, may this cup be taken from me. Nevertheless, not my will but Thine be done." There is no question in each of these cases that there is a real self, a genuine existential subject over against the divine.[4]

Another equally striking example is found in the writings of the twentieth-century mystic, saint, and gnostic Simone Weil, who in her teaching of *Waiting for God* insists on a total suspension of our own thoughts so that we might be "ready to receive in its naked truth the object that is to penetrate it." Warmth of heart, impulsiveness, pity will not make up for a lack of this kind of *attention*. Through it alone can we receive into ourselves the being that we are looking at, "just as he is, in all his truth." Weil goes so far as to demand that it "be publicly and officially recognized that religion is nothing else but a looking"—a curiously strident insistence for one who holds religion to be waiting, openness, and receptivity! There is, indeed something paradoxical in the humility that leads Weil to a complete denial of self in favor of objectivity and at the same time makes possible the most dogmatic and intolerant pronouncements on every subject. Weil wished to destroy her *I* and attain the plane of pure truth and pure objectivity. But there is another *I* that she identified with this plane and, so far from destroying it, she set it no practical limits. She found her *I* by denying it, found it in fact, in a much more absolute way than would be possible for a person who admitted that her own subjectivity entered into her relation to the truth which she possessed.[5]

16

Religion and Ethics:
"The Way to Do Is to Be"

"The way to do is to be."

—Lao-tzu

"What are all *kavvanot* compared with one heartfelt grief!"
—The Baal-Shem-Tov

"He who knows the action that is in inaction, the inaction that is in action is wise indeed."

The *Bhagavad Gita*

Our concern with wholeness and decision and with finding in every situation the right interrelation between structure and spontaneity issues, in the end, into a philosophy of action. One's reason, one's motivation, one's relation to an action determine its very nature, quality, and effectiveness. Karma yoga—the yoga of action—is action without attachment to the fruits of action. You live in the world and act, but you are not acting for the sake of the result. Søren Kierkegaard, in his beautiful book *Purity of Heart Is to Will One Thing*, says that one should be like a person taking aim and that one should concentrate upon the aim and not the goal. In Eugen Herrigel's *Zen and the Art of Archery*, we find the identical point of view as the real secret of the Zen approach to archery: one does not try to attain something by looking at the target, the goal. One concentrates on "the means whereby"—to use the phrase of F. M. Alexander—and the means is no mere technique, but includes the very spirit of the doing.

197

All religious ways of life have ethical implications. For ethics, in the serious sense, is not just a body of external rules. It is the way that we go out to meet what comes to meet us, what impinges on us, what accosts us, what demands us. Much of what we have considered in our dialogue with the religions need only be mentioned for its implications for ethics immediately to spring to mind: the *ahimsa*, or noninjury of the Bhagavad-Gita; Gandhi's *satyagraha*, or nonviolent direct action; the Buddha's refusal to give or accept injury; Lao-tzu's *wu-wei*, or the action of the whole being that flows with the Tao and does not interfere; the love of enemies preached by Jesus and the Hasidim; the importance of *kavana*, or inner intention; "the action that is inaction"; "the way to do is to be."

If there is one thing that is perhaps in common to all of these, it is a philosophy of action that makes doing integral with being and rejects any ethic that is less than a claim on the whole person. This also means that we ought not deny or neglect action for the sake of inwardness. We cannot achieve wholeness by going inward and leaving the outward secondary and inessential, anymore than we can achieve it by going outward and neglecting the inward. If we have such a split between inner and outer, then our so-called "inner, essential self" is going to atrophy, and it will not be a real person at all.

"Who shall stand on God's holy mountain?" asks Psalm 24. "He who has clean hands and a pure heart"—the two together. The wholeness of the human cannot be attained in isolation from other persons and from community. What we do is what we are, and what we are is what we do. There is no concrete reality underlying that way of thinking which sets the individual in conflict with society; for there is no individual who lives outside of society. We are bound into society whether we like it or not, and our contending, if contend we must, is as one part of society confronting another.

There are two, closely related kinds of life that are not worth living, according to Plato's Socrates; an unexamined life and an unjust life. Plato found a link between where you are, what you are, and what you do, based, like the Hindu caste system, on the progression of the soul within the cosmic and the social order. It was obvious for Plato, as it is not for most social scientists and philosophers today, that there is a connection between being, knowing, and valuing—that what we know takes place within what we are and what we do. The teaching of the Bhagavad Gita is closely similar, especially in its central sentence: "He who knows the action that is in inaction, the inaction that is in action is wise indeed." The "inaction that is in action" is that "metalled appetency" that has no purpose or meaning, that chain of cause and effect that is merely driven and has no spiritual freedom.

The Buddha's refusal to deal with metaphysical matters—with "questions that tend not to edification"—focuses us in on what we are doing in the here and now. Zen too stresses that real action and real being have to do with "this moment," the now, with where we are now and what we are doing now. The center of Taoism, similarly, is "The way to do is to be." This statement is entirely misinterpreted if one thinks it means to turn inward and away from the beings with whom one lives. In my own early mysticism there was something inherently disconnected between the means and the end: I thought to reach others by turning away from them. I was, in fact, perpetuating a dualism between the inner and the outer. The more the outer became empty, the richer became my dreams and the more intense my meditation. Lao-tzu, in contrast, teaches a swinging interaction, for the Tao is not located in any particular place. "You do not need a window for better seeing," says Lao-tzu. "Rather abide at the center of your being." But the Tao is never found except through opening one's center to one's fellow beings and the world: "A sound man's heart is not shut within itself."

In contrast to the currently popular dualism between "words" and "feelings," Lao-tzu says, "Real words are not vain and vain words are not real." A *real* word embodies the movement of the Tao between being and being. A *vain* word prevents this movement of the Tao. It shuts the Tao out and hides itself away; for it will not risk itself, it will not give itself. The way of Lao-tzu is *inner* and *outer* both, and it is *between*. In the end no structure is going to take the place of spontaneity. "He who is anciently aware of existence is master of each moment." I do not have to split my existence into a phenomenal "unreal" present as opposed to a "real" but not present essence somewhere transcending it. I can take each moment as it comes. "What more do I need to know of origin than this?"

The injunction of the Hebrew Bible to love God with all your heart, soul, and might implies loving your neighbor as one equal to yourself; for you cannot bring your whole existence into relationship with God minus your relationship to your fellows. We do not love other persons because of God. We meet God in loving other persons. Only in this moment, in this concrete situation can I love you. Even then I may not have the resources to love you; for it is not a matter of what is in me or in you but of what occurs between us. The whole approach customary from Aristotle down—that action is simply *potentia* made actual—is in error. We do not know what our potentials are minus the situation that calls us out and our response to it.

We cannot accomplish real effective action unless we bring the whole of ourself into that action. The whole of ourself is not some mystical or psychological state of being. It is a becoming whole through finding our direction in this moment. Our uniqueness is not *in us*. It is something that comes to be as we respond to what is not ourselves. This sort of love, this sort of relationship takes place *between* persons and cannot be counted on as a social technique at our disposal. Our whole notion of action—that we use this means to that end—is a plain violation of the concrete reality, which is that we do not know what the consequences are going to be of almost any action which we do. We must have social planning and social action, but we cannot string together events in such fashion that they become links in a chain of cause and effect or moves in a chess game. We think that we know what will happen because we imagine it happens *through* us. Yet we do not even know our own resources, much less the situation that will confront us. If we are so well "prepared" that we carry the situation off the way we expected, we may be sure that we have not really been present, that we have not heard the real address of the situation. We have to founder and flounder before we can discover what is asked of us.

When Danilo Dolci spoke at Pendle Hill, a man got up and said, "When you tell us of your work to build community in Palermo, you are talking about little skirmishes, minor tactics. You are not telling us about the larger strategy for revolution." To this Dolci replied, "No, I am concerned about strategy; for what we do in Palermo affects New York, and what is done in New York affects Palermo." It is not a question of a choice between action and cultivating our own garden. It is a matter of saying where we can effectively begin to build community and peace in the situation where we are. Clean hands *and* a pure heart, *kavana*, "the way to do is to be"—all of this takes place within the integument of the family, the group, community, and society. When we succeed in uncovering the concrete reality of the situation, then we shall discover what is asked of us. This approach is neither "evolutionary" nor "revolutionary." It is a call to do what we can in each situation in which we find ourselves.

Ethics is *both* the meeting with the other that comes to you in the situation and it is that turning inward, and perhaps looking upward, that is necessary to find the resources to meet the situation. If we get down to where we really exist, where we live from, we go out from our own ground to meet what is not ourselves. Ethics is grounded in such basic attitudes. This means that we cannot take our values for granted but have to seek the source of these values in the basic attitudes toward reality in which they are rooted.

For more than twenty years, I believed that this insight necessarily implied that modern humanity *cannot* be ethical without being religious. Now I would no longer say that; for I must recognize that there are persons like Albert Camus who face value conflicts at the deepest level without drawing on religion or anything that they would recognize as religious reality. On the other hand, I still believe as strongly as before that moral values do not rest in themselves, that they necessarily presuppose an image of the human—an image of a meaningful direction of personal and social existence—or a basic life-stance. Where they rest, instead, merely on custom, convention, tradition, or inheritance, they cannot stand up before the terrible, the anguished moral problems of our time. For the problem of the ethical is at once, and indistinguishably, the question of the *sources* and the *resources* for answering the question of what *ought I* or *we* do in *this situation*? The crisis of values in our times lies in the manifest inability of most modern persons to find either a ground for moral action or the continual renewal of personal integrity and genuine spontaneity necessary for answering the calls that come to them in their everyday lives.

Twenty years after my own confirmation, I led a post-confirmation discussion group at a liberal temple. One Sunday when the rabbi was called away, he asked me to take over his confirmation class. Informed that each student was reading in preparation for his confirmation speech, I asked each in turn what subject he was studying. One girl said she was studying theology and explained that according to the book she was reading this was really a matter of psychology—what psychological needs cause an individual to believe one religious concept or another. Another girl said that she was studying man and explained that, according to the Bible, man was created in the image of God.

"But if theology is really psychology," I queried, "does that not mean that God was created in the image of man?" Since no one was disturbed by this, I put on the blackboard two propositions, "God is created in the image of man" and "Man was created in the image of God," and went round the room to find in which each individual really believed. I discovered that without a single exception this class believed that God is created in the image of man and that religion is really a matter of psychological needs. Like myself at their age, they considered this in no way incompatible with their being confirmed as Jews. Nor did the loss of God seem to distress them since, as one student said to comfort me, "We still have the Ten Commandments."

One of the consequences of preserving the Ten Commandments without a God who commands is that they are converted into universal and timeless values but they are in no sense commandments addressed to a people at a particular juncture of history, to an individual at a crucial moment of his personal life. We have not taken seriously enough the question of what answer our emotional allegiance to "peace, justice, and brotherhood" can give us when we are confronted by concrete moral dilemmas. We have affirmed the oneness of God in temple and church and denied it in our lives, removing values from the present to the "dawn of a new day" or to a messianic era at the end of history. We have used values as sources of emotional satisfaction or as consolations for the God-forsaken everyday world, rather than as the growing edge of our existence. We have substituted for the judgment of the biblical prophet in the specific historical situation the "progressive revelation" of values that are too self-evident to need to be revealed, too universal to apply to any concrete present. We have lost that demand on the present moment, that judgment on present history which has held the present and future in tension throughout millennia of Jewish and Christian messianism (I cannot speak with authority about the crisis of religious values that undoubtedly exists in the other great religions as well!). We have two sets of values—one that we profess as our "ideals" but relegate to the future as unrealizable at present, another that we live by in the present but do not admit even to ourselves. These latter are the real life-attitudes with which we respond to the situations that confront us. If we are aware of them at all, we assure ourselves that these are practical necessities imposed on us from without. Yet it is only in the perplexity and heartache of trying to discover what it means in practice to deal lovingly with our neighbor as one equal to ourself that our values are tried and we rediscover the Thou who speaks in "Thou shalt."

Society wishes to preserve the Ten Commandments for their socially integrating value. But it translates the personal and specific "Thou shalt" of religion into the impersonal "one must" of morality, and it translates this morality, in turn, into objective law. By then it is neither religious nor moral since it does not help us answer the question, "What *ought I* to do?" but only tells one what *one must* do if one does not wish to pay the penalty.

Many of us have inherited moral values from our parents without having inherited that way of life in which those values were originally grounded. Our children, as a result, do not even inherit our moral values, and it becomes increasingly clear that what we took to be the sure ground of liberal, rational, commonsense morality is really an abyss. In the face of depressions, wars, the Holocaust, the atomic bomb, and Vietnam, the young person of today knows that much of what has been handed down is inadequate for confronting the concrete situations in which one finds oneself. *Or*, to the horror of one's parents, one begins to understand what has been "handed down" not as rhetoric or idealist but as a serious word that speaks to one's condition as one could not before have imagined.

The corollary of the loss of absoluteness in values is that relativism which accepts all moralities as descriptions of the culture of this or that group or subgroup while removing their normative status as values with any binding force from without or any existential reality from within. Moral relativism seems to begin with the simple act of looking around, comparing, and then discovering that the Eskimos do one thing, the Tahitians another, the Samoans a third. Actually it goes beyond that to the position of one who says, "It's all relative" in such a way that one imagines one remains above it. Those who apply the social sciences or anthroprology so naively as to reduce everything to the particular culture and leave themselves out, forget that they too are relative—not only as Americans or Europeans but also as social scientists or anthropologists. Relativism is actually the inverse of absolutism. It is a way of saying, "Unless I can find the same value everywhere, it is nowhere." Thus relativism, which seems to deny universality, is, in fact, the sickness of universalism turned inside out. It does not accept things as they happen in their *uniqueness*; for it knows only *difference*—comparison and contrast in terms of categories.

Moral relativism must be unmasked as not being a moral position at all since it tries to reduce the normative "ought" to a purely descriptive "is" and substitutes a statement of what people *do* value for real valuing from within. For all that, our choice is not, as some contemporary theologians think, between moral absolutes and moral relativism. For any particular individual, this may still be a live option. But for the wide spectrum of individuals from different walks and ways of life who are concerned with contemporary morality, it is not. There is not any one set of moral absolutes on which general agreement could be found. The appeal to unanimity and universality is a thing of the past since we live in dialogue with other individuals and peoples with different cultures and values from our own. This fact has forced persons with a serious moral concern to a deeper searching for a basis for morality that they can really believe and live.

People demand today, and rightly, that values be humanized, that they be really represented and lived by actual human beings in concrete situations. The morality of human wholeness attacks every attempt to separate our life into inner and outer, individual and social, or spiritual and material. It speaks of and from the actual situation—the demand placed on us now—and this cannot be relativized, anymore than it can be absolutized in the metaphysical sense of the term. The morality of human wholeness has precisely the relevance of making present the sustained great refusals in the history of mankind to separate personal integrity and the fight for social justice, inward light and social witness, expanded awareness of the wonder and beauty of nature and active political concern.

Our creaturehood does not mean the denial that we have a ground to stand on—the ground of our created freedom. But it does mean a recognition that we live in perpetual contact with an otherness which we have not created ourselves, with creatures that exist for their own sake and not just for human purposes. In the human sphere, this recognition of otherness means setting a limit to the tendency to regard our own point of view as absolute and the other's as relative. It means the recognition of the other as a brother or sister who is created in the image of the imageless God and whom we cannot deny without denying God. The failure of communication cannot be cured through the simultaneous translations of the United Nations Assembly since the basic obstacle to communication remains—that each people sees itself as absolute and the other peoples as questionable and relative. Without the recognition that in meeting the other we meet a unique person or group that we cannot reduce to a means to our end or to a function of our self-realization, no basis for true social responsibility can possibly exist. Here the true meaning of "love your neighbor" unfolds itself: "Deal lovingly with your neighbor as one equal to yourself" as your fellow creature, your brother, your "Thou."

The morality of human wholeness is not the morality of Dostoevsky's Grand Inquisitor—the morality of compulsory order and compulsory good—but neither is it the morality of the Christ of that legend—the morality of a freely given love which places no demand, which does not ask that we authenticate our existence by becoming genuinely human, the morality which does not demand that we bring our inner feeling and our outer social behavior into one unity but leaves us split in two. It is not the morality of absolute pacifism and liberal perfectionism—it is not the morality of any "ism" at all, but of the concrete historical situation. Yet neither is it the morality of those who make the moral demand relevant to "immoral society" only as a judgment but not as a call to "drive the plowshare of the normative into the hard soil of political fact."

We are created in the image of God. But I do not respect you as a deduction from this premise. On the contrary, I realize you as created in the image of God only when I meet you in your concrete uniqueness as a person. In that relationship which claims my whole being, which I must enter as a person, and in which I find the meaning of my existence, in that relationship which calls me forth and to which I respond, in that relationship of freedom, direction, mutuality, and presentness, there is no room left over to speak of a separate relationship with God. No matter how "inward" I may be, I still live in the world facing my fellows. My relationship to God is not apart from my relationship to other persons but is its very foundation if the latter is understood deeply enough.

The morality of human wholeness implies that we find the absolute ever again in the relative—not as timeless essence or universal, but just in and inseparable from the unique, the unrepeatable, the new. Basic to the morality of human wholeness is hearing and responding— not imposition or obedience in the sense that we have to split ourselves into an obedient and rebellious part, but becoming ourselves in responding to what addresses us in the situation. As Job is confronted with the otherness of nature and of the rain that falls on the land where no man is, so we are called to respond insofar as our resources allow to every other—human or nonhuman—that comes to meet us. This is not because the other is God or contains the essence of God, or "that of God in him," but because the other and we are set in one creation, are creatures who find our access to true existence only through the encounter with and response to genuine otherness

In an age of the "eclipse of God" can we still meet, can we still hear, can we still respond? Or are we like Kafka's scholar-dog in "Investigations of a Dog" who said that in the old days the Word was with the dogs but that now dogs have become so fond of their doggishness that they can no longer hear the Word? The answer to this question is implicit in the words that we have quoted above from Deuteronomy: "It is not in heaven.... But the word is very near you; it is in your mouth and in your heart so that you can do it." If we take this seriously, that means that the word is not simply the possession of those who claim to have unlocked the esoteric mysteries, whether it be the Gnostic elect, Plato's Philosopher King, or those who specialize in the interpretation of the ancient Vedas, the Bible, the Talmud, the Kabbala, the I Ching, or the Buddhist sutras. Certainly the word may come to us through anything we make our own, including the scriptures of any religion. But the word is not tucked away in any special drawer for the privileged. Hearing and responding is a part of our existence itself.

This is the basic trust to which we have pointed, a trust all but obscured in a world in which psychologism so dominates that again and again we miss both the real otherness and the real address of the events that make up our lives, looking only for the byproduct: how the event helps us realize our potentialities or adds to our "growth." We can, nonetheless, hear and respond because the given of our existence cannot be abrogated, namely, that we live meeting situations that place demands upon us. What is really asked may be entirely other, even diametrically opposite, to what some person consciously demands. But we *can* respond to the *real* address of that person.

All ethics rests on a basic attitude toward reality that waits in the depths until it is summoned by a concrete situation. No matter what our religious beliefs or lack of them, we live in an age of the "death of God" in the sense in which I use the term: an age in which we no longer have a direction of meaningful personal and social existence such as gave some sureness and meaning to biblical, Greek, Christian, and Renaissance man, even in the midst of tragedy. Yet two possibilities remain open for us. The first is being ethical within given, inherited structures—the family, the culture, the state—ordinary living that because it *is* within these structures and because it rests on some genuine interhuman contact is ethical in practice, whatever the names by which its source is called or miscalled. The second is the vastly more difficult and painful discovery of the ethical in limit situations, in the "Dialogue with the Absurd," in the age of the "eclipse of God."

The ethical in this second sense takes a deeper grounding, whether one wants to call it religious or not. It means not putting up with the merely surface, and it means the testing of resources. It may mean living with guilt, anxiety, and the absurd. What is common to both types of ethical possibilities is that for them moral values are not authenticated in the abstract through finding rationally consistent positions. It is not in logical consistency but in our withstanding and being true in the situations that confront us that they are authenticated. We do not have to live every moment in a limit situation, and for this we must be grateful; for we do not have the resources to do so. But at times in our lives when we are confronted by the abyss, we *may* have the resources to respond from the depths and become ourselves in responding.

17

World View and Existential Trust

Every lock has its key which is fitted to it and opens
it. But there are thieves who know how to open without keys.
They break the lock. So every mystery in the world can be
unriddled by the particular kind of meditation fitted to it.
But God loves the thief who breaks the lock open: I mean
the man who breaks his heart for God.

I do not beg you to reveal to me the secret of your
ways—I could not bear it! But show me one thing, show it
to me more clearly and more deeply: show me what this,
which is happening at this very moment, means to me, what
it demands of me, what you, Lord of the world, are telling
me by way of it. Ah, it is not why I suffer, that I wish to
know, but only whether I suffer for your sake.

> The surest test if a man be sane
> Is if he accepts life whole, as it is,
> Without needing by measure or touch to understand
> The measureless untouchable source
> Of its images,
> The measureless untouchable source
> Of its substances,
> The source which, while it appears dark emptiness,
> Brims with a quick force
> Farthest away
> And yet nearest at hand
> From olden time unto this day,

207

Charging its images with origin:
What more need I know of the origin
than this?[1]

They build their ark and name it *Weltanschauung* and seal
up with pitch not only its cracks but also its windows in order
to shut out the waters of the living world.
                                        —**Martin Buber,** *Daniel*

The alternation between immediacy and mediacy, between
dialogue and objectification makes up our existence and our religious
way. Ultimately, however, we must choose—whether to enregister
everything in some comprehensive *gnosis* or to take our stand on an
existential trust that cannot pretend to get its arms around the creation
on which it stands.

From the standpoint of existential trust, the oneness of God is
not a superabstraction but the renewed meeting with the ever-unique
and the ever-particular.

"God-talk" is objective; "experience"-talk, whether mystical or
simply religious, is subjective: "I have had these feelings or this
experience." Touchstones of reality have tried to point toward something
that is neither objective nor subjective. For that reason it has a great
deal to do with the way we walk in our daily lives but very little to
do with the way we *think* about this walking since our thinking usually
remains bound up with the objective and the subjective.

In our search for meaning, for touchstones of reality, we sometimes
confuse two quite different things—a comprehensive world-view that
gives us a sense of security and the meaning which arises moment by
moment through our meeting with a reality that we cannot embrace.
Many people when they have a religious or mystical experience move
quickly to a metaphysics and identify their experience with one
particular philosophy of religion or of mysticism. Not content with
having found meaning in immediacy, they want to wrap up reality in
some conceptual totality and use their experience as the guarantor of
that totality. Perhaps one of the most important witnesses which can
be made in our day is that it is not necessary to have a *Weltanschauung*,
a comprehensive world view, in order to be able to live as a human
being. What is more, our "world view" may get in the way of our
confrontation with the concrete at any given point and just thereby rob
us of the real world. This means, in terms of theology, that our stance,
our life-attitude, is more basic than the affirmation or nonaffirmation

of a "Being" or "ground of being." No intellectual construction, not even the philosophy of dialogue, can ever include the real otherness of the other. In meeting the other, I come up against something absurd in the root meaning of the term—something irreducible that I cannot get my arms around or register in my categories. If this is true of the otherness of every concrete other, it is true by the same token of God, whom we meet in the meeting with the other.

A world view is like a geodesic dome. It creates a special atmosphere for you, keeps certain air currents up, and gives you a sense of spaciousness without giving you the real world where the winds blow freely and sometimes uncomfortably. A world view exists within your consciousness, even when you share it with any number of other persons. No matter how adequate the world view is, it leaves out otherness by definition. For that is the very nature of the other—that it cracks and destroys every *Weltanschauung,* that it does not fit into any ensemble of coherences, that it is absurd. You can fit others into your world view, but you cannot do so without robbing them of what makes them really other.

For these reasons I cannot follow Ninian Smart's call to transmute philosophy of religion into a philosophy of world views:

> Since theology is very often the product of struggle at the interface between a religious tradition and secular ideologies; and since the history of religions reveals remarkable contrasts between religions in both belief and practice: it would seem that the opening out of the philosophy of religion to theologies and religions itself pushes us onward in the direction of an even more plural range— the range of both religions and ideologies, the range of *existential worldviews* as they might jointly be called...the philosophy of religion...would be better called something like 'the philosophy of worldviews'...*Weltanschauungs-wissenschaft.*[2]

At the same time Ninian Smart touches our approach in his recognition that religions and ideologies do not merge into "a fuzzy haze—this is neither logically appropriate nor humanly likely; but there is a strong argument for a federalism of persons of good will" and his recognition that "the practical and the theoretical are interwoven in men's systems of belief."[3]

For me, at least, the ground of trust cannot be sought in theology or metaphysics. We cannot step outside the given of our situation and posit a foundation that is conceptually adequate. Once I wrote to Martin Buber and asked him, "Did God have an I-Thou relationship with man in creating him?" "Now you are talking like the theologians!" Buber replied. "How do we know what relationship God had with man in creating him?" There is something about the whole enterprise of theology, metaphysics, and often of philosophy of religion, which tempts the thinker to see God, the human, and the world from above and leave himself out of it. Then one wonders how Bergson got outside the *élan vital* or Whitehead outside the dialectic between God and the world so he could see it as a whole!

There are two different meanings of the word "ground" as we use it in a phrase such as the "ground of being." One of these is found in conceptual, or ontological, formulations. The other is a ground only in the sense of what we can touch on in our situation, in our experience, in our existence—what gives us the courage to take a step forward and then perhaps another step forward and still another. With the former meaning of ground I can have nothing to do because it presupposes removing us from where we are in fact. It presupposes getting behind or above creation. This is the one thing that Job was reproved for and properly so. He was not reproved for questioning God, for contending with God, or for crying out but only, as it says in chapter 40, "Will you condemn me to justify yourself?" Will you, in that witness for your innocence and for your suffering which you have to make, go further and make statements about the whole of reality? This desire for a comprehensive *gnosis* may give satisfaction to our minds when we give in to it, but we cannot live our lives from there. It goes beyond the given of our existence, of our finite freedom and our finite-infinite knowing.

The other meaning of "ground" I can and do affirm, for this is precisely what I mean by "touchstones of reality." Existential trust has to do with this second meaning, but not necessarily and often not at all with the first. Existential trust does not depend upon our affirming that we believe in God or that we have faith in God. What we believe, in the conscious, rational sense of that term, often has little or even a negative connection with our basic life-attitude, our stance. I have never heard a confirmed optimist talk without shuddering. Underneath his words I can sense that he has such a black feeling of what reality is that he constantly has to erect this rosy superstructure over it to avoid having to face it. The confirmed pessimist is in no better case. He enjoys it when things turn out the way he has predicted. He gets a positive ironic pleasure out of being able to gloat, "Well, it is just as I said it would be." Both the optimist and the pessimist put between themselves and the reality they meet a prejudice—an *a priori* emotional or intellectual view that prevents them from seeing reality as it is. If you are really willing to see things as they are, you cannot say in advance whether they will be good or bad. You may even be forced to revise your notions of what is good and what is bad!

The great Protestant theologian Paul Tillich offers an excellent example of *both* uses of ground of being. Sometimes he seems to want to impose acceptance of the term through logic and other times he makes it a witness of faith and trust. Tillich wishes to go beyond the divine Thou that is encountered by Kierkegaard to the transpersonal "ground of being itself." "The theologians who speak so strongly and with such self-certainty about the divine-human encounter should be aware of a situation in which this encounter is prevented by radical doubt and nothing is left but absolute faith." The courage to be takes radical doubt, the doubt about God, into itself, and makes God into a living God—the self-affirmation of Being itself that prevails against nonbeing. Tillich sees the "personal" God of theological theism as "a being beside others and as such a part of the whole of reality." At the same time, this limited God is the subject that makes us into objects and deprives us of our freedom as persons by his omnipotence and omniscience.

The only alternative that Tillich sees to the despair of atheistic existentialism which God's all-powerfulness produces is transcending theism in "absolute faith." Kierkegaard's I-Thou relation to the God of theism cannot enable one to take the anxiety of doubt and meaninglessness into the courage to be. But mysticism, too, must be transcended; for "mysticism does not take seriously the concrete and the doubt concerning the concrete"—the world of finite values and meanings. The divine-human encounter is paradoxical, however; for in it, the God above the God of theism is present, although hidden. It is the Thou, but it is also nearer to the I than the I is to itself. Here, personalism and the transpersonal go hand in hand—so well indeed that one wonders why Tillich need posit the "God above God" as a separate logical or theological category. Knowing for Tillich is knowing in the relationship of faith, but at a still deeper level, it is the knowledge which gives the ground for that relationship. To this extent, Tillich shores up the existential encounter with God with the essentialist *gnosis* that takes refuge in comprehensive concepts.

The question that this faith in a comprehensive system of knowledge raises has never been posed more sharply than by Tillich's disciple and friend, David E. Roberts:

> I have always been mystified as to how he could be so flexible, concrete, vital, and "close to home": on the one hand, and so schematic, abstract, abstruse, and remote on the other....The schematic aspect...is an asset wherever it is used analytically and organizationally, that is, where it is used to clarify concepts and to show their interrelatedness. But it becomes a liability at the point

where existential problems, after being highlighted, are swallowed into an abyss. Somehow Tillich, like God, manages to engulf distinctions without blurring them. He fully realizes (again, no doubt, like God) that such problems are met, insofar as they ever are, by living rather than by constructing systems. But it is a weird experience, which I have undergone many times, to have problems answered with great sensitivity and patience, by being brought into connection with some relevant segment of the system, only to discover later that I do not happen to be the man who carries this system around in his head.[4]

Existentialism, which begins with a reaction against Hegel's universal system, is always in danger—either by way of philosophy or by way of theology—of ending by incorporating its insights into some new Hegelian dialectic. The reaction against system ends in system. The reaction against *Weltanschauung* ends in *Weltanschauung*!

Yet the ground of being for Tillich is not merely a logical, theological, or metaphysical concept. It is also a living presence that undergirds the relation between the I and the Thou, whether the latter be divine or human. In that sense it is identical with touchstones of reality and with existential trust. Thus at the end of *The Courage to Be*, the very book in which he writes about the necessity of going beyond the I-Thou relationship to the God above God, Tillich movingly witnesses:

> Absolute faith, or the state of being grasped by the God beyond God, is not a state which appears beside other states of the mind. It never is something separated and definite, an event which could be isolated and described. It is always a movement in, with, and under other states of the mind. It is the situation on the boundary of man's possibilities. It is this boundary. Therefore it is both the courage of despair and the courage in and above every courage. It is not a place where one can live, it is without the safety of words and concepts, it is without a name, a church, a cult, a theology. But it is moving in the depth of all of them. It is the power of being, in which they participate and of which they are fragmentary expressions.[6]

Although in his book *Biblical Religion and The Search for Ultimate Reality* Tillich says against Pascal (and therefore by implication against Buber) that the God of the Philosophers and the God of Abraham, Isaac, and Jacob are the same God, much that Tillich says in that book is very close to Buber's own understanding of God as the "absolute Person who is not a person but becomes one, so to speak, in order to know and be known, to love and be loved by man." "Man can experience the holy in and through everything," writes Tillich, "but as the holy, it cannot be less than he is; it cannot be a-personal."

It is the unconditional character of the biblical God that

> makes the relation to him radically personal. For only that which concerns us in the center of our personal existence concerns us unconditionally. The God who is unconditional in power, demand, and promise is the God who makes us completely person and who, consequently, is completely personal in our encounter with him.[7]

At the same time, Tillich reaffirms that the God who is a being is transcended by the God who is Being itself, the ground and abyss of every being. But he also asserts, in language very like that of Buber's "absolute Person, that "the God who is a person is transcended by the God who is the Personal-itself, the ground and abyss of every person." His conclusion is that the ground of being is the ground of personal being, not its negation.

> Religiously speaking, this means that our encounter with the God who is a person includes the encounter with the God who is the ground of everything personal and as such not a person. . . .The I-Thou character of the relation never darkens the transpersonal power and mystery of the divine.[8]

Tillich, nonetheless, does not see the necessity of an ultimate choice between existential trust and *gnosis*, as Buber does in his contrast between gnosis and *devotio*. This contrast between Tillich and Buber is not unlike Buber's contrast between Hasidism and the Kabbala. The Kabbalah schematizes the mystery, Buber said, whereas Hasidism stops short, cowers in terror, and lets itself be disconcerted. I can think of no better illustration of this than Rabbi Zusya in a story entitled "The Fear of God":

> Once Zusya prayed to God: "Lord, I love you so much, but I do not fear you enough! Lord, I love you so much, but I do not fear you enough! Let me stand in awe of you like your angels, who are penetrated by your awe-inspiring name." And God heard his prayer, and his name penetrated the hidden heart of Zusya as it does those of the angels. But Zusya crawled under the bed like

a little dog, and animal fear shook him until he howled: "Lord, let me love you like Zusya again!" And God heard him this time also.[8]

Once, without being aware of it, I strove to push Buber into the affirmation of a metaphysical doctrine to underline his trust in redemption. In the Martin Buber section of *Philosophical Interrogations*, I asked him whether the relation to the eternal Thou includes not only the temporal I-Thou relation but the I-It relation, too? What is more, I supported this question with impressive testimony from Buber's own writing in *I and Thou* where he speaks of the primal twofold movement of "estrangement from" and "turning toward" the primal Source:

> Every real relation in the world is consummated in the interchange of actual and potential being, but in pure relation—in the relation of man to God—potential is still actual being. . . . By virtue of this great privilege of pure relation there exists the unbroken world of Thou which binds up the isolated moments of relation in a life of world solidarity.[9]

Does this not mean, I asked Buber, that we relate to the actual and present eternal Thou even when the temporal Thou has again become only past and potential, that is, when it has again become it? Is it not through a *continuing* relation with the eternal Thou that we are able ever again to find the Thou, either with the person who was Thou for us but is now It or with some other whom we have never before met as Thou? If we know the unique value of another only in the I-Thou relationship, is it not the potentiality of his being, or again being a Thou for us, that ultimately prevents our treating the person whom we do not know as Thou purely as a dispensable It? And does not that person's "potential Thou" rest not only on the "actual Thou" of remembered I-Thou relationships but on the actual Thou of Present Reality—the relation to the eternal Thou "in which potential is still actual being"? Is it not our trust in the eternal Thou that gives actuality and continuity to our discontinuous and often merely potential relations to the human Thou?

Buber's response, like that of Zusya, was a drawing back, a stopping short, an allowing himself to be disconcerted. He declined to back up his earlier words in such a way as to allow me to discern a gnosis underlying his existential trust:

> I perceive in this question, from words of mine which have been quoted here, that I have already come close to the limit of what

is accessible to our experience. I hesitate to go a step further with words the full responsibility for which I cannot bear. *In our experience* our relation to God does *not* include our I-It relations. What is the case beyond our experience, thus so to speak, from the side of God, no longer belongs to what can be discussed. Perhaps I have here and there, swayed by the duty of the heart that bids me point out what I have to point out, already said too much.[10]

Does not biblical trust rest upon the belief in the existence of God? I do not think so. We have been hung up for centuries on the question of the existence of God, on proofs and disproofs of his existence. This is not a question that the Hebrew Bible ever asked. A God whose existence could be proved could not be the biblical Creator; for he would be part of an already given order where one thing could be causally or logically related to another since this is the very nature of proof. The person of the Hebrew Bible did not live in such a world of abstractions. He did not know about "nature" as some great whole. He just knew the goats, the war horse, and the clods of dust—all the particulars of things. What he was concerned with was the reality he met in his existence. He was not concerned with metaphysics or even theology. He could not ask the question, for that would mean to turn the world into the given and God into the variable. In Proverbs it is the fool and not the skeptic who "says in his heart there is no God." That does not mean he does not "believe" in God. It means he shuts out the reality of the otherness that meets us in each new situation.

What does this say about God? Abraham Heschel says, "God is of no importance unless he is of supreme importance." That means that a "God" who is just a means to our ends is not really God. Jean-Paul Sartre says, "Even if God did exist, that would change nothing." In contrast to both Heschel and Sartre, the vast mass of people want to keep God around for his usefulness—for the national welfare, for successful living, for positive thinking, for peace of mind or peace of soul. In the face of this situation, the truly religious person, or in our terms the person who is deeply concerned with touchstones of reality, must sometimes, like Albert Camus, have the courage to put the belief in God aside in order to try to make contact once again with existential reality. "I want to live only with what I can know," says Camus. I want to find touchstones of reality that I can live by. In our age this man in his atheism may affirm reality more than those who profess the existence of God but, in the language of T. S. Eliot's "Ash Wednesday," "affirm before the world but deny between the rocks." These latter confess belief in order to keep the social integument together but do not let it matter in the least in their lives.

We meet the "eternal Thou" only in our existence as persons, only in our meeting with the other: we cannot know it as if from outside this existence. If we recognize this, we must renounce the attempt to include God in any conceptual system, even the most creative and organic of process philosophies, whether that of Alfred North Whitehead or Pierre Teilhard de Chardin. To say that one meets God in what transcends oneself does not mean that the other one meets is "supernatural," or even that the "supernatural" is in the "between." The term "natural," however, leads us to forget the reality over against us and to see our existence as entirely included in a conceptual totality that we call "nature," "world," or "universe." In our actual experience, reality, including all other selves, is not only within but over against us. It is not some common, undifferentiated, reality that can be seen from the outside. Much modern thought confuses the subjectivity of the person and the subjectivity of "man": it treats the human as a totality and what is immanent in him as if it were in a single self. In our concrete existence, however, there is no such totality. The Thou confronts us with the unexpected, takes us unawares. We must stand our ground yet be prepared to go forth again and again to meet we know not what. It is not insight into process but trust in existence that enables us to enter into a genuine meeting with the unique reality that accosts us in the new moment.

There is often a correlation between a thinker's approach to ethics and his approach to philosophy of religion. Those thinkers who feel that religion is solidly founded only when it rests on proofs of the existence of God, proofs that by their very nature put God into a rational framework of universal order or law, stand in opposition to the existential trust that receives only what it receives without demanding that God, the human, and the world be installed in any objective, comprehensible totality. The security of the former rests on the cosmos that human understanding has opened to it, the "holy insecurity" of the latter on the trust in the meeting with the reality over against one—the meeting with the God whom one can talk *to* but not *about*. Similarly, those who demand a logical, ordered ethics often do so not because they have reason to believe in the objectivity of the moral order but because they have an almost magic belief that what they posit as fixed, objective, and universal provides security and solidity and protects them against the threat of the romantic, the irrational, and the demonic.

To speak of "touchstones of reality" does not imply that we can define what we mean by "reality." All we can say is that we mean the concrete situation, including whatever enters into it from all that we have been. There is a relation between our various truths—our touch-stones of reality—both those that we experience in our own lives and those that we encounter in the lives of others. But this relation is not one of an abstract consistency. We cannot stand back and look at those events from which we derive our touchstones as if in the moment of reflection we were outside of time. Rather in a new situation it is possible to reaffirm the old touchstones—not in such a way as to say that they are the same as the new, but they are illuminated by them.

If this leaves us with no absolute or truth other than the relation to the moment, into that relation may enter every other truth-relationship that we have made our own. We do not *have* truth. We have a relationship to it. We can affirm certain moments of meeting—not necessarily as having an objectifiable knowledge content but still as not being sheer immersion in the flux. These moment by moment truth-relationships do not yield some higher truth that we can objectify as always the same. All we have is what at any given time we know and what we are not given to know. The notion that we are moving toward omniscience, that science will some day know everything there is to know, simply misunderstands the fact that all human knowing is a mixture of finitude and the infinite. All our knowing is partial ignorance. What we should be concerned about is what it is given us to know at *this* time. In each new discovery or rediscovery, our earlier touchstones of reality are brought into the fullness of the present. Any reference point beyond that would take us out of the only dimension in which we live and think and know—the dimension of time. We must, of course, act as if we were above time when employing our useful abstractions—from mathematics and logic to engineering and even some parts of law. But in the essential matters of our lives, in our concrete existence as whole persons, we must avoid the illusion that we can rise to a reference point above existence itself—an abstract spatiality divorced from events.

If I meet my friend again, I can recognize him, know him again, only if there really is a new relationship. Otherwise I remember him from our past moments of relationship, but he has not come alive to me again as my friend. If I do recognize him in new relationship, then the old has been given new meaning through being brought into the new without destroying its original meaning. Similarly the God that I re-cognize, that I know again, I know in concrete uniqueness, not in any abstract sameness. Objectivizing, structuring, formulating are essential in the carrying forward of our truths. But if you content yourself with them alone, you lose your touchstones of reality. You have to take the further step of bringing the old touchstones into the new.

Therefore, our ultimate criterion of meaning and truth is not the objectification of a structure but the lived new meeting with reality.

We must fight and contend with tradition in order to make an honest witness to our own uniqueness and to all the absurdity and incongruity that has entered into our lives. There are two different Pietas of Michelangelo. The one that was brought from Saint Peter's in Rome to the World's Fair in New York is very beautiful, but it is still the early one in which Michelangelo portrays Mary as a lovely sixteen-year-old girl holding a boyish body of Christ. The later Pieta, which one sees in Florence, is the great one that shows real agony and that was produced in agony out of a genuine wrestling with the marble.

"From wonder into wonder existence opens," says Lao-tzu. To have a touchstone and to touch touchstones means a whole different way of living than is implied by locating the reality "out there" or "in here." Many of us feel that if we only replace the anthropomorphic notion of God with some impersonal concept, we are on the way. But what are we on the way to except another abstraction, unless it lead to greater openness? The only "perennial philosophy" I can espouse is that each of the religions and touchstones that I have entered into dialogue with points toward greater openness. "Alas the world is full of enormous lights and mysteries," says the Baal Shem, "but man hides them from him with one small hand." Prayer is the removal of that hand.

Prayer has to do with discovering each time anew what we can bring and what can be brought—the way we bring ourselves to a poem or a dream or a Hasidic, Zen, or Sufi tale. That is why my former wife, Eugenia, without reducing the religious to the aesthetic, can say in all the seriousness of her open and faithful dialogue with the poems and poets she reads and teaches, "Poetry is the liturgy of our lives." My chief advisor for my doctoral dissertation, Professor Arnold Bergstraesser, amazed me when I had finished it by asking, "Do you know Buber's secret? It is prayer." He did not mean by this that Buber spent so many hours a day praying but that he brought himself into presentness every hour of his life in a real openness. Then Bergstraesser demanded of me, "What will keep you from reading this dissertation ten years later and asking yourself, 'Did I know that then!?' " What he meant, I have realized ever more deeply in the more than forty years since, was that all the marvelous insights that I had gleaned from my study of Buber's thought might become lost, closed over as the waters close over the deep. Not because the insights were untrue but because I might fail to authenticate them and make them real by bringing them in openness into my life. The life of prayer can only be sustained if we bring ourselves to each situation with all that we know and have been. We are all like that Hasid on whom the terrible penance was imposed that for the rest of his life he preserve the full intention of every word of prayer!

The kingdom of God cannot be localized in the immanent or the transcendent, within us or beyond us. It is both the personal—the quality of individual living—and the social—the realization of justice, righteousness, and lovingkindness in lived community. It is dialogue, trust, and grace—moving among us. It is the covenant of peace—the task that demands us and the partnership of existence that sustains and comforts us. It is our touchstones of reality—our discovery and confirmation of and them in the cruel and gracious happenings of our lives.

18

Is Religion the Enemy of Humankind?

A certain man was believed to have died, and was being prepared for burial when he revived.

He sat up, but he was so shocked at the scene surrounding him that he fainted.

He was put in a coffin, and the funeral party set off for the cemetery.

Just as they arrived at the grave, he regained consciousness, lifted the coffin lid, and cried out for help.

"It is not possible that he has revived," said the mourners, "because he has been certified dead by competent experts."

"But I am alive!" shouted the man.

He appealed to a well-known and impartial scientist and jurisprudent who was present.

"Just a moment," said the expert.

He then turned to the mourners, counting them. "Now, we have heard what the alleged deceased has had to say. You fifty witnesses tell me what you regard as the truth."

"He is dead," said the witnesses.

"Bury him," said the expert.

And so he was buried.

"Sati, death of an Indian widow"

An attractive 18-year-old woman, Roop Kunwar. . .was made to sit on the funeral pyre and her husband's body was

221

placed on her lap. A layer of fireworld was erected around her, up to her shoulders, so that she could not get up.

When she tried to speak, members of her late husband's family and some others who had gathered to witness the cremation began chanting *"Jai, jai"* ("Hail, hail"). Within minutes the pyre was lit by her 15-year-old brother-in-law, Pushpender Singh.

Again she tried to get up and speak. The pyre tilted to one side and the fire went out. Dried thorny bushes from the neighbouring field were collected and the pyre was relit. It remained lit from 11:30 a.m. to about 1 p.m., and burnt her to ashes along with her husband's corpse. Initial reports stated that 500 villagers witnessed the event; later estimates were in the thousands.

Roop Kunwar had been married eight months earlier to her husband but had spent only a small part of that time with him, as is Rajput custom....

Her parents were only informed of the death and cremation of their son-in-law and the *sati* of their daughter the day after the event. Roop Kunwar's four brothers and parents rushed to Deorala, suspecting foul play, but it was too late. They were assured that her *sati* had been voluntary and that she had now attained divinity....Funds were already being collected to erect a temple to honour the new *"Mahsati"*, who had brought honour to both families.

Roop Kunwar's family accepted this explanation. When asked some days later what his feelings were, Bal Singh Rathore [her father] replied "bittersweet." He drew consolation, he said, from the fact that his daughter was a martyr to an ancient Hindu custom, and a *devi* (goddess) worshipped by thousands of people. He added that her action had given him social standing and his family had become famous. The *sati* would go down in histroy.

Later, he announced a donation of 100,000 rupees to build a temple to her memory....Roop Kunwar's mother (whose every word now became sacrosanct) began issuing instructions. Many believed these were Roop Kunwar's own words, spoken through her mother's mouth....More than 10,000 pilgrims were streaming in every day to this small village...to make donations, pray at the site of the cremation and seek the blessings of the new *sati Mata* ("Mother *sati*) Roop Kunwar....

Meanwhile, preparations intensified for the 13th-day rites, called the *Chunri Mahotsav*, where 100,000 devotees were expected to be present. On September 16, a cloth, heavily embroidered with gold and called a *chunri*, was brought by Roop Kunwar's parents and carried in a procession by her four brothers, to be offered at the site of the *sati*. . . .

The police decided that they could not prevent the ceremony taking place or arrest those suspected of abetting the *sati*. More than 250,000 people had gathered and a major law and order problem was in the making. Hysterical women prostrated themselves at the site amidst chants extolling the *sati*. The donations swelled to more than 500,000 rupees.

At least four members of Rajasthan's Legislative Assembly, includng a prominent opposition leader, were present to participate in the obsequies. Tens of thousands of photographs of Roop Kunwar were sold and her father-in-law blessed the pilgrims. Pamphlets extolling *sati* circulated and the village was thrust into a religious fervour which was to last nearly a month. Those who had come to offer prayers did not wish to hear any criticism. The practice of *sati*, they said, was part of the glorious Rajput tradition.

On September 18, police arrested Sumer Singh Shekhawat, Roop Kunwar's father-in-law, and four others on the charges of murder and abetting suicide. . . . Rajput representatives presented a memorandum warning the government not to interfere with the religious beliefs of their community. . . . Although *sati* had been outlawed in 1829, some 30 *satis* had taken place in Rajasthan in the 40 years since India had become independent. Now it seemed likely that more such incidents would occur, judging by the size and emotional level of the crowds who had visited Deorala. . . . The Rajasthan High Court had in the meantime ruled that the *sati* custom had "no religious sanction and was neither a religious practice nor a matter of religious faith.". . . During the two weeks of religious fervour following the sacrifice, any attempt they said at arresting those who abetted the *sati* would have led to violence. . . .

Several explanations were advanced for what had occured: Roop Kunwar's dowry would not have to be returned now that she had died; the village stood to benefit enormously if it became a centre of pilgrimage. . . . Sociologists described the events as one of the "many pathologies" which infect Hindu society, caused by the breakdown of traditional ways of life which are torn on all sides by the demands of the modern world.

The Jerusalem Post, January 26, 1988

If someone comes to you and asks your help, you shall not turn him off with pious words, saying: "Have faith and take your troubles to God!" You shall act as if there were no God, as if there were only one person in all the world who could help this man—only yourself.

Whoever says that the words of the Torah are one thing and the words of the world another, must be regarded as a man who denies God.[1]

"Religion," Martin Buber once wrote, "is the great enemy of mankind." He was speaking, of course, of religion when it is used to perpetuate the dualism between the spirit and the everyday and as such becomes a threat to human wholeness. Human wholeness is not simply inner individuation or integration but the wholeness of persons within the partnership of existence, and *that* finds its most meaningful form in what I call the "community of otherness." If we look at our question from this standpoint, we must confess that just as the structures of society more often block the road to genuine community than promote it, so also the structures of religion—creed, cult, and church—more often further a community of affinity, or likemindedness, than they do a community of otherness. What is more, by its very claim to have a corner on the spirit and by the tendency to regard religion as the refuge from the mundane world, religious institutions and groups more often intensify the dualism between spirit and world than overcome it.

After a lecture that I gave on Hasidism to a Jewish audience, I was astonished at the complaint that Hasidism was "mechanistic" and had no room for "love." I had talked of little else but love of God and love of fellowman. "Do you mean by 'mechanistic' 'materialistic?' " I asked the questioner. "Yes," she replied. Then I said, "And do you find what I said materialistic because I spoke of 'hallowing the everyday' and you feel that the spiritual should have nothing to do with the everyday?" Again she replied, "Yes." By some intuition that I cannot explain to myself I understood that she was approaching Hasidism from the very un-Jewish but all too familiar dualism between the spiritual and the material according to which the concern with the everyday automatically signals the exclusion of the truly "spiritual"!

The other side of this paradox is that in a secular society, which in its ever greater complexity is of necessity more and more compartmentalized, religion is perhaps the one human activity and concern that might bring the disparate spheres into healing contact with one another and guard thereby the wholeness of the human. A humanist might protest that this could also be done without religion, and I would not deny it. Yet by and large it is not done. What is more, by and large the problem is not even seen as a problem because people seem quite content to divide their lives into compartments that have little to do with one another.

Many years ago I went to a party at the Greenwich Village apartment of a Harvard classmate and friend. It was not too large an apartment or too large a party, yet it broke up "naturally" into clusters—one of his Harvard friends, one of his high school friends, one of those he knew at summer camp, one of his fellow workers at *Time, Life,* and *Sports Illustrated,* one of Greenwich Village's musicians and composers. My friend moved from group to group talking briefly with each. It struck me at the time that this was an exact microcosm of New York City itself with its many cultures that pass by one another without meeting. In a considerably smaller city, such as San Diego, one might imagine that there would be only one culture. Yet I was similarly struck recently when I emerged from a breathtakingly beautiful performance of the Bach B Minor Mass in the wonderful Immaculata Cathedral of the University of San Diego and passed by the San Diego Stadium where the Padres or the Chargers were enacting a very different sort of rite! What, I wondered, could bring these two cultures together?

If this is true among groups of people, it is also true within individuals themselves. Each of us has so many different associations in so many different contexts that without realizing it we become accustomed to shifting gears with each one. Occasionally I have difficulty recognizing not only voices over the telephone but also names unless I can place first the context of the person who is speaking. Not so long ago I wrote a doctoral student at the University of Utah, whom I had met only once, asking her if she could send me a picture of herself with her next chapter. An image of another woman had intervened, and I could neither locate the image nor get it out of my mind. In endeavoring to place it, I methodically went over what turned out to be an incredible number of different places and contexts with which I had been associated in the last 20 years only to realize finally that the image was of someone I knew in the present!

Neither human existence nor religion can exist in pure immediacy. The history of religion is far more a history of objective structures of creed, cult, and grouping than of direct revelations, theophanies, ecstasies, or dialogues between the human and the divine. To acknowledge this dialectic still leaves unanswered the question of which is the master and which the servant, which the end and which the means. Insofar as religions become bastions to protect the spirit against defilement by the world or to protect the community of believers from contact with those who do not believe in the same way, then we must say that structure and objectification are the master and that religion is, indeed, the enemy of humankind. This is not just a question of how we define religion but of what is the prevailing tendency or direction within any given religious life, group, institution, or tradition.

In response to the question whether one should pay taxes to the Roman government, Jesus asked whose picture was on the coin and then answered, "Render unto Caesar the things that are Caesar's and unto God the things that are God's." Assuming this to be an authentic saying growing out of a specific historical, political, and economic context, we cannot fail to note how often the same question has been asked in effect in the ages since. Not long after the death of Jesus, Rabbi Akiba was burned at the stake by the Romans for his persistence in practicing and teaching Judaism, which the Romans had outlawed in Palestine. When his disciples exclaimed at the look of joy on his face, he said, "All my life I have wanted to recite the *Sh'ma* [Hear O Israel, the Lord Our God, the Lord is One.] in the right way, and now I can do so!" This became the origin of the designation of martyrdom within Judaism as the *Kiddush Ha-Shem*, the sanctification of the name of God, a sanctification that not only means declaring God's oneness but also *Yihud*, the practical task of unification in the face of the monstrous contradictions of life.

Not long after the martyrdom of Akiba and other Jewish rabbis, countless Christians were martyred in Rome for their insistence on continuing their Christianity and for their refusal to take part in the army or own slaves or otherwise serve the Roman Empire, which they identified with the Great Beast of the Apocalypse. Yet from the time of Constantine on, the Church and the State became identified and Jesus' saying about the tribute money was increasingly used as a justification for that very dualism between spirit and life that made Buber speak of religion as the great enemy of humankind.

What seems the self-evident meaning of the saying is not necessarily the real one, however, as Buber himself has printed out in "The Validity and Limitations of the Political Principle," a speech that he gave at the German universities at the time when he first consented to appear publicly in the postwar Germany which until then had appeared to him "faceless" because of the twelve years of Nazi totalitarianism. In the two millennia since Jesus answered this question, the particular situations out of which it arises have become ever more difficult and contradictory, even though they are often not ones of foreign rule but one's own and not of a government sustained by force but one willingly submitted to. In an age when everything else is made relative, the political principle and with it the sovereignty of each separate nation has been made absolute. In the political state and especially in its highest fulfillment, the totalitarian state, what man owes to Caesar is simply himself and what is left over for God is virtually nothing. Hegel, Marx, and Heidegger each in his own way have absolutized history and the historical state and have attributed to the state the legitimately unconditional determining force. As a result, the state comes to occupy the divine seat of authority—until, as inevitably happens, the plurality of states and the uneasy balance of power set a limit from without to the absolutism within.

The choice is not between being a "Single One" in the style of Kierkegaard or submerging oneself in a party or a state, but rather between serving a Mammon that swallows up the soul and leaves nothing of it free and serving the group *quantum satis*—as much as is possible and desirable at any one time and in any given conflict without surrendering to it once and for all. "In each situation that demands decision the demarcation line between service and service must be drawn anew—not necessarily with fear, but necessarily with that trembling of the soul that precedes every genuine decision." One can serve God within the party and the state, but only by drawing the demarcation line ever anew and that means above all by not giving over the integrity of oneself and one's cause in the name of the end justifying the means:

> What is at stake here is shown most clearly when means are proposed whose nature contradicts the nature of the goal. Here, too, one is obliged not to proceed on principle, but only to advance ever again the responsibility of the line of demarcation and to answer for it not in order to keep one's soul clean of blood—that would be a vain and wretched enterprise—but in order to guard against means being chosen that will lead away from the cherished goal to another goal essentially similar to those means; for the end never sanctifies the means, but the means can certainly thwart the end.[2]

What Buber concludes from this is that those who, however various their goal, are united in their fidelity to the truth of God, must unite to give to God what is God's, or what, in our day may come to the same thing—to give to the human what is human in order to save it from being devoured by the political principle.

If we look closely at what Buber has said, we shall see that he has proceeded by a different logic than those who take it for granted that Jesus meant that one should give one part of human existence, the material, to Caesar, and another part, the spiritual, to God. The real contrast here is between the part and the whole; for the structures of economics and the state are always structures of the part, structures of indirectness and mediacy, whereas the realm and claim of God is always the whole that, if anything can, legitimizes those partial structures and imparts meaning to them.

Looked at in this way, the question of whether religion is an enemy to humankind is not a question that can be answered in general, academically, or once for all, say, from the outside by its opponents or from within by its proponents. It can only be answered again and again, in each situation of trust and contending anew, by those of us who fight on whatever front, within whatever group, or even—like Luther, Socrates, and Amos—alone! It is we who decide in each new battlefield whether the prevailing direction of religion is toward a dualism in which the spirit has no binding claim upon life and life falls apart into unhallowed segments or toward the continual overcoming of that dualism by taking up again and again the task of hallowing the creation that has been given to us. Every rung of human existence can be a ground of hallowing if we put off the habitual. The religious person meets God, not in the aseity of the philosophers, but in the events and meetings of concrete life, in the Dialogue with the Absurd.

Each religious person has his or her own touchstones and the emphasis that his or her tradition and situation make necessary. No philosopher of religion has the right to prescribe ideal requisites for the coming of the kingdom. There is, nonetheless, a direction of movement within each tradition and between and among traditions, groups, and individual persons that might enhance the partnership of existence.

The first element of that direction is fervor. We do not need a "religious revival" nor certainly any turning away from study or from the full and, where possible, improved, use of our powers of reason. But we do need genuine fervor if religion is to call to the wholeness of the person and the community and help them to find the ever-renewed direction toward God amid the complexities and contradictions of the present.

A second element is genuine community, the movement toward a community of otherness, first within the religious group itself, and then between group and group, culture and culture, nation and nation, people and people—openhearted dialogue that confirms the other in his or her otherness and does not demand that the word or way of the other conform to one's own.

A third element is the overcoming of dualism by the insistence in each human and social sphere anew, that the spirit be relevant to life and that life be open to the demand of the spirit. Only thus can the mediate and indirect structures of our existence be brought into the immediate and be given meaning by the whole.

Lastly, and perhaps in this hour most important, is the recovery of existential trust through the courage to address and the courage to respond.[3] This is the *via humana* in which our dialogue with one another and our dialogue with the absurd issues ever anew into our meeting with the eternal Thou. The awareness of the ineffable is included within this dialogue: for it means nothing other than true openness to the wonder met in every moment. The *via humana* opens to us a different way of living, a greater wholeness, than the compartmentalization of our lives into inner and outer, feeling and thought, subjective and objective, individual and society can ever do.

Only we can remove from our eyes that one small hand that shuts off from us the enormous lights and mysteries which fill the world. Only we can bring to light the hidden human image—the image of the imageless God.

> Whoever says that the words of the Torah are one thing and the words of the world another must be regarded as a person who denies God.

NOTES

Chapter 1—Religion and the Religions

1. Kenneth W. Morgan, *Reaching for the Moon: On Asian Paths* (Chambersburg, Pa.: Anima Publications, 1990), p. 2.

2. *Ibid.*, p. 5.

Chapter 2—My Dialogue with the Religions

1. Maurice Friedman, *Touchstones of Reality: Existential Trust and the Community of Peace* (New York: E. P. Dutton, 1972), p. 52.

2. John Hick, *An Interpretation of Religion: Human Responses to the Transcendent* (New York: Macmillan Press, 1989), pp. 252 f.

3. Quoted in Louis Fischer, *Gandhi: His Life and Message for the World* (New York: Signet Key Book, 1954).

4. E. A. Burtt, ed., *The Teachings of the Compassionate Buddha* (New York: New American Library, Mentor Books, 1955), pp. 195–198, italics mine.

5. The passages from Lao-tzu's teaching that I have quoted as the springboard for my interpretation are from *The Way of Life according to Lao-tzu*, trans. with an introduction by Witter Bynner (New York: Capricorn Books, 1961), nos. 1, 81, 21, 14, 10, 47, 7, 49, 55, 57, 56, 63, 76, 81 respectively.

6. Sardar Sir Jogendra Singh, *The Persian Mystics: The Invocations of Sheikh Abdullah Ansari of Herat, A.D. 1005–1090* (London: John Murray, Albemarle Street, 1939), pp. 22–29, 34.

7. Jelaluddin Rumi, *This Longing: Poetry, Teaching Stories, Seletted Letters,* trans. by Coleman Barks and John Moyne (Putney, Vt.: Threshold Books, 1988), pp. 23, 30f., 37, 42, 52, 61, 64, 66, 105.

231

8. John Moyne and Coleman Barks, *Unseen Rain: Quatrains of Rumi* (Putney, Vt.: Threshold Books, 1986), pp. 13, 27, 32, 35, 63 f., 75, 83.

9. Martin Buber, *The Legend of the Baal-Shem*, trans. by Maurice Friedman (New York: Schocken Books, 1969), pp. 49 f. This passage from "The Life of the Hasidim" can also be found in Martin Buber, *Hasidism and Modern Man*, ed. and trans. with an introduction by Maurice Friedman (Atlantic Highlands, N.J.: Humanities Press International, 1988), book 1, part 4.

10. For the fruit of my years of dialogue with Hasidic tales, see Maurice Friedman, *A Dialogue with Hasidic Tales: Hallowing the Everyday* (New York: Human Sciences Press, 1988).

11. For a fuller discussion of my way and of my response to these religions, see Maurice Friedman, *Touchstones of Reality*, chap. 1 to 6 and 10.

Chapter 3—The Biblical Covenant: Exile, Contending, and Trust

1. For a fuller interpretation of Job and biblical faith, see Maurice Friedman, *Problematic Rebel: Melville, Dostoievsky, Kafka, Camus*, 2nd rev., enlarged, and radically reorganized ed. (Chicago: The University of Chicago Press and Phoenix Books, 1970), pp. 3–22.

Chapter 4—Jesus: Image of the Human or Image of God?

1. Cf. Henry Sharman, *The Records of the Life of Jesus* (New York: Harper & Bros., 1937), and *Jesus as Teacher* (New York: Harper & Bros., Student's revised edition, 1944).

2. Martin Buber, *Two Types of Faith*, trans. by Norman P. Goldhawk (New York: Harper Torchbooks, 1961), p. 160.

3. Martin Buber, *Eclipse of God. Studies in the Relation between Religion and Philosophy* with an introduction by Robert Seltzer (Atlantic Highlands, N.J.: Humanities Press International, 1988), "Religion and Philosophy," trans. by Maurice Friedman, p. 36.

4. Martin Buber, *Tales of the Hasidim: The Early Masters*, trans. by Olga Marx (New York: Schocken Books, 1961), pp. 212f.

Chapter 5—Hasidism

1. Buber, *Tales or the Hasidim: The Early Masters*, p. 135—"Originality."

2. *Ibid.*, p. 313—"The Way."

3. *Ibid.*, p. 316—"Alien Thoughts."

4. *Ibid.*, p. 104—"The Strong Thief," italics added.

5. Martin Buber, *Tales of the Hasidim: The Later Masters*, trans. by Olga Marx (New York: Schocken Books, 1961), p. 214.

6. *The Early Masters*, p. 174—"The Rope Dancer."

7. *The Later Masters*, p. 170—"Everywhere."

8. *Ibid.*, p. 70—"Of Modern Inventions."

9. Martin Buber, *The Tales of Rabbi Nachman*, trans. by Maurice Friedman (New York: Horizon Books, 1969; Avon Books—Discussion Books, 1970), p. 36.

10. *Ibid.*, p. 40.

11. *The Later Masters*, p. 145—"The Secret Prayer."

12. *Ibid.*, pp. 66f.

13. *Ibid.*, p. 57.

14. *The Early Masters*, p. 66.

15. Martin Buber, *The Origin and Meaning of Hasidism*, ed. and trans. with an introduction by Maurice Friedman (Atlantic Highlands, N.J.: Humanities Press International, 1988), "God and the Soul," pp. 190–98.

Chapter 7—The *Via Humana*

1. Buber, *Tales of the Hasidim: The Early Masters*, p. 107—"To Say Torah and to Be Torah."

2. *The Later Masters*, p. 281—"Holiness."

Chaptr 8—Religious Symbolism and "Universal" Religion

1. John Hick, *An Interpretation of Religion*, pp. 264–266.

Chapter 9—Legend, Myth, and Tale

1. *The Early Masters*, Preface, pp. vf.

2. Ernst Cassirer, *Language and Myth*, trans. by Suzanne Langer (New York: Harper & Bros., 1946), pp. 11, 18, 27.

3. H. and H. A. Frankfort, et. al., *The Intellectual Adventure of Ancient Man: An Essay on Speculative Thought in the Ancient Near East* (Chicago: University of Chicago Press, 1946), pp. 4f., and concluding chapter, "The Emancipation of Thought from Myth," which is also found in H. and H. A. Frankfort, et. al., *Before Philosophy*, chap. 8 (New York: Penguin Books), pp. 241–248.

4. Martin Buber, *The Prophetic Faith*, trans. from the Hebrew by Carlyle Witton-Davies (New York: Harper Torchbooks, 1960), p. 46.

5. Martin Buber, *Hasidism and Modern Man*, ed. & trans. with an introduction by Maurice Friedman (Humanities Press Intnl., 1988), p. 26.

6. Harry M. Buck, Jr. "From History to Myth: A Comparative Study," *The Journal of Bible and Religion*, vol. 29, July 1961, pp. 219f.

7. Mircea Eliade, *Cosmos and History: The Myth of the Eternal Return*, trans. by Willard Trask (New York: Horper Torchbooks, 1959), p. 85.

8. *Ibid.*, pp. 106f.

9. *Ibid.*, p. 156.

10. *Ibid.*, p. 162.

11. *Ibid.*, pp. 154f.

12. Martin Buber, *Two Types of Faith*, trans. by Norman P. Goldhawk (New York: Macmillan, 1986), p. 160.

13. Wilfred Cantwell Smith, *On Understanding Islam: Selected Studies* (The Hague: Mouton Publishers, 1981), pp. 149–151, 156, 161.

14. Eliade, *Cosmos and History*, p. 132.

15. Martin Buber, *Pointing the Way*, trans. & ed. by Maurice Friedman (New York: Schocken Books, 1974), "Prophecy, Apocalyptic, and the Historical Hour," p. 200. See pp. 192–207.

16. Martin Buber, *Israel and the World: Essays in a Time of Crisis* (New York: Schocken Books, 1963), "The Two Foci of the Jewish Soul," p. 36.

17. Eliade, *Cosmos and History*, pp. 158f.

Chapter 10—Religion and Literature

1 Martin Buber, *A Believing Humanism: Gleanings*, trans. with an introduction and explanatory comments by Maurice Friedman (New York: Simon & Schuster Paperbacks, 1969), "The Demonic Book," pp. 46f.

2. Maurice Friedman, *To Deny Our Nothingness: Comtemporary Images of Man*, 3rd. ed. with new preface and appendix (Chicago: University of Chicago Press Phoenix Books, 1978, Midland Books), p. 27.

3. Walter Stein, *Criticism as Dialogue* (London and New York: Cambridge University Press, 1969), pp. 12–16, 29, 31, 33f., 42, 44.

4. Walter J. Ong, S.J., *In the Human Grain: Further Explorations of Contemporary Culture* (New York: The Macmillan Co., 1957), pp. 37f.

5. Walter J. Ong, S.J., *The Barbarian Within: And Other Fugitive Essays and Studies* (New York: The Macmillan Co., 1961), pp. 52 f., 55, 62, 65 f.

6. Maurice Friedman, *Problematic Rebel: Melville, Dostoievsky, Kafka, and Camus,* pp. 439ff.

7. *Ibid.,* p. 482.

8. *Martin Buber: Briefwechsel aus sieben Zahrzehnten,* Vol. III: *1938–1965* (Heidelberg: Verlag Lambert Schneider, 1975), #294 Martin Buber to Herman Kasack, Jerusalem, December 22, 1953, p. 357, my translation.

9. Martin Buber, *Tales of the Hasidim: The Early Masters,* "How to Say Torah," p. 107.

Chapter 11—Solitude and Community

1. Raymond Bernard Blakney, *Meister Eckhart. A Modern Translation* (New York: Harper Torchbooks, 1957), p. 14; Paul Reps, *Zen Flesh, Zen Bones: A Collection of Zen and Pre-Zen Writings* (New York: Doubleday, Anchor Books, 1961), "True Friends," pp. 70f.; *Tales of the Hasidim: The Early Masters,* p. 26—"When Two Sing."

2. Kenneth Boulding, *The Naylor Sonnets* (Nyack, New York: Fellowship Publications).

3. Martin Buber, *The Knowledge of Man: A Philosophy of the Interhuman,* ed. with an introduction essay (chap. 1) by Maurice Friedman (New York: Harper Torchbooks, 1966), "What Is Common to All," trans. by Maurice Friedman, pp. 95f.

4. Burtt, ed., *The Teachings of the Compassionate Buddha,* p. 136

5. *Lao Tzu/Tao Teh Ching,* trans. by John C. H. Wu, ed. by Paul K. T.Sih, Asian Institute Translation, no. 1 (New York: St. John's University Press, 1961), p. 17; *Chuang Tzu: Basic Writings,* trans. by Burton Watson (New York: Columbia Univeristy Press, 1964), pp. 56f.

6. *The Analects of Confucius,* trans. and annotated by Arthur Waley (New York: Vintage Books), pp. 162, 181, 189.

Chapter 12—Peter Pan's Shadow: Tradition and Modernity

1. John O. Voll, "Renewal and Reform in Islamic History: *Tajdid* and *Islah*," chap. 2 of John L. Esposito, ed., *Voices of Resurgent Islam* (New York: Oxford University Press, 1983), pp. 32–37, 40f., 43f.

2. Mordecai Kaplan, *The Future of the American Jew* (New York: Macmillan, 1948), pp. 35f.

3. C. G. Jung, *Psychology and Alchemy, Collected Works*, vol. 12 (New York: Pantheon Books, 1953), p. 36.

4. C. G. Jung, *Aion: Researches into the Phenomenology of the Self, Collected Works*, vol. 9 (2) (New York: Pantheon Books, 1959), p. 70.

5. C. G. Jung, *Psychology and Religion: East and West, Collected Works*, vol. 11, trans. by R. F. C. Hull (New York: Pantheon Books, 1958), pp. 82, 96, 157, italics added.

6. C. G. Jung, *Two Essays on Analytical Psychology, Collected Works*, vol. 12 (New York: Pantheon Books, 1953), p. 237.

7. C. G. Jung, *Answer to Job*, trans. by R. F. C. Hull (Cleveland and New York: World Publishing Co., 1960), pp. 179, 186.

8. For a full-scale treatment of Jung, see Maurice Friedman, *To Deny Our Nothingness*, chap. 9, pp. 146–167.

Chapter 13—The Dialectic Between Spirit and Form

1. Thomas Merton, *The Way of Chuang Tzu* (New York: New Directions, 1965), "Three Friends," pp. 54f.

2. Paul Arthur Schlipp and Maurice Friedman, eds., *The Philosophy of Martin Buber* volume of *The Library of Living Philosophers* (LaSalle, Illinois: Open Court, 1967), Martin Buber, "Replies to My Critics," trans. by Maurice Friedman, p. 731.

3. Martin Buber, *Hasidism and Modern Man*, p. 25.

4. Martin Buber, "Interpreting Hasidism," ed. & trans. by Maurice Friedman, *Commentary*, vol. 36, no. 3 (September 1963) pp. 218–25.

5. Israel J. Kazis, "Hasidism Reexamined," *The Reconstructionist*, vol. 23, no. 8 (May 31, 1957), pp. 7–13.

Chapter 14—The Paradox of Religious Leadership

1. Thomas Merton, *The Way of Chuang Tzu*, "The Sacrificial Swine," p. 108; Idries Shah, *The Way of the Sufi* (New York: E. P Dutton [paperback], 1970), pp. 79f., 149f., 169; Buber, *Tales of the Hasidim: The Early Masters*, p. 48—"Themselves."

2. Based on Maurice Friedman, *To Deny Our Nothingness*, pp. 104–108.

3. F. Rahman, *Prophecy in Islam: Philosophy and Orthodoxy* (London: George Allen & Unwin, 1958), p. 57.

4. Rumi, *This Longing*, p. 70. See also p. 41.

5. Annemarie Schimmel, *Mystical Dimensions of Islam* (Chapel Hill: University of North Carolina Press, 1975), pp. 101, 103f.

6. *Ibid.*, pp. 193, 204f., 212.

7. *Ibid.*, pp. 236–239. I am indebted to Professor Marcia Hermansen for the quotition from Muhammad Iqbal.

8. Martin Buber, *Israel and the World*, "Biblical Leadership," p. 126.

9. *Ibid.*, p. 131.

10. *Ibid.*, p. 133.

11. Martin Buber, *Meetings*, ed. and trans. with an introduction by Maurice Friedman (LaSalle, Ill.: Open Court Publishing Co., 1973), pp. 37f. Also found in Schilpp and Friedman, eds., *The Philosophy of Martin Buber*, p. 19.

12. Based on Maurice Friedman, *To Deny Our Nothingngess*, p. 110.

13. *Ibid.*, pp. 111f.

14. Paul Reps, *Zen Flesh, Zen Bones*, "Right and Wrong," pp. 41 f.

15. *Tales of the Hasidim: The Later Masters*, p. 217—"Every Rabbi Is Good."

16. Merton, *The Way of Chuang Tzu*, "Means and Ends," p. 154.

17. *Tales of the Hasidim: The Later Masters*, p. 126—"Refusal"; *Zen Flesh, Zen Bones*, "What Are You Doing! What Are You Saying!" p. 59 f.

18. *Zen Flesh, Zen Bones*, "The Real Miracle," p. 68.

19. Buber, *Tales of the Hasidim: The Early Masters*, pp. 53f.—"The Strength of Community."

Chapter 15—Spontaneity, Decision, and Personal Wholeness

1. Merton, *The Way of Chuang Tzu*, "When Life Was Full there Was No History," p. 76; *Tales of the Hasidim: The Early Masters*, p. 153—"The Hair Shirt"; *The Later Masters*, p. 189—"The Enemy"; Martin Buber, *For the Sake of Heaven: A Chronicle*, trans. by Ludwig Lewisohn (New York: Atheneum, 1969), p. 6.

2. Maurice Friedman, *Touchstones of Reality: Existential Trust and the Community of Peace* (New York: E. P. Dutton, 1972; Dutton Books [paperback], 1974), p. 70.

3. Leslie H. Farber, *The Ways of the Will: Essays Toward A Psychology and Psychopathology of the Will* (New York: Basic Books, 1966); Leslie H. Farber, *lying, despair, jealousy, envy, sex, suicide, drugs, and the good life* (New York: Harper Colophon Books, 1978).

4. Based on Maurice Friedman, *To Deny Our Nothingness*, pp. 104ff.

5. *Ibid.*, Chap. 8, pp. 135–145.

Chapter 17—World View and Existential Trust

1. Martin Buber, *Tales of the Hasidim: The Early Masters*, "The Strong Thief," p. 104; "Suffering and Prayer," pp. 212f.; Witter Bynner, *The Way of Life according to Lao-Tzu*, no. 21, p. 37.

2. Ninian Smart, *Concept and Empathy: Essays in the Study of Religion*, ed. by Donald Wiebe (New York: Macmillan, 1986), pp. 74, 76.

3. *Ibid.*, pp. 84f.

4. David E. Roberts, "Tillich's Doctrine of Man" in Charles W. Kegley, and Robert W. Bretall, eds., *The Theology of Paul Tillich*, vol. 1 of *The library of Living Theologians* (New York: Macmillan, 1956), p. 130. Cf. Tillich's reply to Roberts on pp. 329f.

5. Paul Tillich, *The Courage to Be* (New Haven: Yale University Press, 1952), pp. 188f.

6. Paul Tillich, *Biblical Religion and the Search for Ultimate Reality* (Chicago: University of Chicago Press, 1955), p. 27.

7. *Ibid.*, pp. 81-85.

8. Martin Buber, *Tales of the Hasidim: The Early Masters*, p. 246.

9. Martin Buber, *I and Thou*, 2nd ed. with a postscript by author added, trans. by Ronald Gregor Smith (New York: Charles Scribner's Sons, 1958), p. 100.

10. Sydney and Beatrice Rome, eds., *Philosophical Interogations* (New York: Harper Torchbooks, 1970), Martin Buber section conducted by Maurice Friedman, Buber's replies trans. by Friedman, pp. 82f.

Chapter 18—Is Religion the Enemy of Humankind?

1. Idries Shah, *The Way of the Sufi*, "When Death Is Not Death," p. 120; *Tales of the Hasidim: The Later Masters*, p. 89—"When It Is Good to Deny the Existence of God"; *The Early Masters*, p. 134—"The Man Who Denies God."

A reader for the SUNY Press wrote concerning my citing the article on "Sati, death of an Indian widow": "I dislike this use of *sati* as an example abstracted completely from its traditional context and with no contextualizing discussion." I shall, therefore, quote without comment two sources on the subject provided me by Professor Lance Nelson, a distinguished scholar of Hinduism, and let the reader judge for his or her self whether the article on Sati quoted at the beginning of chap. 18 is an example of religion as an enemy of humankind (Although I confess that my belief in karma ["Karma," I have quipped, "is the word we use to console ourselves for the misfortunes of others!"] is not strong enough for me to view sati in general as anything other than distasteful and a violation of the humanity of women [which low esteem of women carries over today into the burning of thousands of young brides in India in order that the husband may get a better dowry through a second marriage!] my concern here is for this contemporary "example" of sati that, to read the report, seems like nothing short of murder and is in no way "voluntary," even in the sense of leaving the woman to accede to it through social pressure.):

"In classical times, if her husband died before her, a woman theoretically had the extreme option either to perform sati, self-immolation on the funeral pyre of her husband, or, more commonly, to undergo the rite of passage to widowhood...[sati] was viewed as auspiciousness par excellence, whereas the *vidhava*...was considered not only unfortunate but positively inauspicious, an "ogress who ate her husband with her karmic jaws"....By entering the fire, she [the *sati* purified] herself [expressing equanimity and courage and radiating benevolence on the family, those present, and generations to come]....Some acts of sati were more suicidal than religious, especially since widowhood, with its severe norm, was the only alternative....A man had total freedom of choice whether to become a yogi or not. A woman, on the contrary, could only choose between being a sati or a widow (no remarriage was possible)." Katherine K. Young, "Hinduism" in Arvind Sharma, ed. *Women in World Religions* (Albany, N.Y.: SUNY Press, 1987), pp. 83–86.

"A widow was inauspicious to everyone but her own children. Wherever she went her presence cast a gloom on all about her. She could never attend the family festivals which played so big a part in Hindu life, for she would bring bad luck on all present. She was still a member of her husband's family, and could not return to that of her father. Always watched by the parents and relatives of her lord, lest she broke her vows and imperilled the dead man's spiritual welfare, shunned as unlucky even by the servants, her life must often have been miserable in the extreme.

"In these circumstances it is not surprising that women often immolated themselves on their husbands' funeral pyres. . .

"The living cremation of the sati was always in theory voluntary, but, if we are to judge from later analogy, social and family pressure may have made it virtually obligatory on some high-caste widows, especially those of the warrior class. The 15th-century traveller Nicolo dei Conti states that as many as three thousand of the wives and concubines of the kings of Vijayanagara were pledged to be burnt with their lord on his death. . . .The widow herself, if she had no young children, might well prefer even a painful death, in the hope of reunion with her husband, to a dreary life of hunger, scorn, and domestic servitude. It is thus not surprising that satis were so common in medieval Hindu society." A. L. Basham, *The Wonder That Was India* (New York: Hawthorn Books, 1963), pp. 188–190.

2. Martin Buber, *Pointing the Way*, "The Validity and Limitation of the Political Principle," p. 218.

INDEX